STRATEGIC PREEMPTION

US Foreign Policy and Conflict in the Islamic World

Series Editors:
Tom Lansford
The University of Southern Mississippi-Gulf Coast, USA
Jack Kalpakian
Al Akhawayn University, Morocco

The proliferation of an anti-US ideology among radicalized Islamic groups has emerged as one of the most significant security concerns for the United States and contemporary global relations in the wake of the end of the Cold War. The terrorist attacks of September 11, 2001 demonstrated the danger posed by Islamic extremists to US domestic and foreign interests. Through a wealth of case studies this new series examines the role that US foreign policy has played in exacerbating or ameliorating hostilities among and within Muslim nations as a means of exploring the rise in tension between some Islamic groups and the West. The series provides an interdisciplinary framework of analysis which, transcending traditional, narrow modes of inquiry, permits a comprehensive examination of US foreign policy in the context of the Islamic world.

Other titles in the series

Balancing Act
US Foreign Policy and the Arab-Israeli Conflict
Vaughn P. Shannon
ISBN 0 7546 3591 0

A Bitter Harvest
US Foreign Policy and Afghanistan
Tom Lansford
ISBN 0 7546 3615 1

US-Indonesian Hegemonic Bargaining
Strength of Weakness
Timo Kivimäki
ISBN 0 7546 3686 0

Crossing the Rubicon
Ronald Reagan and US Policy in the Middle East
Nicholas Laham
ISBN 0 7546 3961 4

Strategic Preemption
US Foreign Policy and the Second Iraq War

ROBERT J. PAULY, JR.
Norwich University

TOM LANSFORD
The University of Southern Mississippi-Gulf Coast

ASHGATE

Published by
Ashgate Publishing Limited
Gower House
Croft Road
Aldershot
Hants GU11 3HR
England

Ashgate Publishing Company
Suite 420
101 Cherry Street
Burlington, VT 05401-4405
USA

Ashgate website: http://www.ashgate.com

British Library Cataloguing in Publication Data
Pauly, Robert J.
  Strategic preemption : US foreign policy and the second
  Iraq war. - (US foreign policy and conflict in the Islamic
  world)
  1. Iraq War, 2003 2. United States - Foreign relations -
  2001- 3. United States - Foreign relations - Iraq 4. Iraq -
  Foreign relations - United States
  I. Title II. Lansford, Tom
  327.7'30567

Library of Congress Cataloging-in-Publication Data
Pauly, Robert J., 1967-
  Strategic preemption : US foreign policy and the second Iraq war / by Robert J.
Pauly, Jr., and Tom Lansford.
     p. cm. -- (US foreign policy and conflict in the Islamic world)
  Includes bibliographical references and index.
  ISBN 0-7546-3975-4 (hardback) -- ISBN 0-7546-4357-3 (pbk.)
  1. Iraq War, 2003. 2. United States--Foreign relations--2001- I. Title: US
foreign policy and the second Iraq war. II. Title: United States foreign policy and
the second Iraq war. III. Lansford, Tom. IV. Title. V.
Series: US foreign policy and conflict in the Islamic world series.

  DS79.76.P34 2004
  327.730567'09'0511--dc22   2004012585

ISBN 10: 0 7546 3975 4 (Hbk)   ISBN 13: 978 0 7546 3975 6 (Hbk)
ISBN 10: 0 7546 4357 3 (Pbk)   ISBN 13: 978 0 7546 4357 9 (Pbk)

Reprinted 2006

Printed and bound in Great Britain by MPG Books Ltd, Bodmin, Cornwall

Contents

Acknowledgements

As is true with any project of this nature, it could only have been completed with the help and support of a number of individuals. The authors wish to thank Ms Kirstin Howgate of Ashgate Publishing for her guidance and patience through the preparation of the manuscript. They would also like to especially thank Mr Jack Covarrubias of Old Dominion University for his editing assistance. Robert J. Pauly, Jr., would like to express his thanks to his parents, brothers and sister-in-law, for their love and support. I would also to thank my graduate students at Norwich University for their instructive feedback and suggestions. Finally, I thank Kelly Whitlock for her friendship, kindness and hospitality.

Tom Lansford is extremely grateful to Mr James D. Buffett for assistance with the writing process. I would also like to express my deep thanks to Dr Denise von Herrmann for her support during his project and also wish to thank Dr Elliott Pood for providing the release time which allowed me to complete this work. I wish to acknowledge Kyle Bromwell, Drew Lucas, Mike Pappas and Ross Rutt. I would further like to extend a special note of thanks to Mr John Shinn, "Go Saints!" Finally, as always, I must thank Amber for the past, present and future.

For the servicemen and women of
Operation Iraqi Freedom

Introduction

The Legacy of the Past

Post-Cold War US Security Policy and Iraq

Since the end of the Cold War, US security policy in the Persian Gulf has been dominated by the issue of Iraq. During the waning days of the superpower conflict, Iraq was a pawn in the great bipolar struggle for influence in the region. Iraq emerged as a diplomatic battleground between the United States and the Soviet Union, and it became a key ingredient for US strategies to contain Iran and the growth of anti-American fundamentalism in the Gulf. Saddam Hussein's invasion of Kuwait quickly proved that his interests did not necessarily match those of Washington and the subsequent international conflict to liberate Kuwait came to be only the first step in a decade long effort by the United States to contain Iraq. Hence, instead of using Iraq to contain Iran, US policy evolved into one of dual containment of both Iraq and Iran.

US-Iraqi relations through the 1990s were marked by constant strife, both rhetorical and physical, which escalated into a struggle for regional power between the world's sole remaining superpower and a weakened, but still respected and potentially potent, former regional hegemonal contender. Throughout these contests, Saddam was often able to achieve short-term victories or to turn defeats into public relations successes through adroit maneuvering and manipulation of popular perceptions in the Gulf states and the broader Middle East. In doing so, he emerged by the end of the 1990s as a leading figure of pan-Arab nationalism, in spite of his brutal repression of Iraqi Shiites. Meanwhile, moderate Arab leaders, such as Hosni Mubarak of Egypt or King Hussein of Jordan (and later, his son, Abdullah II) have been increasingly viewed as too pro-American or too tied to the West in general.

The Grand Coalition

While positive perceptions of Saddam's reputation grew in the Arab street in the post-Cold War era, the United States faced increased criticism and greater constraints on its role in the Middle East in general, and specifically in the Persian Gulf. To some degree, the highwater mark for US influence was exemplified by the 1990-1991 anti-Saddam coalition. The first anti-Saddam military coalition or "Grand Coalition" reflected the unparalleled military and diplomatic strength of the United States at the dawn of the post-Cold War period. The administration of George H.W. Bush was able to draw together a broad and multifaceted coalition of traditional American allies and a range of states that had adversarial relations with Washington.

Ultimately the success of the Grand Coalition in achieving its immediate and stated goals was primarily due to the broad nature of the Bush-led anti-Saddam alliance. In the aftermath of the first Bush administration, the two subsequent presidents tried to emulate the success of the Grand Coalition and either maintain or develop coalitions that combined military, economic and diplomatic partners. However, the administrations of Bill Clinton and George W. Bush were unable to replicate the breadth and depth of the Grand Coalition. Sweeping changes in the global system and recalculations of national security priorities by individual states eroded the cohesion of the anti-Saddam efforts. In addition, both administrations pursued increasingly unilateral security policies in response to both domestic and international events.

The United States and Coalition Warfare

Military coalitions have been a central feature of US security policy in the post-World War II era. Successive US administrations have been able to utilize international organizations, coalitions and military alliances as a means to enhance American national security and to lessen the costs of superpower status. For instance, John Gerard Ruggie contends the growth of multinational institutions, such as the United Nations, North Atlantic Treaty Organization (NATO) and the World Trade Organization, were the result of very specific American preferences for the post-World War II "world order."[1] As cooperation in security issues became institutionalized, even the demise of the West's Cold War nemesis did not initially threaten the habits of collaboration.[2] By the end of the Cold War, security cooperation had become a policy priority for nations on both sides of the Atlantic and was generally not regarded as only a means to secure other security goals.[3]

The American preference for international security cooperation has its roots in the initial Cold War administrations. John Lewis Gaddis notes that in the immediate aftermath of World War II, many US policymakers feared that America alone could not contain the Soviets and that "the United States would also need the manpower reserves and economic resources of the major industrialized non-communist states."[4] Secretary of State John Foster Dulles even asserted that military cooperation could provide greater security than nuclear deterrence and since military alliances were the "cornerstone of security for the free nations."[5]

US policymakers pursued the creation of, and American participation in, a range of security organizations. Most common were the coalition and formal military alliance. Both arrangements can be collectively defined as "a formal or informal arrangement for security cooperation between two or more sovereign states."[6] The main difference between the two types of security structures involves the level of formality. Alliances are generally rigid, lasting arrangements created to deal with general or long-term threats. Alliances have formal rules, procedures and decision-making hierarchies, all based on recognized international agreements, such as treaties. Conversely, a coalition tends to be temporary and forms in reaction to a specific, often temporary threat.[7] Once the threat is defeated or significantly diminished, the coalition tends to break apart.[8] NATO is an example of an alliance while the collection of nations brought together against Iraq in 1990-1991 is an example of a coalition.

In the post-World War II era, the majority of military coalitions deployed by successive US administrations were "coalitions of the willing." Instead of negotiating in order to gain the full range of capabilities and resources available through formal military alliances, American presidents often deliberately chose to develop an informal coalition of those nations willing to bandwagon on a particular issue. This strategy was designed to minimize possible leadership issues or problems of mission scope. Such coalitions of the willing generally increased the effectiveness of the US-led arrangements, although not all problems were eliminated.[9]

Key to the success of coalitions of the willing is the role and importance of leadership by the major powers.[10] As G. John Ikenberry points out, leadership in the international arena is really about "power": "To exercise leadership is to get others to do things that they would not otherwise do."[11] Throughout the Cold War period, the US exercised considerable hard and soft power.[12]

A core issue of leadership is the potential for free-riders undermining the cohesion of the coalition. Within any coalition there is the potential that certain members will not do their share (they become free-riders). Since states always seek to maximize their interests, so they often seek methods to "cheat" in terms of burdensharing.[13] It is therefore incumbent on the coalition leadership to provide disincentives to cheat or "undercontribute."[14] One way to do this is through the "shadow of the future." If states perceive that they will have to cooperate again in the future, even if on different issues, they are much less likely to cheat.[15] Recalcitrant states may also find themselves shut-out of decision-making procedures in the current coalition or alliance or have their influence curtailed in other ways.[16]

With the end of the superpower conflict, US leadership increasingly faces challenges from other states and from international organizations seeking to balance against American primacy. This reflects the nature of the international system, which is neither unipolar nor multipolar, but instead a "uni-multipolar" configuration in which there is one superpower and a number of major powers.[17] Because the United States lacks clear hegemony, it must rely on coalitions with some combination of the major powers.[18] The post-Cold War era began with the formation of one of the largest and most successful coalitions in history as the first Bush administration was able to bring together a range of former and contemporary adversaries to oppose the regime of Saddam Hussein.

The First Bush Administration and the Gulf War

The Persian Gulf War has come to be cited as a shining example of coalition diplomacy and US leadership.[19] In the wake of the Iraqi invasion of Kuwait, the first Bush administration was able to develop an informal coalition of the willing whose goals were subsequently endorsed by a variety of international bodies, including the UN. For instance, in quick response to the invasion, the UN Security Council voted 14-0 in United Nations Security Council Resolution (UNSCR) 660 to condemn the invasion and call for an immediate Iraqi withdrawal.[20] Significantly, as Colin Powell, then Chairman of the Joint Chiefs of Staff, notes, the Soviet Union did not treat the "crisis as another East-West confrontation, with the Soviet Union willy-nilly lining up behind its onetime friend Saddam."[21] For the first time since World War II, the United States and the Soviet Union would be on the same side during a major military conflict.   Before it commenced military action, the Bush administration sought a Security Council Resolution which would authorize the use of force if the Iraqis did not retreat.   On 29 November 1990, in Resolution 678 the council voted 12-2 to authorize the removal of Iraqi forces by "all necessary means to uphold and implement resolution 660."[22] In order to secure the support of the council, the US was willing to tone-down the original language of the draft (Secretary of State Jim Baker wanted the resolution to specifically include the phrase "the use of force") and to include one last chance for Saddam to withdraw.[23]

Developing the Coalition

The development of the coalition was made easier by the high threat quotient posed by Saddam whose invasion threatened not only regional stability but the main tenets of the international order. As a result, states lined up to bandwagon with the United States. Concurrently, the coalition was strengthened by the extraordinary steps that the Bush administration was willing to undertake in order to affirm US leadership. In late August 1990, administration officials launched an intensive campaign to publicize what they perceived to be appropriate contributions from each of the major allied powers. Various figures, including Deputy Secretary of State Lawrence Eagleburger and Treasury Secretary Nicholas Brady were dispatched to capitals to secure or reaffirm support as needed.[24] The US officials also worked to gain support for allied states from other allied states. For instance, Great Britain only contributed troops (it was the largest British deployment since World War II). The Bush administration helped secure funds from Germany and Japan to cover part of the costs of the British forces. These two states provided the British $55 million per day during the height of the campaign.[25] Bush would also use financial incentives for other states. On 1 September 1990, Bush initiated a plan, approved two months later, to forgive Egypt's $7 billion debt to the US.[26]

In order to secure as broad a coalition as possible, the administration did not seek substantial military resources and commitments from each of the allies. Instead, the administration proceeded along two tracks: first, it sought to gain diplomatic pledges of support from as wide an array of states as possible; and second, it endeavored to gain military support from a much smaller group of states who could provide either assets needed to bolster American forces or soldiers whose presence would enhance the credibility of the coalition.[27]

The coalition ultimately consisted of an inner and outer band of nations. At the heart of the anti-Saddam coalition were those states which provided military assets and formed the inner band. However, even these states can be divided into two broad categories. First, the "inner core" included those states that made major contributions to the military effort and whose withdrawal would have created significant fiscal or manpower problems. The interests and preferences of these states were carefully considered and taken into account. Second, the "outer core" consisted of states that provided token military forces or whose participation caused problems for the coalition as a whole. For instance, several states were referred to as "fire alarm" states, ones which consistently threatened to withdraw from the coalition if they perceived the US led allies were violating some principle or norm which undergirded the consensus.[28] The outer band of states were those such as Japan which offered financial or diplomatic support, but not troops.[29] Those states and actors, including Jordan and the Palestine Liberation Organization, that did not bandwagon with the US suffered a loss of both prestige and diplomatic clout.

Although the level and degree of support varied significantly, the US-led coalition of the willing was the "largest and most capable international military coalition in a generation."[30] For example, ships from 60 different nations participated in the naval blockade of during Operations Desert Shield and Desert Storm and coalition states provided some 200,000 troops, sailors and airmen. The inner band of states totaled 26 states and included 13 of the NATO allies, and newly democratizing states in Eastern Europe such as Bulgaria, Czechoslovakia and Poland. Arab states such as Syria and Egypt provided some 50,000 troops. Even developing countries such as Bangladesh, Senegal and Zaire provided some forces as members of the outer band. After the liberation of Kuwait, formal hostilities ceased on 27 February 1991, and Saddam accepted all of the UN conditions the following day.

Coalition Lessons

The success of the grand coalition against Saddam was attributable to a variety of factors. First, Bush accomplished the main priority that any US leader must during a foreign policy crisis: he had to ensure domestic support for his foreign policy agenda. As Richard Rose notes, to "take charge in an international crisis, a president must do three things more or less simultaneously: act effectively in the international arena, mobilize public opinion [in the US], and maintain support in Washington."[31] Second, Bush expended considerable time and energy in personal or "Rolodex diplomacy" to ensure foreign support. This included 35 calls to foreign leaders and summits with leaders of a range of countries, including the Soviet Union, Canada, Jordan and Great Britain.[32] Third, Bush offered considerable incentives for states to join the coalition. For instance, the US softened its stance toward China in the aftermath of the Tiananmen Square massacre and lobbied nominal American enemy Syria to join the coalition.[33] Fourth, because Bush was able to convince both his domestic audience and foreign leaders that the Iraqi invasion was a substantial threat to world stability, the coalition had a high degree of cohesion and solidarity. Bush made several compromises, including the scope and goals of the military, in order to maintain that cohesion. Fifth and finally, Bush took advantage of the fact that most of the major powers perceived it to be in their interest to bandwagon with the US. The shadow of the future seemed to hold the promise of continued cooperation under the auspices of benign American primacy. Many states that were formerly enemies of, or at least antagonistic toward, the US participated in the coalition in the hope that US leadership would help ensure regional and global stability through continued engagement with multilateral organizations such as the UN.

As testament to the success of the original coalition, Bush was able to maintain the core elements of the anti-Saddam alliance beyond its original impetus (the invasion of Kuwait). Even after Saddam accepted the truce, Bush was able to implement a containment strategy toward Iraq with broad international support. The main elements of this strategy were international economic sanctions, UN weapons inspections, the imposition of a UN protectorate over the Kurdish regions of northern Iraq and the establishment of no-fly zones over northern and southern Iraq.[34]

On the other hand, during the Gulf operations, a number of problems emerged which highlighted the problems inherent in coalition warfare. This was especially true in regard to the actual military operations. For instance, many states resisted US efforts to develop a unified command and control structure. France and Italy specifically sought separate roles for the West European forces in an effort to enhance the autonomy of European security structures. A British officer serving in the naval blockade noted wryly that "political games were going on which had less to do with efficient execution of the blockade and rather more to do with eroding American domination of NATO and the newly formed Coalition."[35] Because of ongoing problems of this nature, the campaign to oust Saddam and subsequent coalition actions during the 1990s would undermine the confidence of the US military in broad, multilateral campaigns.

The "New" Bush Administration

In the aftermath of the 11 September 2001 attacks, the George W. Bush administration sought to develop a coalition of coalitions. The ultimate success of the administration's Afghan policy set the stage for its actions with respect to Iraq. In practice, Bush's policy choices in regard to Iraq all bore the imprint of both the administration's recent experiences in Afghanistan and the broader trends toward unilateral (or perhaps selectively multilateral) action that were manifested during the Clinton years.

In describing the coalition against Al Qaeda and the Taliban, Deputy Secretary of State Richard Armitage told the European nations that "in this coalition building there is a continuum from, on the one hand, rhetorical or political support for activities ... and at the far end of the continuum is the possibility of some military activity either together or unilaterally."[36] In some respects, Bush's strategy toward Afghanistan reflected that of his father whose coalition had various levels and degrees of participation. A key difference, however, is that while the first Bush administration endeavored to develop as broad a diplomatic coalition as possible, it purposely formed a very narrow military coalition. While the administration sought and gained pledges of support from all of the major international organizations, including the UN, NATO, Organization of American States (OAS) and the European Union (EU), the overriding priority was to secure enough assistance so that the US could "pick and choose among its allies, fashioning the moral authority of an international coalition without having to deal with the problems of the whole alliance."[37]

In the end, the Bush administration pursued policies designed to produce a global counterterrorism coalition which "would assign different tasks to different countries, with many of the players involved in intelligence-gathering, police work, and bushwacking on money trails—but perhaps few actually joining in the military phase."[38] National Security Advisor Condoleezza Rice described the effort in the following manner: "This is a broad coalition in which people are contributing on very different and very many fronts. The key to the broad coalition is to remember that, while everybody understandably wants to focus on military contributions, this is not the Gulf War."[39] The nature of the coalition encouraged many states to bandwagon with the US since the terrorist threat was potentially quite high and the Bush administration offered a number of inducements for states to cooperate.[40]

It was not until after the military phase of Operation Enduring Freedom that the Bush administration made its major requests for troop assistance. As Philip Gordon summarized, the US saw multilateral

> support as politically useful but not particularly significant militarily. In this case it was reinforced by what many Americans saw as a key 'lesson' of Kosovo. Whereas many in Europe saw the Kosovo air campaign as excessively dominated by the United States and American generals, most Americans—particularly within the military—saw just the opposite: excessive European meddling, with French politicians and European lawyers interfering with efficient targeting and bombing runs, and compromising operational security. This time, the Bush team determined, would be different.[41]

The use of precision weaponry during the campaign reinforced the exclusivity of the military operation. For instance, more than 70 percent of the aerial ordnance used in the Afghan campaign was precision-guided. In contrast, 30 percent of the munitions used in Kosovo were precision-guided, while only 10 percent of the ordinance in the Gulf War was precision-guided.[42]

Although the coalition only provided minimal troops for the Afghan campaign, the allies provided the bulk of the peace-keeping troops after the fall of the Taliban. Furthermore, the UN forces would actually be under the operational command of the US The British government, which initially commanded the UN mission, stated that the UN operations would be conducted "in cooperation with the Americans, they are the big brother."[43] Other nations were less pleased. Berlin protested the arrangement and called for autonomous command.[44] Meanwhile Paris objected to having to "clean-up" after the Americans. French policymakers claimed that Washington seemed to say "We'll do the cooking and prepare what people are going to eat, then you will wash the dirty dishes."[45]

Iraq and the "Axis of Evil"

In his State of the Union address on 29 January 2002, Bush identified Iran, North Korea and Iraq as members of an "axis of evil." The administration concurrently began to lay the groundwork to mark Iraq as the next target in the US-led war on terror. Bush also stated that he would take preemptive military action.[46] This doctrine of preemption would later be codified in the National Security Strategy (NSS).[47] The promulgation of the NSS marked a rejection of the traditional policy of containment which had proven to be both popular and effective during the Cold War. Indeed in the aftermath of the bipolar struggle, containment remained popular as a means to avoid confrontation and aggressive action. During the 1990s, the Clinton administration applied the strategy to both Iraq and Iran through a policy of "Dual Containment."

In concrete terms, Bush authorized increases in covert aid to anti-Saddam elements while his national security team worked through the late summer of 2002 to develop specific policy options. Secretary of State Colin Powell emerged as the foremost advocate for building a strong coalition, while Vice President Dick Cheney and Secretary of Defense Donald Rumsfeld argued for immediate action, even if it meant unilateral military strikes. Powell was able to sway the President, who used a 12 September 2002 UN speech to launch the diplomatic effort.[48]

The emerging doctrine of preemption was a response to changes of threat perception in the United States. The bipolar superpower struggle had dominated US politics for most of the post-World War era, as the main American security strategy was the containment of the Soviet Union. However, containment was never a passive policy and it was often marked by aggressive attempts to "rollback" Soviet gains. This included the judicious use of American military and economic power, but it also was marked by preemptive strikes to forestall, or counter, Soviet expansion as was the case in the invasion of Grenada in 1983. Just as President Ronald Reagan sought victory in the bipolar Cold War struggle by a renewed policy of rollback toward the Soviet Union, the administration of George W. Bush sought to "rollback" international terrorism through assertive and aggressive action. The first manifestation of the new Bush policy would be Iraq.

The terrorist attacks of 11 September 2001 forced the Bush administration to recalculate its security policy in regard to terrorism. Throughout most of modern history, the most significant threat to nationstates was the potential for war and the conquest of national territory by foreign powers. The threat of invasion was countered through the development of significant offensive and defensive military capabilities, and the power to project these capabilities through a robust navy. The Cold War altered the security threat quotient since the exchange of nuclear weapons could allow an enemy to destroy and conquer territory without exposing its military to large-scale direct casualties (as in the case of the US bombing of Hiroshima and Nagasaki at the end of World War II). As both rival superpowers developed considerable nuclear arsenals, the need for large standing armies declined as nuclear exchanges made conventional warfare potentially catastrophic because of the risk of escalation. Because of the potential devastation of a first strike, methods were developed which provided the President with the ability to launch a nuclear assault without congressional approval and as a preemptive action if necessary. Hence, as the specific threats to the US changed during the course of the Cold War, so too did the strategic response.

With the demise of state actors as direct threats to American security and the concurrent rise of substate actors, mainly international terrorist groups, as the chief threat to American interests, US security policy had to again evolve. Terrorist groups routinely violate international law by intentionally attacking civilian targets, and states have a recognized right to self defense. With the NSS, the evolution of American strategy to allow the US to act before harm could be done to the civilian population or infrastructure demonstrates the continuing maturation of US policy in order to counter emerging new threats. The preemptive invasion of Iraq is the operationalization of the new security posture.

The US-led invasion of Iraq did place considerable strains upon the institutions which framed the post-World War II and the post-Cold War world. The Bush administration was roundly criticized by both domestic and foreign politicos for its pursuit of unilateral military action. Yet, the invasion of Iraq had the tacit or formal support of a range of nations, just not those states that had formed the core of US-led multilateralism during the Cold War period. Instead, the states of Eastern Europe, who suffered the most from the containment policy of the bipolar Cold War struggle, joined the US in its rejection of a neo-containment, status quo policy toward Iraq.

Within Europe, it would be the traditional Atlanticist states such as Great Britain, the Netherlands and Denmark, joined by Spain and Italy (both led by conservative governments, and both with a lengthy history of terrorist activity), who joined with the Eastern European states to support US action and force into public debate the longstanding differences between the pro-and anti-Eurocentric states. For France, the episode undermined the two institutions through which successive post-World War II French governments had used to maintain French global power and influence, even as the military and economic strength of the nation declined in proportion to the rising superpowers and its own European neighbors.

Methodology

In its efforts to disarm Saddam's regime, the Bush administration pursued policies which tested Cold War alliances and strained the global consensus that developed in the aftermath of the 2001 terrorist attacks on the United States. Through the course of the diplomatic wrangling and the military action that followed, the US demonstrated that it remains the primary military power, but that other states such as Russia and France seek to develop a counter pole to American power. In this fashion, the remainder of this book places the Iraq conflict in the context of emerging trends in international security.

In line with the aims of the series in which this book is included, the work examines the broad framework of US policy toward Iraq under the administration of George W. Bush. The war with Iraq marks the second time in the young twenty-first century that the United States has invaded a Muslim-majority country and the book seeks to detail not only the specifics of the conflict, but the war's broad impact on US relations with Muslim states both in a regional and global context. The book also examines the tensions created between the US and its main European allies over the military conflict.

The first chapter of the book, "US Iraq Policy and September 11," specifically analyzes the impact of the 11 September attacks and the subsequent military victory in Afghanistan on US-Iraq policy. Central to the chapter is an exploration of the evolution of US terrorist policy and Iraq since the 9/11 attacks. This section also uses a comparative framework to contrast the responses of the Clinton and Bush administrations to Al Qaeda and the broader threat of international terrorism, while also presenting the major differences between the two administrations in regard to Iraq. It reviews and evaluates the evidence that was presented to link Al Qaeda and Iraq (and broader evidence of Iraqi support for international terrorism). Finally, the chapter covers the transition of the Bush administration from pursuing Al Qaeda to confronting Iraq.

Chapter Two, "The Doctrine of Preemption," explores preemptive war in the context of international law and the traditions of US security policy. The utility of preemption to US security policy is evaluated in the context of costs and benefits. In addition, the full range of the NSS, as it relates to preemption and US strategy, is also analyzed in the context of the full spectrum of applications. Finally, the chapter examines the immediate and future consequences of preemption in the framework of longstanding trends in US foreign policy.

"Diplomacy and Brinksmanship," the third chapter, the Bush administration's diplomacy is presented against the larger history of US global relations. Specifically, the chapter seeks to explore the charges of "unilateralism" which emerged during the Iraq crisis and delve into the true place that multilateralism has in US foreign policy. The chapter both examines the domestic pressures exerted on the nation's foreign policy and the powers of the presidency. Against this backdrop, the chapter relates the role of brinksmanship in modern diplomacy and what role the tactic played in the build-up to the war with Iraq.

Chapter Four, "A Coalition of the Willing," provides an overview of the administration's efforts to assemble a coalition of nations to first confront and then ultimately attack Iraq. Central to this exploration is an understanding of the role of the United States in the post-Cold War world, and the place of multilateralism in US policy. It further explores the diplomatic maneuvering of Washington and the international community during the war's prologue. The heart of the chapter traces the efforts of the Bush administration to gain allies and the counter-efforts of opponents of military action against Iraq to balance against or break-apart the US-led coalition. The role and motivations of France, Germany, and Russia are examined, as are the interests of the main US allies, including the Atlanticist states of Western Europe and the new democracies of Eastern Europe.

In Chapter Five, "Operation Iraqi Freedom," the narrative of the military action against Iraq is presented against the developing trends in US military strategy. Longstanding constraints on the exercise of US military power, including the

Weinberger-Powell Doctrine are analyzed along with emerging influences in military doctrine. The specifics of the "shock and awe" strategy are placed in the context of military evolution and the overall effectiveness of the campaign is assessed against both expectations and the success of the 1991 Iraq War.

Chapter Six, "Rebuilding and Reconstruction," largely explores that notion that the US "won" the war, but "lost" the peace. The chapter explores the efforts of the US at nation building in Iraq and analyzes the American reconstruction program in light of its advantages and constraints. The section further explores the potential damage that the Iraqi insurgency has on the immediate and long-term future of post-war Iraq. The chapter details the Bush administration's plans to reconstruct Iraq as a model for other Arab states in the context of the continuing ethnic and religious conflict within Iraq and the broader Persian Gulf region. Finally the long range consequences of US success in nation building and the stabilization of Iraq are presented along with their possible impact on the region and the world.

The conclusion of the book seeks to bring together the often disparate threads of US Iraq policy to tie the past to both the present and the future. In order to do so, the impact of the attacks of 11 September are emphasized in terms of their importance to US foreign and security policy. Furthermore, the lessons of coalition-building are integrated with the military lessons of the Iraq war. In addition, the US objectives in regards to post-war Iraq are explored in the context of the obstacles to achieving those goals. To conclude the book, the authors develop specific policy prescriptions to facilitate the future of US foreign and security policy toward Iraq and the broader Islamic world.

Notes

[1] See John Gerard Ruggie, "Third Try at World Order? America and Multilateralism After the Cold War," *Political Science Quarterly*, 109 (Fall 1994): 553-570.

[2] See Robert J. Lieber, "No Transatlantic Divorce in the Offing," *Orbis*, 44/4 (Fall 2000): 571-85.

[3] Gunther Hellmann and Reinhard Wolf, "Neorealism, Neoliberal Institutionalism, and the Future of NATO," *Security Studies* 3/1 (Autumn 1993), 20.

[4] John Lewis Gaddis, *Strategies of Containment: A Critical Appraisal of Postwar American National Security Policy* (New York: Oxford University Press, 1982), 152.

[5] John Foster Dulles, "Policy for Security and Peace," *Foreign Affairs* 32 (April 1954), 355-57.

[6] Stephan M. Walt, *The Origins of Alliances* (Ithaca: Cornell University Press, 1987), 12.

[7] For a broader examination of the differences between alliances and coalitions, see Glenn H. Snyder, "Alliance Theory: A Neorealist First Cut," *International Affairs*, 44 (Spring 1990): 103-24.

[8] See Wayne A. Skillet, "Alliance and Coalition Warfare," *Parameters*, 23 (Summer 1993): 74-85.

[9] Mark Schissler, *Coalition Warfare: More Power or More Problems?* (Newport: US Naval War College, 1993).

[10] For an examination of theories on international leadership, see David P. Rapkin, ed., *World Leadership and Hegemony* (Boulder: Lynne Rienner, 1990).

[11] G. John Ikenberry, "The Future of International Leadership," *Political Science Quarterly*, 111/3 (Fall 1996), 388.

[12] Hard power is "a country's economic and military ability to buy and coerce" while soft power is "the ability to attract through cultural and ideological appeal"; Joseph S. Nye, Jr., "Redefining the National Interest," *Foreign Affairs*, 78/ 4 (July/August 1999), 24. Nye notes that in the post-Cold War "information age soft power is becoming more compelling than ever before," ibid., 25.

[13] Michael Hechter, "Karl Polanyi's Social Theory: A Critique," *Politics and Society*, 10/4 (Winter 1981), 403.

[14] Charles Lipson, "Is the Future of Collective Security Like the Past?" in Downs, *Collective Security*, 115.

[15] Arthur A. Stein points out that collective groupings of states and international organizations "may be required again in the future, and destroying them because of short-term changes may be very costly in the long run. Institutional maintenance is not, then, a function of a waiving calculation; it becomes a factor in the decision calculus that keeps short-term calculations from becoming decisive," Arthur A. Stein, *Why Nations Cooperate: Circumstance and Choice in International Relations* (London: Cornell University, 1990), 52.

[16] One example of such sanctions would be the French withdrawal from NATO's integrated military command in which Paris essentially became a free rider. As a result, the French found themselves locked out of many of the major military policy decisions; for more detail, see Michael M. Harrison and Mark G. McDonough, *Negotiations on the French Withdrawal From NATO: FPI Case Studies, No. 5* (Washington, D.C.: Johns Hopkins, 1987).

[17] Samuel Huntington, "The Lonely Superpower," *Foreign Affairs*, 78/2 (March/April 1999), 36.

[18] Huntington identifies several regional powers, including "the French-German condominium in Europe, Russia in Eurasia, China and potentially Japan in East Asia, India in South Asia, Iran in Southwest Asia, Brazil in Latin America, and South Africa and Nigeria in Africa," ibid. These regional powers "are preeminent in areas of the world without being able to extend their interests and capabilities as globally as the United States," ibid.

[19] See Mashhud H. Choudhry, Coalition Warfare: Can the Gulf War-91 Be the Model for Future? (Carlisle Barracks: US Army War College, 1992); or James P. Dunnigan, and Austin Bay, From Shield to Storm: High-Tech Weapons, Military Strategy, and Coalition Warfare in the Persian Gulf (New York: Morrow, 1992).

[20] The resolution specifically stated that the Security Council "demands that Iraq withdraw immediately and unconditionally all of its forces to the positions in which they were located on 1 August 1990," UN, Security Council Resolution 660, S/RES/660 (2 August 1990).

[21] Colin Powell, with Joseph E. Persico, *My American Journey* (New York: Random House, 1995), 463.

[22] UN, Security Council Resolution 678, S/RES/678 (29 November 1990). Yemen and Cuba voted against the resolution, while China abstained.

[23] The Security Council required that "Iraq comply fully with resolution 660 (1990) and all subsequent relevant resolutions, and decides, while maintaining all its decisions, to allow Iraq one final opportunity, as a pause of goodwill, to do so," and gave the Iraqi leader until 15 January 1991 to comply; ibid.

[24] See Alan Riding, "US Officials Begin Tour to Seek Financial Backing for Gulf Force," *The New York Times* (5 September 1990); and Patrick Tyler and David Hoffmann, "US Asking Allies to Share the Costs," *Washington Post* (30 August 1990).

[25] "Making 'Em Pay," *The Economist* (26 January 1991), 18.

[26] Patrick E. Tyler, "Bush to Forgive $7.1 Billion Egypt Owes for Military Aid," *Washington Post* (1 September 1990); and William Claiborne, "Mubarak Sets Summit, Seeks All Arab Force," *Washington Post* (9 August 1990).

[27] On US efforts to promote burdensharing among the allies, see Andrew Bennet, Joseph Lepgold and Danny Unger, "Burden-sharing in the Persian Gulf War," *International Organization*, 48/1 (Winter 1994): 39-75.

[28] Lake, 152.

[29] Ultimately, Japan contributed some $13 billion toward the cost of the war, while Germany contributed $12 billion; John M. Goshko, "Germany to Complete Contribution Toward Gulf War Costs Thursday," *Washington Post* (27 March 1991). Both nations also dispatched minor naval forces after the end of the war to assist in the ongoing naval blockade; Steven R. Weisman, "Breaking Tradition, Japan Sends Flotilla to Gulf," *The New York Times* (25 April 1991).

[30] Gary G. Sick and Lawrence G. Potter, "Introduction," in Gary G. Sick and Lawrence G. Potter, eds., *The Persian Gulf at the Millennium: Essays in Politics, Economy, Security, and Religion* (New York: St. Martin's, 1997) 1.

[31] Richard Rose, *The Post Modern President* (Chatham, NJ: Chatham House, 1991), 333.

[32] Bush also traveled to the Middle East and had leading figures in the administration also engage in personal diplomacy; see Colin Campbell and S.J. and Bert A. Rockman, *The Bush Presidency: First Appraisals* (Chatham, NJ: Chatham House, 1991) or Rose. On Rolodex or telephone diplomacy, see Brigitte Lebens Nacos, "Presidential Leadership During the Persian Gulf Conflict," *Presidential Studies Quarterly*, 24/3 (Summer 1994): 543- 62.

[33] Bush received the Chinese foreign minister in the White House and relaxed US policy toward China and in return, the Chinese did not veto any of the UN Security Council Resolutions. In addition, Bush offered inducements for Syrian President Hafiz Assad to join the coalition and thereby helped prevent the impression that the coalition was an anti-Arab entity. The US also allowed Turkey to increase textile exports to the US and as mentioned, forgave Egypt's debt.

[34] For more on US containment strategy toward Iraq, see Alexander George and William E. Simmons, eds., *The Limits of Coercive Diplomacy* (Boulder: Westview Press, 1994): Zalmay Khalilzad, "The United States and the Persian Gulf: Preventing Regional Hegemony," *Survival* 37, no. 2 (Summer 1995): 95-120; and Richard Haass, ed., *Economic Sanctions and American Diplomacy* (New York: Council on Foreign Relations, 1998).

[35] Theodore Craig, Call for Fire: Sea Combat in the Falklands and the Gulf War (London: John Murray, 1995), 168.

[36] NATO, "Press Availability: US Deputy Secretary of State Armitage and NATO Secretary General Lord Robertson," Brussels (20 September 2001).

[37] Ibid.

[38] Howard LaFranchi, "Despite Talk of Coalition, US Mostly Goes it Alone," *The Christian Science Monitor* (29 October 2001).

[39] Condeleezza Rice, Press Briefing, Washington, D.C. (8 November 2001).

[40] For example, Bush issued Presidential Determination 2001-28 which ended arms sanctions on Pakistan and India "in the interest of the national security of the United States," US, White House, "Presidential Determination 2001-28" (22 September 2001). In addition, Pakistan received a $1 billion non-military aid package (this made Pakistan the second largest recipient of foreign aid after Israel); Rory McCarthy, "US to Reward Pakistan With Billions in Aid," *The Guardian* (20 September 2001).

[41] Philip H. Gordon, "NATO After 11 September," *Survival*, 43/4 (Winter 2001-2002), 4.

[42] Joseph Fitchett, "High-Tech Weapons Change the Dynamics and the Scope of Battle," *International Herald Tribune* (28 December 2001).

[43] James Meek, Richard Norton-Taylor and Michael White, "No. 10 Retreats on Plan to Send More Troops," *The Guardian* (20 November 2001).

[44] Carola Hoyos and Gwen Robinson, "Multinational Peacekeeping Force Approved," *Financial Times* (21 December 2001); and Carola Hoyos, Andrew Parker and Hugh Williamson, "Anti-terrorist Coalition Threatened With Split," *Financial Times* (20 December 2001).

[45] Joseph Fitchett, "US Allies Chafe at 'Cleanup' Role," *International Herald Tribune* (26 November 2001).

[46] Bush stated that "I will not wait on events, while dangers gather. I will not stand by, as peril draws closer and closer. The United States of America will not permit the world's most dangerous regimes to threaten us with the world's most destructive weapons," George W. Bush, "The President's State of the Union Address" (29 January 2002), online at http://www.whitehouse.gov/news/releases/2002/01/20020129-11.html.

[47] The policy document notes that "While the United States will constantly strive to enlist the support of the international community, we will not hesitate to act alone, if necessary, to exercise our right of selfdefense by acting preemptively against such terrorists, to prevent them from doing harm against our people and our country," US, National Security Council, *The National Security Strategy of the United States* (17 September 2002), online at http://www.whitehouse.gov/nsc/nss.html.

[48] Powell met with Rice and Bush on 5 August and was able to convince the President of the importance of a coalition effort. Rice even noted that she felt the "headline" from the meeting should have been "Powell Makes Case for Coalition as Only Way to Assure Success," Bob Woodward, *Bush At War* (New York: Simon and Schuster, 2002), 334. On 14 August, Powell met with other members of the national security council (though not the President) and argued to make the September speech about Iraq. The others, including Rice, Cheney and Rumsfeld, agreed; ibid., 335.

Chapter 1

US Iraq Policy and September 11

Introduction

There are few defining days in the history of any nation-state, irrespective of its internal economic, political and cultural composition. When one does occur, it is typically labeled in that fashion on the basis of an event or series of events that deliver an unanticipated shock to that state's political leadership and its citizenry and lead to a subsequent reevaluation of their collective interests. On 11 September 2001, the United States of America was subjected to precisely such a shock. That morning, 19 members of a terrorist organization known as Al Qaeda hijacked four American commercial airlines, which they proceeded to use to launch the most devastating assault on targets within the territory of the United States since the Japanese surprise attack on Pearl Harbor on 7 December 1941. Two of the planes struck the North and South towers of the World Trade Center in New York, resulting in the collapse of both structures as millions of Americans watched on live television. A third plane flew into the Pentagon on the outskirts of Washington, D.C., and a fourth crashed in a field in Western Pennsylvania after a struggle between the hijackers and a courageous group of passengers on board. Ultimately, the attacks resulted in the loss of nearly 3,000 lives, most, but not all, those of American citizens.

The events of 9/11 raised two immediate questions in the minds of President George W. Bush administration, the members of his national security team and, for that matter, in capitals across the globe. First, precisely who was responsible for the attacks? And second, how should the United States respond—in terms of both means (diplomatic, economic, judicial, military and political) and timing? Each question, in turn, demanded both short- and longer-term consideration, followed by the articulation of rhetorical statements and the subsequent planning and application of substantive action, including, if necessary, the use of military force. Bush's initial responses, delivered the day of the attacks, focused in general terms on both queries. At midday, for example, the President pledged that the United States "will hunt down and punish those responsible for these cowardly acts."[1] Later, in an evening address to the nation, he reiterated that point, then added another that would foreshadow the nature of the American-led Global War on Terrorism that has unfolded in the months and years since then, noting that "we will make no distinction between the terrorists who committed these acts and those who harbor them."[2]

Over the ensuing days, evidence implicating Al Qaeda, a transnational terrorist organization based in Afghanistan under the leadership of Osama bin Laden and harbored by the ultra-orthodox Islamic regime of the Taliban, mounted quickly. In short, that evidence suggested that bin Laden had planned and orchestrated the attacks from Afghanistan, where he trained and then dispatched the hijackers responsible for carrying out the operation on 9/11.[3] The United States, in turn, responded by building an international "coalition of the willing" to confront Al Qaeda and its Taliban hosts. Ultimately, in response to Taliban leader Mullah Muhammad Omar's refusal to hand bin Laden over to Bush administration to answer for the attacks, the United States launched Operation Enduring Freedom in October 2001. With limited logistical and combat assistance from fellow North Atlantic Treaty Organization (NATO) allies such as France, Germany and the United Kingdom, along with somewhat more substantial support from the opposition Afghan Northern Alliance, American forces removed the Taliban from power and reduced markedly bin Laden's capacity to organize and direct future terrorist operations on the scale of the assaults on the World Trade Center and Pentagon. It did so over a period of less than two months that was followed by ongoing nation-building operations to develop a functioning democratic Afghanistan.[4]

Above all, Operation Enduring Freedom demonstrated that the United States was willing to carry out the promise Bush made just hours after the events of 9/11: namely that it would seek to punish not only the terrorists responsible for the attacks but also those states or regimes willing to cooperate with or harbor bin Laden and his ilk. In reiterating that pledge in an address to Congress just over two weeks prior to the launch of operations against Taliban and Al Qaeda forces in Afghanistan, Bush had warned, "we will pursue nations that provide aid or safe haven to terrorism. Every nation, in every region, now has a decision to make. Either you are with us, or you are with the terrorists. From this day forward, any nation that continues to harbor or support terrorism will be regarded by the United States as a hostile regime."[5] Put simply, Bush's stance reflected a changing perception among the members of the administration's inner circle (and, arguably, within the American populace) of the nature of the dangers to US interests at home and abroad posed by terrorism generally and Al Qaeda specifically and a corresponding willingness to take a more proactive approach to reducing and eventually eliminating those threats.

Bush's predecessor, President William J. Clinton, also recognized that terrorism presented a growing danger. His administration, however, was more cautious, relying on limited cruise missile strikes on bin Laden's training camps in Afghanistan in response to Al Qaeda attacks such as those on the US Embassies in Nairobi, Kenya, and Dar-es-Salaam, Tanzania, in August 1998 and the USS *Cole* in October 2000 rather than the more robust approach reflected in Operation Enduring Freedom. As military historian Victor Davis Hanson contends, on 11 September 2001, "in a blink the old idea of easy retaliation by using cruise missiles or saber-rattling press conferences seems to have vanished. With the end of that mirage, the two-decade fear of losing a single life to protect freedom and innocent civilians also disappeared. Past ideas of restraint, once thought to be mature and sober, were now in an instant revealed to be reckless in their naiveté and derelict by their disastrous consequences."[6]

Clinton's unwillingness to sanction the use of anything but token force against Al Qaeda paralleled his stance toward perhaps the most persistent US adversary of the

1990s: Iraqi President Saddam Hussein. As opposed to Clinton, whose only substantial—and somewhat sustained—response to Saddam's consistent unwillingness to adhere to a series of United Nations (UN) Security Council Resolutions to which he acceded at the conclusion of the 1990-91 Persian Gulf War (including, most notably, prohibitions against the development of nuclear, chemical and biological weapons of mass destruction [WMD] and sponsorship of terrorist groups) was a brief flurry of cruise missile strikes in the context of Operation Desert Fox in December 1998.[7] Those strikes, which came after Saddam's expulsion of UN weapons inspectors the previous month, did not result in the inspectors' return. Rather, once completed, they left Saddam free to defy the United States without repercussions until the events of 9/11 contributed to the expression of a renewed American willingness to take bold action against Iraq.

Bush articulated that shift in tone, if not formal policy (as the Clinton administration had also repeatedly stressed verbally that it was committed to regime change in Iraq), through the promulgation of a broader approach to the issue of the state sponsorship of terrorism in the context of his January 2002 State of the Union Address. In the wake of the successful completion of Operation Enduring Freedom the previous month, Bush used the address to impress upon those states with a history of support for terrorism that the United States would no longer tolerate such behavior. In particular, the President characterized three states (Iraq, Iran and North Korea) as members of "an axis of evil, arming to threaten the peace of the world." Furthermore, he made a connection between the threats posed by states determined to develop WMD and maintain relationships with terrorists, including, but not limited to, bin Laden and his global network, concluding that Iraq, Iran and North Korea "pose a grave and growing danger. They could provide these arms to terrorists, giving them the means to match their hatred. They could attack our allies or attempt to blackmail the United States. In any of these cases, the price of indifference would be catastrophic."[8]

Essentially, that address provided the rhetorical foundation for the planning and conduct of the Second Iraq War, which is the general topic under consideration in this monograph. The present chapter, on the other hand, is concerned primarily with the degree to which the Bush administration's policy toward Iraq from 2001-03 was related to the war on terrorism broadly and the events of 9/11 in particular. The balance of the chapter examines those issues through the presentation of six related sections that unfold in the following manner. The first section discusses in detail the altered perception of threats to US interests in the aftermath of 9/11. The second section examines the relationship between Al Qaeda and the United States during both the Clinton and Bush administrations from 1993-2004. The third section examines the relationship between Saddam's Iraq and the United States during the Clinton and Bush administrations from 1993-2004. The fourth section evaluates the extent to which credible linkages existed between Saddam's regime and Al Qaeda prior to the 9/11 attacks on one hand and whether Iraq played any role whatsoever in the planning and conduct of those assaults on the other. The fifth section assesses the Bush administration's prudence—or lack thereof—in confronting Iraq in the context of the war on terror given the evidence examined in the previous three sections. The sixth section presents a set of concluding observations on the chapter's most significant findings.

Changing Perception of Threats to US Interests in the Aftermath of 9/11

American presidents have employed a variety of different tools in the interrelated conduct of foreign and national security policy over the past two and one-quarter centuries. In general terms, the approaches they choose to pursue are typically conditioned by the changing nature and perception of the threats they face and the contemporary domestic and foreign crises to which they must respond. Nonetheless, irrespective of the historical circumstances, three rules have consistently proven indispensable to the effective formulation and implementation of policies designed to safeguard American interests within and outside of the United States. It is essential first to define a state's national interests, second to prioritize those interests and third to take policy decisions accordingly. More pointedly, the policies that grow out of such decisions are the product of an admixture of three elements—interests, commitments and capabilities. States develop their interests on the basis of a range of factors, including economics, politics, security, geography, history, individual leadership, culture (most notably ethnicity and religion) and the unpredictability of unfolding events. Consequently, leaders make commitments that are, in turn, contingent on the state's economic, military and political capabilities at a particular historical juncture.

During the Cold War, the United States developed and implemented foreign policies that responded primarily, if not always exclusively, to its bipolar struggle against the Soviet Union. Notwithstanding their individual particularities, the presidential administrations serving in office between the conclusion of World War II in August 1945 and the implosion of the Soviet Union in December 1991 each defined American interests relative to those pursued by the leadership in Moscow at a given point. Most such policies were based at least in part on the containment doctrine outlined by seminal Cold War strategist George F. Kennan in the aftermath of World War II. The Harry S. Truman administration, for example, opened the Cold War by committing itself to the economic prosperity, political integration and military security of Western Europe (through Marshall Plan grants and the establishment of the North Atlantic Treaty Organization [NATO], respectively) in order to limit the Soviet sphere of influence to Eastern and Central Europe. The Ronald W. Reagan administration, by contrast, successfully pursued the rollback of Soviet influence at the global level by increasing US military spending during the 1980s to a level at which Moscow could no longer compete and elected to release the vice grip it had previously held on its sphere of influence. The George H.W. Bush administration was left to orchestrate, if not preside over, the opening act of the restoration of democracy across Eastern and Central Europe in 1989-90 culminating in the reunification of Germany in October 1990. While by no means unchallenging, the policies each of these leaders and their advisors crafted were a product of an all but identically structured international system. In short, they each had a familiar bipolar model to use as a point of departure in developing and implementing their respective policies.

The first post-Cold War administration—that run by Clinton and his advisors—had no such initial blueprint to consult. Instead, Clinton's foreign policy team (along with, for that matter, myriad scholars of international relations) struggled to develop a model to fit a system no longer conditioned by the actions of two superpowers grappling for power and influence across the world. For their part, scholars offered five general paradigms with potential applicability to the emerging post-Cold War order. The first model, of which Francis Fukuyama was the principal advocate, predicted a diminution of, if not an end to, conflict as a byproduct of the victory of the American-led West over the Soviet-sponsored East in the Cold War.[9] The second, put forward by Samuel P. Huntington, mirrored the Cold War system but replaced the ideological confrontation pitting the United States against the Soviet Union with cleavages rooted in religious, economic and cultural differences, which, he predicted, would divide the world between North and South, Christianity and Islam, and Orient and Occident.[10] The third reflected the self-help world of neo-realists such as Kenneth Waltz and John Mearsheimer, with states striving to advance their interests unilaterally in an anarchical international environment.[11] The fourth, proposed by Zbigniew Brzezinski and Robert Kaplan among others, focused on the intensification of ethnic conflict manifested in a proliferation of failed states in regions as geographically diverse as Central Africa and the former Yugoslavia.[12]

Above all else, the promulgation of such a dissimilar set of models reflected the uncertainty prevalent within the international system in the aftermath of the Cold War. That uncertainty complicated the foreign policy construction process to such an extent that the Clinton administration failed to develop a clear blueprint to help guide American engagement abroad during either of its two terms. Rather than prioritize US interests consistently on the basis of a particular region of the globe or issue area, the administration launched and pursued a wide variety of initiatives, ranging from military intervention in the Balkans to often overbearing mediation in the context of the Israeli-Palestinian peace process, few of which it followed through to completion. As Richard Haass, President of the Council on Foreign Relations and former head of policy planning under Secretary of State Colin Powell, has argued, "Clinton inherited a world of unprecedented American advantage and opportunity and did little with it. ... A foreign legacy can result either from achieving something great on the ground (defeating major rivals or building major institutions, for example) or from changing the way people at home or abroad think about international relations. Clinton did neither."[13]

There were two causes for the Clinton administration's lack of strategic vision, neither of which was entirely the President's fault. First, Clinton's longevity in the White House detracted from his ability to maintain a foreign policy team whose members shared the same viewpoints throughout his tenure. He had two National Security Advisors (Anthony Lake and Samuel Berger), three Secretaries of Defense (Les Aspin, William Perry and William Cohen) and two Secretaries of State (Warren

Christopher and Madeleine Albright) in eight years, most of whom had at least subtly different ideas of how to define and pursue US interests. Albright and Berger, for instance, tended to have a greater affinity for the use of military force—albeit still of a limited nature—than either Lake or Christopher. Second, Clinton assumed office in the immediate aftermath of the Cold War, a period during which the American public had no appetite for the expression of grand strategic visions or the expenditure of tax dollars abroad given that the threats previously presented by the either the Soviet behemoth or Saddam Hussein were at least perceived to have been eliminated. Clinton's personal interest in domestic as opposed to foreign policy—and the primacy he often ceded to the former at the expense of the latter—only complicated matters further.

Even once Clinton did decide to focus on foreign and security policy—in the context of his second term in particular—he and his advisors elected to try to do everything rather than concentrate on one or two initiatives. Consider, for instance, Berger's characterization of the President's legacy in January 2001: "Today ... America is by any measure the world's unchallenged military, economic and political power. The world counts on us to be a catalyst of coalitions, a broker of peace [and] a guarantor of global financial stability."[14] Berger's vision was also reflected in the Clinton administration's National Security Strategy (NSS) of December 1999. That document promulgated three fundamental objectives. First, "to enhance America's security." Second, "to bolster America's economic prosperity. And third, "to promote democracy and human rights abroad."[15]

None of those three broad goals suggested the existence of any one clear threat to American security, in response to which a robust defense was necessary. By contrast, the Bush administration's initial NSS, which was issued in September 2002 just over a year to the day of the anniversary of the 9/11 attacks and will be addressed in greater depth in Chapter 2, articulated three clear national interests—the defense, preservation and the extension of the peace by way of collaboration with the world's great powers at the expense of its terrorists and tyrants—on behalf of which Bush promised to employ America's unparalleled economic, military and political assets. However, it cleverly framed those interest-based objectives in principled rhetoric, explaining that the United States would endeavor to promote a "balance of power that favors ... political and economic freedom, peaceful relations with other states and respect for human dignity."[16] As Yale University historian John Lewis Gaddis, perhaps the most authoritative scholar of American national security strategy over the past half-century, has pointed out, the differences between the Bush NSS and the 1999 Clinton NSS "are revealing. The Bush objectives speak of defending, preserving, and extending the peace; the Clinton statement simply seems to assume peace. ...Even in these first few lines, then, the Bush NSS comes across as more forceful, more carefully crafted, and— unexpectedly—more multilateral than its immediate predecessor."[17]

The principal difference in the Clinton and Bush administrations' respective approaches to national security was related primarily to the changing nature of the threats to US interests, which grew directly out of Al Qaeda's assaults on the World Trade Center and Pentagon. Although the Bush administration waited a year to articulate a formal NSS through which it would confront transnational terrorist organizations (primarily, but not exclusively, Al Qaeda) and their state sponsors (most notably Iraq and Iran), the fundamental tenets of that strategy quickly became apparent in the immediate aftermath of the attacks and over the subsequent weeks and months. Upon learning of the attacks, one thing was clear in Bush's mind: in striking their targets in New York and Washington, the hijackers had committed an act of war against the United States, one that would require a response that extended far beyond a domestic law enforcement investigation (Clinton's preferred means to deal with Al Qaeda during his two terms). As Bush recalled, "I ... realized we're under attack. This is a war and it took me no time to realize it was a war."[18]

Although Bush did not use the word "war" in describing the attacks in his address to the nation on the evening of 11 September, the President and his advisors wasted little time in framing the struggle against Al Qaeda that was to follow in precisely such terms in the ensuing days, weeks and months. Less than 48 hours after his nationally televised address, Bush issued a statement in which he stressed explicitly, "on September 11, 2001, terrorists attacked America in a series of despicable *acts of war* [emphasis added]."[19] Similarly, at a prayer service at the National Cathedral in Washington the next day, the President declared, "war has been waged against us by stealth and deceit and murder. This nation is peaceful, but fierce when stirred to anger. This conflict was begun on the timing and terms of others. It will end in a way, and at an hour, of our choosing."[20] By describing the attacks as acts of war, Bush was essentially providing the pretext for the conduct of military operations against Al Qaeda and its state and non-state partners in response as opposed to an approach focusing only on the use of domestic law enforcement bodies to bring the perpetrators to justice.

Next, in the context of his 23 September address to Congress, Bush began preparing the public for the conduct of a global war against terrorism he suggested would be as pivotal to America's future as was true of the ideological struggle pitting the United States against the Soviet Union between 1945 and 1991. In laying out the scope of the conflict Washington stood prepared to wage, the President noted that "our enemy is a radical network of terrorists, and every government that supports them. Our war on terror begins with Al Qaeda, but it does not end there. It will not end until every terrorist of global reach has been found, stopped and defeated." Furthermore, he cautioned, "our response involves far more than instant retaliation and isolated strikes. Americans should not expect one battle, but a lengthy campaign, unlike any other we have ever seen. It may include dramatic strikes, visible on TV, and covert operations, secret even in success. We will starve terrorists of funding, turn them one against another, drive them from place to place until there is no refuge or no rest. And we will pursue nations that provide aid or safe haven to terrorism."[21] The struggle Bush described was one triggered by the events of 9/11, but also one that could have begun and been conducted much more vigorously when Al Qaeda first emerged as a legitimate threat to US interests—both at home and abroad—under Clinton's watch during the 1990s.

Al Qaeda and the United States: From Clinton to Bush

When the Clinton administration entered office in January 1993, the principal security threats it would face in the future were understandably unclear. However, Clinton's failure to mitigate, if not eliminate, one such threat—that posed by Al Qaeda—over the ensuing eight years, was arguably his greatest shortcoming as president, particularly given the devastating nature of the attacks that organization staged on 9/11. Ultimately, Clinton and his advisors made two sets of errors with respect to the manner in which they chose to confront bin Laden's organization. First, they were late to recognize the severity of the dangers posed by Al Qaeda, choosing to treat terrorism as a law enforcement rather than national security issue.   Second, even after acknowledging the grave threats presented by bin Laden, they remained reluctant to take decisive military action against either Al Qaeda or those regimes upon which it was suspected of relying for support.

In order to assess the extent to which the Clinton administration should be faulted for its inability, or perhaps unwillingness, to weaken, if not liquidate Al Qaeda, it is necessary to review the opportunities it had to respond to terrorist acts carried out by bin Laden and his supporters, how effectively or ineffectively it handled those chances and why that was the case in each instance. Given that this discussion is only one component of the broader chapter and manuscript, assessments of the following four such examples are sufficient: the February 1993 bombing of the World Trade Center in New York; the foiled plot to detonate bombs aboard 11 airliners over the Pacific Ocean and subsequent failure to secure bin Laden's extradition from Sudan in 1995-96; the August 1998 bombings of the American Embassies in Nairobi, Kenya, and Dar-es-Salaam, Tanzania; and the October 2000 bombing of the USS *Cole*. The subsequent paragraphs address each case in turn.[22]

The Clinton administration's first opportunity to deal with an act of terrorism directed against the United States came on 26 February 1993. That morning, a group of terrorists led by a man named Ramzi Yousef parked a rental van packed with explosives in a garage beneath the North Tower of the World Trade Center. They then lit the fuses attached to the bomb and fled. The resulting explosion caused limited damage to the infrastructure of the tower, killing six people and injuring 1,000 more.[23]

Yousef, who was traveling on an Iraqi passport at the time and not apprehended until February 1995, later boasted to Federal Bureau of Investigation (FBI) agents that the objective of the operation had been to collapse the foundation of the North Tower, causing it to topple into the adjacent South Tower in hopes of killing up to 250,000, a catastrophe that would have dwarfed the losses entailed in the 9/11 attacks.[24] The subsequent FBI investigation of the bombing uncovered considerable evidence linking Al Qaeda to the operation, a development that proved a indicator of the rising threats bin Laden was to present to US interests in the years to come.[25]

Clinton based his 1992 presidential campaign primarily, if not exclusively, on domestic rather than foreign policy issues, most notably those associated with economic and social programs. He had minimal experience in international security affairs and the chief foreign policy advisors he chose (Christopher and Lake among others) were skeptical of the robust use of military force to back diplomatic overtures. Viewed against that backdrop, Clinton's response to the 1993 bombing of the World Trade Center was hardly surprising. He chose to view the attack as an isolated act carried out by a loosely affiliated group of individuals as opposed to a coordinated assault planned and orchestrated by a transnational terrorist organization, let alone one with any state backing whatsoever. As a result, the administration limited its response to a criminal investigation carried out unilaterally by the FBI, an approach that left national security institutions such as the Central Intelligence Agency (CIA) and Department of Defense largely out of the equation. This lack of collaboration reduced the potential to uncover Al Qaeda's misdeeds in an expeditious fashion, one that cost the administration valuable time in identifying bin Laden as a credible national security threat.[26]

Gradually, Clinton did come to recognize the pressing nature of the rising dangers presented by Al Qaeda. However, he remained reluctant to take decisive action to counter those threats, most emphatically so during his initial term in office. In January 1995, for example, a collaborative effort between US and Filipino domestic law enforcement agencies uncovered a second terrorist plot involving Yousef, an individual named Abdul Hakim Murad and an Al Qaeda agent called Khalid Shaikh Mohammed. The plan called for the planting and detonation of bombs aboard 11 commercial airplanes bound from points in Asia to sites in the United States, with the explosions to occur over the Pacific Ocean and result in the deaths of some 4,000 Americans.[27] Fortunately, the plan never came to fruition. Instead, the Filipino police apprehended Murad in Manila in January 1995, and Yousef was taken into custody by Pakistani Special Forces and FBI agents in Islamabad, Pakistan, the next month. Mohammed, on the other hand, remained at large.[28]

Yousef's apprehension and conviction for his role in the World Trade Center bombing in a subsequent trial in New York in 1996 contributed to the development of an increased emphasis within the Clinton administration on dealing with the bin Laden problem. Regrettably, Clinton and his national security team proceeded to squander repeated opportunities to secure bin Laden's extradition from Sudan to the United States over the course of the 1996 election year. Bin Laden had set up a base of operations in Sudan following his expulsion from Saudi Arabia in the wake of his repeated criticisms of the political leadership in the Kingdom in 1991. Notwithstanding denials by some Clinton administration officials, published reports that have emerged in recent years indicate that Sudan offered to deliver bin Laden to the Americans—either directly or by way of a third country—on repeated occasions during 1996. Such offers were made to contacts in the CIA, the Department of State and in the US private sector.[29] Whether or not the Sudanese would actually have delivered bin Laden remains open to question. What is clear is that the political leadership in Khartoum eventually forced him to leave the country in May 1996, at which point he relocated to Afghanistan, where he reconstituted the Al Qaeda infrastructure that he used to orchestrate the events of 9/11.

Had the Clinton administration elected to engage Sudan more vigorously, the attacks bin Laden carried out in subsequent years could perhaps have been prevented.

One explanation as to why Clinton did not choose to pursue bin Laden any more vigorously at that juncture was that he wanted to maintain a positive focus rather than panic the public prior to the November 1996 Presidential Election, which he won convincingly over former Republican Senator Robert Dole. Dick Morris, one of Clinton's top domestic political advisors during his initial term, for example, notes that, "on issues of terrorism, defense and foreign affairs, generally, [Clinton] was always too wary of criticism to act decisively."[30] Unfortunately, the trend Morris points out continued throughout Clinton's final four years in the White House as well, a period during which the President had two clear opportunities to respond decisively to attacks carried out by Al Qaeda on American civilian and military targets—the August 2001 African embassy bombings and the October 2000 bombing of the USS *Cole*.

In May 1998, bin Laden called a press conference of sorts at an undisclosed site near Khost in Afghanistan, the vast majority of the territory of which was under the control of the Taliban. He used the occasion to publicly declare war against the United States for the fifth time since October 1996.[31] Three months later, Al Qaeda carried out bombings of the US Embassies in Nairobi, Kenya, and Dar-es-Salaam, Tanzania. The attack in Kenya killed 256 people and injured another 4,500; the strike in Tanzania left 11 dead. Among the casualties were several American diplomats. Clinton responded as forcefully as he had to any previous Al Qaeda assault to that point, authorizing cruise missile strikes on an alleged chemical weapons factory in Khartoum, Sudan (which the administration suspected of collaboration in the embassy bombings) and Al Qaeda training camps in Afghanistan.[32] It remains unclear whether the factory in Khartoum ever actually produced chemical weapons of any sort rather than pharmaceutical supplies (as the Sudanese claimed). And the missiles directed at the training camps in Afghanistan neither resulted in bin Laden's death nor reduced markedly Al Qaeda's capacity to threaten US interests. In short, pinprick strikes sent the wrong message to bin Laden: that Washington lacked the political will to use the full extent of its military assets against Al Qaeda. As Mike Rolince, former chief of the international terrorism division at the FBI, asserted in an interview with *National Review* editor Rich Lowry, "What you told bin Laden is that he could go and level two embassies, and in response, we're going to knock down a few huts. If you're bin Laden, that sounds like a real legitimate cost of doing business."[33]

Bin Laden continued conducting the business to which Rolince refers with tragic repercussions in the context of the October 2001 bombing of the USS *Cole*. Al Qaeda operatives carried out the attack by guiding a small explosives-laden boat across the harbor in the port of Aden, Yemen, to the side of the *Cole*, where they detonated it. The resulting explosion ripped a hole in the side of the *Cole*, killing 17 American sailors and severely wounding 39 more in the process. Clinton dispatched a team of FBI investigators to Yemen and considered a military response against Al Qaeda once reliable evidence as to its involvement in the attack was uncovered, but ultimately decided not to use force.[34] There are two interrelated reasons why it stands to reason that Clinton chose to act the way he did. First, he was within three months of the end of his final term and preoccupied with forging an enduring foreign policy legacy.

Second, he had spent much of the previous year attempting to base that legacy upon the achievement of a lasting peace between the Israelis and Palestinians. Put simply, launching missile strikes against bin Laden—who was viewed favorably by many Palestinians and Muslims in the broader Middle East—let alone a war on terror, would have undermined his last-ditch, albeit ultimately futile efforts, at resolving the Israeli-Palestinian conflict.

When Bush took office in January 2001, he was left with the Clinton administration's legacy of relative inactivity in dealing with the perpetually rising security threats posed by Al Qaeda. Rather than pressure the Taliban, which harbored bin Laden in Afghanistan from 1996-2001, diplomatically or consider the deployment of military forces in that context, Clinton chose to pursue bin Laden primarily through domestic law enforcement bodies and weaken Al Qaeda to the limited extent possible through one flurry of limited cruise missile strikes. As Morris contends, "All our [present] terrorist problems were born during the Clinton years. It was during his eight years in office that [Al] Qaeda began its campaign of bombing and destruction aimed at the United States. ... Bill Clinton and his advisors were alerted to the group's power and intentions by these attacks. But they did nothing to stop [Al] Qaeda from building up its resources for the big blow on 9/11."[35] And, regrettably, although perhaps somewhat more understandably, the Bush administration's approach to the issues of terrorism generally and Al Qaeda specifically proved no more robust than Clinton's as the President and his advisors worked to craft an effective foreign and security policy blueprint in the weeks and months preceding the events of 9/11.

Prior to assuming office, Bush joined Vice President-elect Dick Cheney and National Security Advisor to be Condoleezza Rice at a briefing conducted by Clinton's third Director of Central Intelligence, George Tenet. In the context of the briefing, Tenet—who retained his position when Bush took office—warned all three that bin Laden represented a "tremendous threat" to American interests at home and abroad, one that was "immediate."[36] Over the ensuing months, the CIA issued several more warnings, including 34 communications intercepts in the summer of 2001 indicating that Al Qaeda was planning a major operation against the United States by issuing subtly coded statements such as "Zero hour is tomorrow" or "Something spectacular is coming."[37] These warnings stirred the Bush administration to action, albeit of a sort that had not extended beyond the planning stage when Al Qaeda launched its attacks on the World Trade Center and Pentagon. Rice, for example, was in the process of preparing a National Security Directive (NSD) on the issue on September 10, one that built on lower-level National Security Council discussions on the construction of a strategy to eliminate Al Qaeda.[38] That planning, of course, shifted rapidly into concrete military action against both Al Qaeda and the Taliban in the aftermath of 9/11. And the conduct of Operation Enduring Freedom proved to be just the initial battle in the Bush administration's conduct of a broader war against transnational terrorist groups and their state sponsors. Ultimately, that war came to include the confrontation and elimination of an American adversary that—similar to bin Laden's Al Qaeda—the Clinton administration had failed to deal with decisively: Saddam Hussein's Iraq.

Saddam Hussein and the United States: From Clinton to Bush

Over the course of Clinton's two terms in office, his administration sought to mitigate Saddam's potential to develop nuclear, chemical and biological WMD and, perhaps, eventually transfer those munitions to terrorist organizations by relying upon the UN to dispatch weapons inspectors to Iraq and oversee Baghdad's use of proceeds from the sale of its petroleum resources for essential items such as food and medicine. It also employed limited military force against Iraq on several occasions from 1993-98, the most robust of which came in response to Saddam's expulsion of the weapons inspectors in December 1998. According to Kenneth Pollack, the point man on Iraq in Berger's NSC, "Bill Clinton was certainly not looking to make Iraq the centerpiece of his foreign policy. And when the President found himself in domestic political turmoil as a result of the Monica Lewinsky affair, avoiding foreign policy crises became an even greater priority."[39] Consequently, Clinton attempted to contain the threats posed by Iraq on the cheap in terms of both economic and political capital, domestically as well as internationally. As journalists and public policy analysts Lawrence Kaplan and William Kristol assert, the "Clinton administration avoided confronting the moral and strategic challenge presented by Saddam, hoping instead that an increasingly weak policy of containment, punctuated by the occasional fusillade of cruise missiles, would suffice to keep Saddam in his box."[40]

As was the case with the evaluation of Clinton's handling of the threats posed by Al Qaeda, which appeared in the previous section, an assessment of his administration's management of US policy toward Iraq from 1993-2001 is best achieved through a review of the most significant crises that defined the relationship between Washington and Baghdad during that period. Four such imbroglios stand out above the rest: foiled spring 1993 plot by the Iraqi intelligence service (Mukhabbarat) to assassinate former American President George H.W. Bush during a trip to Kuwait to commemorate the coalition victory in the 1990-91 Persian Gulf War; the brief mobilization of Iraqi forces along the Kuwaiti border in October 1994; stillborn US-backed plots to overthrow Saddam's regime in March 1995 (by Kurdish and Iraqi National Congress [INC] forces) and June 1996 (by rogue military officers); and a 1997-98 showdown between Saddam and the Clinton administration that ended with the formal expulsion of UN weapons inspectors from Iraq in the aftermath of the conduct of Operation Desert Fox in December 1998.

In April 1993, former President George H.W. Bush planned a visit to Kuwait to commemorate the American-led expulsion of Iraqi invaders from that state in the context of the 1990-91 Persian Gulf War. A day before Bush's arrival, the Kuwaiti authorities announced that they had uncovered and foiled a Mukhabbarat plot to assassinate him. The Mukhabbarat had planned to detonate a bomb in the center of Kuwait City as Bush's motorcade drove through. The bomb had already been planted and was uncovered by the Kuwaitis, who passed the information on to the Clinton administration. Subsequent CIA and FBI investigations confirmed that the explosives indeed had the markings of the Mukhabbarat. [41] Two months later, Clinton retaliated against Iraq by authorizing the launch of 23 cruise missiles into the Mukhabbarat headquarters in Baghdad, an attack that occurred in the middle of the night when the building was largely deserted and thus destroyed potentially valuable intelligence files but killed few operatives.[42] By Clinton's standards, it was a relatively forceful response. To Saddam, who had retained power despite the Gulf War and ruthlessly crushed domestic revolts by the Kurds in the north and Shiites in the south following that conflict, it was likely perceived as a sign of weakness, one he would attempt to exploit with gradually but consistently increasing degrees of success in subsequent years. As former CIA Director James Woolsey recalled in one published report: after an exhaustive two-month investigation, Clinton "fired a couple of dozen cruise missiles into an empty building in the middle of the night, which is a sufficiently weak response to be almost laughable."[43]

However, while it stands to reason that the nature of Clinton's response to the assassination plot against Bush may have emboldened Saddam, the second confrontation between the two was resolved in a manner more beneficial to the United States. At the conclusion of the Persian Gulf War, Saddam agreed to abide by restrictions on WMD development and also to accept economic sanctions regulating Baghdad's income from its oil resources—both subject to UN oversight and verification—in the context of Security Council Resolution 687. Annoyed by American insistence that the sanctions remain in place indefinitely, Saddam challenged Clinton by amassing approximately 80,000 troops along the border between Iraq and Kuwait. The United States countered with Operation Vigilant Warrior, a reinforcement effort that quickly raised American troop strength in the Persian Gulf region from 13,000 to 60,000. Clinton's reaction, along with an explicit warning from US and British military officers that they would strike the Iraqis if they did not pull their forces back from the border region, forced Saddam to back down.[44] Thus, in this instance, Clinton's approach proved effective. Unfortunately, the President did not prove nearly so resolute over the long term.

During the run-up to the 1996 Presidential Election, Clinton was willing to allow his advisors some latitude in the development of plans to weaken, if not eliminate, the Iraqi regime from within. A more direct use of US military force, on the other hand, was deemed too risky in an election year. Saddam, for his part, focused concurrently on limiting the damage the UN Special Commission for the Disarmament of Iraq (UNSCOM) could inflict on his WMD programs and maintaining firm political control at the domestic level through the ruthless repression of any and all who sought to defy his regime. Against this backdrop, the Clinton administration generally and the CIA specifically set about planning two insurgency operations: one a collaborative effort with Kurdish Democratic Party head Mazud Barzani and exiled INC leader Ahmed Chalabi in 1995 and the second a coup under the leadership of an anti-Saddam faction in the upper levels of the Iraqi security services and military. Regrettably, but perhaps not unexpectedly, given Saddam's penchant for survival over the years, neither plot came to fruition. A March 1995 offensive by Kurdish forces near the northern city of Irbil appeared promising initially but the dispatch of reinforcements from the Iraqi Republican Guard in Baghdad caused the United States (which itself was unprepared to provide substantial military support should the situation sour) to caution the Kurds to stand down, which they did. The coup was also stillborn. The Mukhabbarat uncovered the plot and liquidated the conspirators in June 1996.[45] Ultimately, neither operation proved particularly damaging to Clinton politically, which was probably one of the principal reasons he approved both to begin with.

Not surprisingly, Clinton proved increasingly unwilling to take any marked political risks in confronting Iraq over the final four years of his tenure in the White House. Similar to the President's restrained approach to dealing with Al Qaeda, he limited himself to one relatively small-scale military operation in the face of Saddam's perpetual defiance of UNSCOM inspectors in 1997 and 1998 prior to their final departure from Iraq in the run-up to Operation Desert Fox. The start of Clinton's second term in January 1997 coincided with the commencement of a campaign by Saddam to gradually frustrate UNSCOM's efforts, while reconstituting at least some of his WMD capabilities with proceeds siphoned from the oil proceeds allowed by the UN in order to (theoretically but by no means practically) provide food and medicine to the Iraqi people. Differences within the Security Council between the United States and the United Kingdom on one hand, and France, Russia and China on the other, who favored strict and loose enforcement of the UN's resolutions, respectively, only strengthened Saddam's hand. As Pollack explains, Saddam's "goals were to impede UNSCOM's progress, exacerbate the growing differences within the Security Council, and antagonize the United States without presenting enough of a provocation to justify a major military response. However, he was also looking to fight back against the inspectors' efforts to penetrate the security of his regime."[46]

Ultimately, it was Iraq's repeated provocations in the latter issue area that led to an American military response in the context of Operation Desert Fox. In the months preceding that operation, Saddam had repeatedly denied UNSCOM inspectors access to many of his presidential palaces, mammoth structures, where many suspected he had hidden WMD. In February 1998, UN Secretary General Kofi Annan traveled to Baghdad, where he negotiated a temporary compromise through which the inspectors were granted "unrestricted access" to all sites in Iraq. However, by November, Iraqi officials were still routinely turning inspectors away from a variety of sensitive "presidential sites." The next month, the United States conducted four days of air and cruise missile strikes on a range of Iraqi targets, just 11 of 97 of which were directed at suspected WMD sites.[47] When the operation was complete, Iraq permanently expelled the inspectors and Saddam remained free of anything but token diplomatic pressure to comply with the UN resolutions over the balance of Clinton's term. As Kaplan and Kristol conclude, the "whole business reflected the administration's refusal to employ measures of genuine strategic effectiveness. The Clinton policy toward Iraq may have comforted the sensibilities of its architects—but not nearly so much as it comforted Saddam Hussein, who, by the time Clinton left office, was out of the box whose confines had been mostly imaginary to begin with."[48]

As was the case with Al Qaeda, Clinton left George W. Bush to deal with an increasingly threatening Iraq at the start of the latter's tenure as President in January 2001. Similar to its approach toward Al Qaeda, the Bush administration's overt campaign to confront Saddam and eventually liquidate his regime (which will be discussed in detail later in the monograph) did not pick up steam until after the terrorist attacks of 9/11 in general and the conduct of Operation Enduring Freedom in particular. In short, Bush used his January 2002 State of the Union address to put Saddam on notice that his administration would not allow Iraq nearly so much latitude vis-à-vis compliance with UN resolutions as did Clinton's. Ultimately, the Bush administration made Iraq the focal point of its preemptive National Security Strategy. In each instance, Bush's decisions were based on the threats posed both by Iraq itself and the potential dual dangers posed by Baghdad's collaboration with transnational terrorist groups such as Al Qaeda.

Evaluation of the Linkages Between Al Qaeda, Iraq and the Events of 9/11

One of the most controversial aspects of the case the Bush administration put forward in the months preceding the Second Iraq War was the extent to which Saddam's regime had a relationship with Al Qaeda and played a role in the events of 9/11, either directly or indirectly. A central element of that case, for example, was the suggestion forwarded by several members of the administration that the United States could no longer afford to take a chance that a state such as Iraq would transfer WMD to a terrorist organization like Al Qaeda, which, as demonstrated by the attacks on the World Trade Center and Pentagon, had the capacity and the will to strike civilian as well as military targets with any means at its disposal. In order to assess the probability of the emergence of that type of threat, in turn, it is first essential to review the evidence indicating Iraq's willingness to support terrorism. This section conducts that assessment through the presentation of subsections that address the following three issues: Saddam's relationship with terrorist organizations in general since assuming power as Iraqi President in July 1979; the linkages between Saddam's regime and Al Qaeda in the 1990s and 2000s; and the role, if any, Iraq played in the planning and conduct of the 9/11 assaults.

Linkages Between Saddam and Terrorism in General

Evidence of relationships between Saddam and terrorist organizations dates back to the 1970s. In particular, Saddam first expressed an interest in supporting international terrorism in the aftermath of the October 1973 Yom Kippur War, the last of a series of Arab-Israeli Wars that left Israel in control of territory in the West Bank, Golan Heights, Gaza Strip and Suez Canal corridor abutting Jordan, Syria and Egypt, respectively. Put simply, Palestine Liberation Organization (PLO) Chairman Yasser Arafat's refusal to openly denounce Egyptian President Anwar Sadat's subsequent willingness to pursue a peace dialogue with Israel—the first step on the road to the negotiation of the 1979 Camp David Accords—infuriated Saddam, who was not yet Iraqi President but held considerable power in the inner circle of the political leadership in Baghdad. As a result, Saddam ordered the closure of the PLO's offices in Baghdad and began to pursue relationships with a number of other radical Palestinian groups, who were equally disgruntled over Arafat's acquiescence to the warming state of affairs between Egypt and Israel. The most notable individual associated with these groups was the Palestinian terrorist Sabri al-Banna, more commonly known as Abu Nidal.[49]

Nidal first moved to Baghdad in 1970 as a representative of Arafat's Fatah organization, but it was not until his split with the PLO that he began to rely directly on support from Saddam to fund his increasing array of terrorist activities. Those endeavors ranged from attacks on political figures within the PLO and neighboring states (most notably Syria) with which the Iraqi leadership had grievances to spectacular strikes on Western civilians such as the bombing of the Israeli airline El Al's ticket counters at the Rome and Vienna airports that killed 18 and injured 110, including many American tourists in December 1985. In addition to Nidal, Iraq played host to Popular Front for the Liberation of Palestine (PFLP) figures including Dr Wadi Haddad and Dr George Habash during the 1970s and, according to one Iraqi defector, Saddam continued to harbor some 50 PFLP members into the 1990s.[50] Saddam's support for men such as Nidal, Haddad, Habash and their respective operations is the principal reason Iraq was first placed on the US Department of State's list of state sponsors of terrorism in the late 1970s. As David Mack, who served as political officer at the American Embassy in Baghdad at the time, recalled in one published report, "we all knew precisely where Abu Nidal's house was located, although, of course, we weren't allowed to go there. Saddam liked to keep these groups there for show."[51] Saddam himself admitted as much in a July 1978 interview with *Newsweek*, acknowledging that, "regarding the Palestinians, it's no secret: Iraq is open to them and they are free to train and plan [terrorist attacks] here."[52]

When Arafat engaged in negotiations with Israel in the context of the 1993 Oslo Process, resulting in the establishment of the Palestinian Authority and subsequent ceding of limited governmental control to that entity over the administration of territory in the Gaza Strip and West Bank, Saddam did what he could to destabilize that process—and, by association—the broader Middle East by offering financial inducements for suicide attacks organized by groups such as Hamas, Islamic Jihad and the Al Aqsa Martyr's Brigade. In particular, Saddam made a habit of paying $25,000 to the families of individuals who carried out suicide bombings against targets in Israel during the 1990s and 2000s, a bounty he eventually increased to $50,000.[53] These initiatives served both to improve Saddam's image in the Arab and broader Islamic worlds in the aftermath of the 1990-91 Persian Gulf War given the widespread support for the Palestinian cause that exists in those regions and also to complicate the Clinton administration's attempt to forge a lasting settlement in the Israeli-Palestinian peace process. Ultimately, Clinton's efforts to achieve that objective collapsed amidst the eruption of the Al Aqsa *intifada* in the fall and winter of 2000-01, an outcome Saddam can claim to have played at least a marginal role in producing.

Linkages Between Saddam's Regime and Al Qaeda

Notwithstanding the relevance of the relationships Iraq built with the aforementioned terrorist groups in the 1970s and 1980s, allegations of linkages between Saddam's regime and Al Qaeda during the 1990s are considerably more germane to this study. A wide range of published reports appearing prior to—and, even more so, since—the events of 9/11 reveal evidence suggesting the existence of clear ties linking Iraq to Al Qaeda generally and to a range of terrorist operations directed against targets both within and outside of the United States from 1993-2003. In order to assess that evidence rationally, this section will examine it in two interconnected clusters (those relating to Iraqi funding and training of bin Laden's operatives and the extent to which Saddam's regime was directly involved in attacks on American targets at home and abroad) as a foundation for a discussion of the linkages (or lack thereof) between Baghdad and Al Qaeda's 9/11 strikes on the World Trade Center and Pentagon.

The most credible evidence of linkages between Saddam Hussein's regime and Al Qaeda that has appeared in the public record to date pertains to individual contacts between the two and the funding, logistical support and training provided by officials associated with the former to members of the latter. The sources from which the evidence under consideration here is drawn range from speeches delivered by Bush and his advisors and declassified intelligence reports delivered by CIA officials to Congress to a range of American and international media reports and exhaustively researched monographs addressing the relationships cultivated between Iraq and Al Qaeda during the 1990s and 2000. Collectively, these sources lay out in detail the existence of contacts between representatives of the Iraqi government and Al Qaeda that began as early as 1990 and continued into 2003.[54] An October 2002 letter to the Senate Intelligence Committee from CIA Director Tenet is one notable case in point. In that letter, Tenet stressed that "we have solid reporting of senior level contacts between Iraq and Al Qaeda going back a decade," including "credible reporting that Al Qaeda leaders sought contacts in Iraq who could help them acquire WMD capabilities."[55]

One of the most comprehensive accounts of the Iraq-Al Qaeda relationship to date appeared in *Weekly Standard* reporter Stephen F. Hayes' article on a leaked secret memo from Bush administration officials to the Senate Intelligence Committee in October 2003. According to Hayes' reporting, the 50-point memo makes the following points: First, contacts between Saddam's regime and Al Qaeda commenced in 1990 and continued until days before the start of the Second Iraq War in March 2003, including notable bursts of activity coinciding with the showdown pitting Baghdad against Washington from February-December 1998. Second, such contacts, which were both direct and indirect in character (some within Iraq and some in other states, including Afghanistan, Pakistan, Sudan and the Czech Republic), led to the cultivation of a mutually beneficial relationship in the context of which Saddam offered financial backing to Al Qaeda, and bin Laden reciprocated by criticizing the American-backed UN sanctions on Baghdad in repeated *fatwas* declaring war on the United States. Third, while the memo is inconclusive regarding direct links connecting Saddam to Al Qaeda's attacks on US targets at home and abroad during the 1990s and 2000s, it does suggest that Iraq regularly trained Al Qaeda operatives in the conduct of terrorist operations.[56]

Among the contacts Hayes has cited in his reporting on the links between Saddam's regime and Al Qaeda was a 1994 meeting between an Iraqi intelligence agent named Farouk Hijazi and bin Laden in Sudan. Hijazi was captured by American troops near the Syrian border following the fall of Baghdad in April 2003.[57] Another newspaper report suggested that Hijazi had traveled to the mountains near Kandahar, Afghanistan, in December 1998 to offer bin Laden asylum in Iraq.[58] The Bush administration also believes that a senior Al Qaeda operative—Abu Musab al-Zarqawi—received medical treatment in Baghdad after he was wounded in fighting with US troops during Operation Enduring Freedom, a claim the President himself made in his January 2003 State of the Union address.[59] In addition to these examples, Iraq itself identified an individual named Abd-al-Karim Muhammad Aswad as the "official in charge of the regime's contacts with [bin Laden's] group and currently the regime's representative in Pakistan" in a November 2002 article in *Babil*, a newspaper run by Saddam's son Uday.[60]

As to Iraq's involvement in attacks carried out by Al Qaeda against American targets, the most compelling case to date has been made by scholar Laurie Mylroie, a former campaign advisor to Clinton who now publishes a weekly online newsletter entitled *Iraq News*. In a masterfully researched 2001 work entitled *Study of Revenge: The First World Trade Center Attack and Saddam Hussein's War against America*, Mylroie argued that the February 1993 bombing of the North Tower of the World Trade Center was orchestrated by Iraq and carried out by Yousef (also known as Rashid the Iraqi), who has since been linked directly to Al Qaeda as well as Saddam's regime. In particular, Mylroie echoes an assessment she contends was the consensus among senior FBI agents who investigated that attack: that it "is best understood as a 'false flag' operation run by Iraq, leaving the Muslim extremists who participated in the conspiracy behind, to be arrested." She also contends and provides considerable documentary evidence linking Iraq to Yousef's foiled attempt to plant and detonate bombs aboard 11 airliners bound for the United States over the Pacific Ocean in 1995.[61] While perhaps not definitive, Mylroie's assertions appear all the more credible when one considers the contacts between Iraq and Al Qaeda denoted above.

Iraq's Role—or Lack Thereof—in the Events of 9/11

While no member of the Bush administration has never argued publicly that Iraq was directly involved in either the planning or conduct of the 9/11 attacks on the World Trade Center and Pentagon, it is possible to construct a limited circumstantial case that suggests the existence of precisely such a linkage. It is perhaps most appropriate to begin articulating that case with an examination of Saddam's own behavior on the morning of the attacks and over the ensuing days. In the hours prior to Al Qaeda's strikes in New York and Washington, Iraq placed its military forces on their highest level of alert since the outbreak of the 1990-91 Persian Gulf War. Saddam himself retreated into the depths of one of his fortified bunkers in Tikrit, the northern Iraqi city from which he first emerged as a powerful figure in the Baath Party.[62] Nor did Saddam's regime indicate any sign of even token disapproval of the attacks, which resulted in the loss of nearly 3,000 lives, most of them civilians, including some from the Greater Middle East. Iraq, for instance, was the only state among the 22 members of the Arab League not to condemn the strikes. Instead, it issued a statement claiming that the United States deserved the attacks.[63]

There are, of course, at least two contrasting explanations for Iraq's behavior concurrent with, and in the aftermath of, the events of 9/11. One, the most conservative of the two, is that Saddam approved of, but was not involved in, the attacks and nonetheless figured he would be a convenient target for retaliatory strikes by the United States given the consistently adversarial nature of the relationship between Washington and Baghdad from 1990-2001. Another, for which there is limited—albeit by no means definitive—evidence, is that Iraq was directly involved in the planning of the assaults and training of at least some of those Al Qaeda operatives who carried them out. Con Coughlin, who has written one of the more comprehensive recent biographies of Saddam's life, sums up these alternate explanations nicely, noting that the "intense secrecy and security that surrounded Saddam's every move meant it was impossible to say for sure why the Iraqi leader had placed his country on high alert and retreated to a bombproof shelter, but the timing alone was sufficient to raise suspicions."[64]

Three pieces of evidence in particular indicate that Iraq may indeed have played a role in the 9/11 attacks. First, two Iraqi defectors who were debriefed by Western intelligence officials in late 2001 claimed that Iraq had established a terrorist training camp at the Salman Pak military base south of Baghdad for use in training groups of Islamic fighters from Saudi Arabia, Yemen and Egypt. Furthermore, the camp's features included an old Boeing 707, which was employed to "teach the recruits how to hijack a plane using only their bare hands or knives, techniques similar to those used by the September 11 hijackers."[65] Second, the transitory Iraqi coalition government established after the elimination of Saddam's regime in the context of the Second Iraq War has produced a memo it claims documents a visit by 9/11 ring leader Mohammed Atta to that Salman Pak training camp in July 2001.[66] Third, Czech officials have asserted repeatedly that Atta met with Iraqi intelligence agent Ahmed al-Ani in Prague several times in 2000 and 2001.[67] While these pieces of evidence are circumstantial at best and have never been cited publicly by Bush administration officials, they certainly raise suspicions worthy of at least some consideration, particularly considering both Saddam's enmity toward the United States and his long history of support for terrorist organizations over the years.

Connecting the Dots: From 9/11 to the "Axis of Evil"

In the immediate aftermath of, and subsequent weeks and months following Al Qaeda's attacks on the World Trade Center and Pentagon, the Bush administration pursued two objectives that were initially distinctive and gradually grew more and more interconnected: confronting bin Laden and his Taliban hosts in Afghanistan on one hand and putting Saddam on notice that he was also in Washington's sights on the other. The administration pursued these objectives in two stages, the central elements of which were the conduct of Operation Enduring Freedom from October-December 2001 and the articulation of the "Axis of Evil" approach in the context of Bush's January 2002 State of the Union address, respectively. This section addresses each of these issues briefly, reiterating some of the most significant points raised in the opening two sections of the chapter.

Bush used his initial speeches in response to the events of 9/11—most notably those to the American public on the night of the attacks and before Congress on 23 September—to focus primarily on Al Qaeda and secondarily on those states willing either to cooperate with or directly harbor members of bin Laden's organization and other terrorist groups. During this period, the United States reformulated its strategy to counter threats posed by terrorists from one reliant on judicial measures and the occasional—and always limited—use of military force (the Clinton approach) to one drawing on all available diplomatic, economic, military and political means (the Bush approach). Ultimately, once the Taliban had refused to comply with American demands to turn over bin Laden to answer for Al Qaeda's attacks, the Bush administration used Operation Enduring Freedom to demonstrate credibly to terrorist groups and their state sponsors that the United States would henceforth back its policymakers' rhetoric with resolute military action that, when necessary, would extend beyond the pinprick air strikes that had been Clinton's weapon of choice.

Although some high-level advisors within his administration (most notably Secretary of Defense Donald Rumsfeld) pressed for the inclusion of military operations against Iraq in the initial American response to events of 9/11, Bush personally chose to deal with Al Qaeda and the Taliban in Afghanistan first, before enlarging the war on terror to include Saddam's regime and those presided over by the mullahs in Iran and Kim Jong-il in North Korea.[68] Once the United States had sent the necessarily forceful message to bin Laden and Mullah Omar by way of Operation Enduring Freedom, he turned to the threats posed by Iraq, Iran and North Korea generally and Iraq specifically. In the aforementioned State of the Union, he left no doubt that Washington would not hesitate to take action against any of the three but placed a particular emphasis on Saddam. Most significantly, he asserted that "Iraq continues to flaunt its hostility toward America and to support terror. The Iraqi regime has plotted to develop anthrax, and nerve gas, and nuclear weapons for over a decade" and cautioned that "all nation's should know: America will do what is necessary to ensure our nation's security."[69] In delivering this warning, Bush essentially fired the first rhetorical volley suggesting that the United States would in the future take action to preempt threats to American interests before such dangers had progressed to a stage at which they would prove difficult, if not impossible, to eliminate.

Conclusions

At its core, this chapter addressed five fundamental issues. First, it considered the changing nature of the perception of threats to the security of the United States since the events of 9/11. Second, it examined the dangers posed by Al Qaeda to American interests at home and abroad between 1993 and 2003, and the manners in which the Clinton and Bush administrations responded to those threats. Third, it assessed the distinctive policies pursued by the Clinton and Bush administrations toward Iraq during that period. Fourth, it reviewed and evaluated the evidence that has appeared in the public record suggesting the existence of linkages between Saddam's regime and terrorist organizations such as Al Qaeda generally and the extent to which it is likely that Iraq played a role in the planning and conduct of the 9/11 attacks on the World Trade Center and Pentagon specifically. Fifth, it discussed the Bush administration's subsequent transition from confronting Al Qaeda and the Taliban in the context of Operation Enduring Freedom in Afghanistan to building a case to eliminate Saddam's regime in Iraq.

The presentation, discussion and evaluation of these issues lead to the following conclusions. First, the 9/11 strikes demanded that the United States reformulate its approach to fighting terrorism such that all available economic, military and political options would be considered and, if necessary, utilized. Given the loss of life in New York and Washington those assaults entailed and the potential for even greater losses in the future, any other course of action would have been imprudent. Second, Clinton's approaches to confronting both Al Qaeda and Iraq from 1993-2001 proved ineffective in that they did not reduce appreciably the threats posed by either to US interests at home and abroad. Third, after reflecting on Clinton's limited use of force against bin Laden's organization and Saddam's regime during the 1990s, Bush and his advisors determined correctly that a more assertive approach was essential. The administration then used Operation Enduring Freedom as the first example of the application of that new strategic formula to what it defined as a long-term war on terrorism that it would carry out across the globe. Fourth, Bush served notice that he would extend the war against terrorist groups to their state sponsors and did so in the articulation of a sweeping new doctrine of preemption that is the principal topic of Chapter 2. Notwithstanding the inconclusive nature of the connections between Saddam's regime and the events of 9/11, the existence of consistent linkages between Iraq and terrorist groups since the 1970s suggest that allowing it to continue to cultivate such relationships in the future was simply a chance the United States could not afford to take.

Notes

[1] George W. Bush, "Remarks by the President upon Arrival at Barksdale Air Force Base," 11 September 2001, excerpted in *We Will Prevail: President George W. Bush on War Terrorism and Freedom* (New York: Continuum, 2003), 2.

[2] George W. Bush, "Presidential Address to the Nation," 11 September 2001, excerpted in ibid., 2.

[3] Bob Woodward, *Bush at War* (New York: Simon & Schuster, 2002), 42-57.

[4] For a detailed examination of the organization and conduct of Operation Enduring Freedom, see Tom Lansford, *All for One: Terrorism, NATO and the United States* (Aldershot, UK: Ashgate Publishing Limited, 2002).

[5] George W. Bush, "Presidential Address to a Joint Session of Congress," 23 September 2001, excerpted in *We Will Prevail*, 15.

[6] Victor Davis Hanson, *Ripples of Battle: How Wars of the Past still Determine How we Fight, How we Live and How we Think* (New York: Doubleday, 2003), 12.

[7] Kenneth M. Pollack, *The Threatening Storm: The Case for Invading Iraq* (New York: Random House, 2002), 87-94.

[8] George W. Bush, "President's State of the Union Address," 29 January 2002, excerpted in *We Will Prevail*, 108.

[9] See Francis Fukuyama, *The End of History and the Last Man* (New York: Avon, 1993).

[10] See Samuel P. Huntington, *The Clash of Civilizations and the Remaking of World Order* (New York: Simon & Schuster, 1996).

[11] See Kenneth N. Waltz, "The Emerging Structure of International Politics," *International Security* 18 (Fall 1993): 44-79; John J. Mearsheimer, "Back to the Future: Instability in Europe After the Cold War," *International Security* 15 (Summer 1990): 5-56.

[12] See Zbigniew Brzezinski, *Out of Control: Global Turmoil on the Eve of the Twenty-first Century* (New York: Touchstone Books, 1993); Robert D. Kaplan, "The Coming Anarchy," *Atlantic Monthly* 281 (Summer 1994).

[13] Richard N. Haass, "The Squandered Presidency: Demanding More From the Commander-in-Chief," *Foreign Affairs* (May/June 2000): 137.

[14] Samuel R. Berger, "A Foreign Policy for the Global Age," Remarks to the United States Institute of Peace (17 January 2001).

[15] William Clinton, "A National Security Strategy for a New Century," *White House Office of the Press Secretary*, December 1999, iii.

[16] George W. Bush, "National Security Strategy of the United States," *White House Office of the Press Secretary* (17 September 2002).

[17] John Lewis Gaddis, "A Grand Strategy of Transformation," *Foreign Policy* (November/December 2002): 50-51.

[18] Quoted in Bill Sammon, *Fighting Back: The War on Terrorism—from Inside the Bush White House* (Washington, D.C.: Regnery Publishing, Inc., 2002), 102.

[19] George W. Bush, "Presidential Proclamation Declaring National Day of Prayer and Remembrance for the Victims of the Terrorist Attacks," 13 September 2001, excerpted in *We Will Prevail*, 4.

[20] George W. Bush, "Remarks by the President from Speech at National Day of Prayer and Remembrance Ceremony," 14 September 2001, excerpted in ibid. 6.

[21] George W. Bush, "Presidential Address to a Joint Session of Congress," 23 September 2001, excerpted in ibid., 14-15.

[22] The following works provide in-depth examinations of the William J. Clinton administration's handling of the threats posed by Al Qaeda to US interests at home and abroad between January 1993 and January 2001: Richard Miniter, *Losing Bin Laden: How Bill Clinton's Failures Unleashed Global Terror* (Washington, D.C.: Regnery Publishing, Inc., 2003); Peter L. Bergen, *Holy War, Inc.: Inside the Secret World of Osama bin Laden* (New York: The Free Press, 2001); and Laurie Mylroie, *Study of Revenge: The First World Trade Center Attack and Saddam Hussein's War against America* (Washington, D.C.: The AEI Press, 2001).

[23] Miniter, *Losing Bin Laden*, 1-39; Mylroie, *Study of Revenge*, 78-87.

[24] Mylroie, *Study of Revenge*, 48-50, Miniter, *Losing Bin Laden*, 84-85.

[25] Miniter, *Losing Bin Laden*, 34-39.

[26] Ibid., 32-34, 87-92. Complicating matters further, as Miniter notes, was the fact that Clinton never met with Director of the Central Intelligence Agency Director James Woolsey on a one-on-one basis during Woolsey's tenure in that position from 1993-95.

[27] Miniter, *Losing Bin Laden*, 71-76; Mylroie, *Study of Revenge*, 198-207.

[28] Miniter, *Losing Bin Laden*, 83-87.

[29] Miniter, *Losing Bin Laden*, 99-149; Rich Lowry, *Legacy: Paying the Price for the Clinton Years* (Washington, D.C.: Regnery Publishing, Inc., 2003), 314-17. For example, Miniter contends that a Pakistani-American businessman by the name of Mansour Ijaz attempted to convince several Clinton administration officials to entertain offers from Sudan to pass bin Laden along to the United States in 1996.

[30] Dick Morris, *Off With Their Heads: Traitors, Crooks & Obstructionists in American Politics, Media & Business* (New York: ReganBooks, 2003), 97-98.

[31] Miniter, *Losing Bin Laden*, 161-64.

[32] Ibid., 170-86.

[33] Quoted in Lowry, *Legacy*, 318.

[34] Miniter, *Losing Bin Laden*, 216-29.

[35] Morris, *Off With Their Heads*, 70.

[36] Woodward, *Bush at War*, 34-35.

[37] Ibid., 4.

[38] Ibid., 34-36.

[39] Kenneth M. Pollack, *The Threatening Storm: The Case for Invading Iraq* (New York: Random House, 2002), 86-87.

[40] Lawrence F. Kaplan and William Kristol, *The War Over Iraq: Saddam's Tyranny and America's Mission* (San Francisco: Encounter Books, 2003), 37.

[41] Pollack, *The Threatening Storm*, 66-67; Con Coughlin, *Saddam: King of Terror* (New York: HarperCollins, 2002), 289; Lowry, *Legacy*, 288.

[42] Pollack, *The Threatening Storm*, 67.

[43] Quoted in Lowry, *Legacy*, 288.

[44] Pollack, *The Threatening Storm*, 69-71.

[45] Ibid., 72-81.

[46] Ibid., 87.

[47] Ibid., 87-94.

[48] Kaplan and Kristol, *The War Over Iraq*, 62.

[49] Coughlin, *Saddam: King of Terror*, 140-41.

[50] Ibid., 141-43.

[51] Quoted in ibid., 142.

[52] Quoted in *Newsweek* (17 July 1978). Reference made in ibid., 143.

[53] Miniter, *Losing Bin Laden*, 233.

[54] Sources consulted in the research and writing of the section of the chapter addressing the relationship between Saddam Hussein's Iraqi regime and Al Qaeda included: Coughlin, *Saddam: King of Terror*, xxv-xxxiv; Miniter, *Losing Bin Laden*, 231-41; Mylroie, *Study of Revenge*, 1-9, 106-260; Stephen Hayes, "An Intelligent Democrat," *The Weekly Standard* (15 December 2003); Hayes, "Case Closed," *The Weekly Standard* (24 November 2003); Hayes, "Osama's Best Friend," *The Weekly Standard* (3 November 2003); Hayes, "The Al Qaeda Connection," *The Weekly Standard* (12 May 2003); Mansoor Ijaz, "Saddam and the Terrorists," *National Review* (30 June 2003).

[55] Quoted in Hayes, "An Intelligent Democrat."

[56] Hayes, "Case Closed."

[57] Hayes, "The Al Qaeda Connection"; Ijaz, "Saddam and the Terrorists."

[58] Julian Borger, "Saddam: 'Forging Links with bin Laden'," *Guardian Weekly* (14 February 1999). Reference made in Miniter, *Losing Bin Laden*, 235.

[59] Hayes, "The Al Qaeda Connection."

[60] Ibid.

[61] Mylroie, *Study of Revenge*, 119-260.

[62] Coughlin, *Saddam: King of Terror*, xxv-xxvi.

[63] Miniter, *Losing Bin Laden*, 239-40.

[64] Coughlin, *Saddam: King of Terror*, xxv.

[65] Ibid., xxvii.

[66] Con Coughlin, "Does This Link Saddam to 9.11," *Daily Telegraph* [London] (14 December 2003).

[67] Coughlin, *Saddam: King of Terror*, xxvi.

[68] Woodward, *Bush at War*, 49-50.

[69] Bush, "State of the Union Address," 29 January 2002, excerpted in *We Will Prevail*, 108.

Chapter 2

The Doctrine of Preemption

Introduction

Upon assuming office, any American presidential administration faces three fundamental challenges in formulating and implementing its national security policy. First, a given president and his advisors must define and prioritize the nation's interests at that historical juncture—both domestically and internationally. Second, they must determine the present and potential future dangers most likely to threaten those interests. Third, on the basis of their assessment of all such prospective threats, they must decide what measures to take in order to safeguard US interests at home and abroad while in power. What, in turn, typically renders each of these challenges either extraordinarily daunting, relatively easy to overcome or somewhere in between these two extremes, is the extent to which unanticipated events alter an administration's initial interest and threat calculations over the balance of its term or terms in Washington.

While generally reflective of the above definition, the private formulation and public articulation of American national security policy—or, in some cases, lack of one or both—has varied from administration to administration over the course of the history of the United States generally and since the end of World War II specifically. During the Cold War, for example, most administrations build their security policies toward the Soviet Union around the strategy of containment originally conceived by American diplomat George F. Kennan in the aftermath of World War II and articulated under the pseudonym "X" in the pages of the journal *Foreign Affairs* in the summer of 1947. Although some US presidents were more forceful than others in dealing with Moscow both rhetorically and practically, each focused primarily on ensuring that the Soviet Union did not extend the physical presence of its military forces far beyond its sphere of influence in Eastern and Central Europe. Only one—Ronald Reagan—elected to shift from a strategy of containment to one that sought to "roll back" Soviet influence across the globe, a move that helped to convince political leaders in Moscow (President Mikhail Gorbachev in particular) that they could no longer compete with the United States economically and, ultimately, politically or militarily either. In the end, that realization led to the conclusion of the Cold War by way of the collapse of Communist regimes throughout the Warsaw Pact in 1989-90, the reunification of Germany in October 1990 and the implosion of the Soviet Union itself in December 1991.

Notwithstanding the utility of the policies formulated and implemented by Cold War presidents from Harry S. Truman to Reagan—or lack thereof—the strategies they pursued were only occasionally articulated in the context of a publicly released blueprint. Put simply, the principal reason behind this dearth of documentation was the lack of a formal requirement to act otherwise. That, however, changed dramatically near the end of the Reagan administration. In 1986, the 99th US Congress passed the Goldwater-Nichols Act, which mandated that from that point forward, each administration would have to submit an annual National Security Strategy (NSS) to the legislative branch. While the requirements that such a report be produced and submitted each year and within six months of the start of a given administration's initial term have each been interpreted loosely since the enactment of Goldwater-Nichols, Presidents George H.W. Bush, William J. Clinton and George W. Bush all released one prior to the end of their first four years in office.[1]

Ultimately, the latter Bush administration's NSS proved to be the most significant of the three, both in terms of the revolutionary—and thus controversial—nature of its content and the shifts in the strategic environment in response to which it was drafted. In particular, the Bush NSS was unveiled a year after Al Qaeda's 11 September 2001 attacks on the World Trade Center in New York and the Pentagon on the outskirts of Washington, D.C. Furthermore, its promulgation coincided with Bush's then ongoing rhetorical efforts to confront Iraqi President Saddam Hussein over Baghdad's weapons of mass destruction (WMD) programs and sponsorship of terrorist organizations. Those efforts, in turn, were part of a dozen year diplomatic, economic—and, at times, military—struggle pitting America against Iraq, one that began when the United States and its allies negotiated a United Nations (UN) sponsored cease-fire with Baghdad at the conclusion of the 1990-91 Persian Gulf War. Most significantly, that settlement stipulated that Saddam discontinue the acquisition and production of WMD and the requisite medium- and long-range missile systems to use such munitions to attack his adversaries and refrain from supporting terrorist groups, agreements that he violated repeatedly between 1991 and 2002.[2]

Iraq's record of defiance prompted Bush to issue a firm set of dictates to Saddam in a speech before the UN General Assembly in New York on 12 September 2002. In the context of that address, which was delivered symbolically just over 12 months to the day of the 9/11 attacks, the President made three unequivocal points. First, he demanded that Iraq comply immediately with all of the promises it made to the international community at the end of the Persian Gulf War, noting that Saddam had ignored 16 separate UN Security Council resolutions in the previous decade.[3] Specifically, the President emphasized that because it was continuing to pursue the acquisition of WMD and long-range missile systems, Iraq remained "a grave and gathering danger" to international security.[4] Second, he challenged the UN to carry out its responsibilities by impressing upon Saddam the need to disarm in an internationally-verifiable manner, asking members of that body's General Assembly: "Will the United Nations serve the purpose of its founding, or will it be irrelevant?"[5] Third, he pledged that the United States would indeed take action to eliminate the threats Iraq posed to American interests—with the UN's help if possible, but also unilaterally if necessary—noting that "we cannot stand by and do nothing while dangers gather."[6]

Five days after Bush's UN speech, his administration released its first NSS since assuming office, the timing of which was certainly not coincidental. Designed in large part as a means to warn American adversaries in general and Iraq in particular that the United States would not tolerate either the development and proliferation of WMD or the state sponsorship of terrorism, Bush's NSS is built around three pledges. First, the United States "will defend the peace by fighting terrorists and tyrants." Second, it "will preserve the peace by building good relations among the great powers." And third, it "will extend the peace by encouraging free and open societies on every continent."[7] At its core, the NSS represented a shift in strategic thinking from a reliance on the deterrent containment doctrine of the Cold War to a willingness to use preemptive policy-making when necessary to safeguard American national interests. It was a shift necessitated by the changing nature—and severity—of the threats posed to those interests as evidenced by the events of 9/11. As National Security Advisor Condoleezza Rice, one of the principal architects of the innovative new strategy, has asserted, "some threats are so potentially catastrophic—and can arrive with so little warning, by means that are untraceable—that they cannot be contained. ...So as a matter of common sense, the United States must be prepared to take action, when necessary, before threats have fully materialized."[8]

Bush's address to the UN General Assembly and his subsequent release of the NSS set the stage for concurrent—and equally vigorous—domestic and international debates over the need to disarm Iraq, which led to the passage of two measures: a US Congressional Resolution authorizing the use of force against Iraq[9] and a UN Security Council Resolution demanding that Saddam readmit and grant unrestricted investigative access to UN inspectors charged with determining the extent to which his regime has disarmed.[10] The balance of this chapter examines the Bush administration's NSS broadly and its application in the context of the run-up to and conduct of the Second Iraq War through the presentation of the following six sections: an assessment of the historical basis and contemporary rationale for a doctrine of preemption; a review of the central tenets of the NSS; an evaluation of the strengths of the NSS; an evaluation of the weaknesses of the NSS; a discussion of the application of the NSS to the case of Iraq; and a set of conclusions on the overall utility of Bush's NSS with respect to the conduct of the war on terror and the long-term democratization of the Greater Middle East.

Historical Basis and Contemporary Rationale for a Doctrine of Preemption

Prior to engaging in a discussion of the merits of any strategy based primarily on preemptive relative to reactive measures, it is first necessary to define the terms upon which that debate focuses. Put simply, policymakers use preemptive tools to prevent the emergence of a threat to the interests of a distinct actor or actors, whether an individual, state, institution—or, in some cases, a combination of one or more of these entities—before it becomes imminent and thus exceedingly difficult, if not impossible, to eliminate without bearing unacceptable costs. Given that basic definition, the word preemptive is, at least some cases, interchangeable with preventive and preventative, as are policies and strategies articulated through the use of such rhetorical devices. In addition, there are a variety of different means through which to achieve preemptive, preventive and preventative objectives. For the purposes of this study, those means are best defined as military and non-military in nature. The former include both the limited and unlimited use of military force by one or more states, whether acting with or without the imprimatur of an international organization such as the UN, North Atlantic Treaty Organization (NATO) or European Union (EU). The latter, for their part, range from the issuance of rhetorical warnings to the imposition of economic, judicial and political sanctions.

Historical examples of states taking preemptive action, whether military or non-military in character, are myriad and include ancient as well as contemporary cases drawn from every corner of the globe. However, in light of the fact that the principal issues under consideration here involve modern rather than more historically distant events, this section will be limited to the examination of twentieth and twenty-first century examples subdivided contextually into four temporal categories: the pre-Cold War era, the Cold War era, the post-Cold War era and the post-9/11 era. Those categorical discussions, in turn, provide a necessary foundation for an analytical discussion of the rationale for the Bush administration's NSS, which is itself examined in detail in the ensuing section.

Pre-Cold War Era

Notwithstanding the devastating nature of World War II, which cost more lives than any other conflict in the world's history, its conclusion was ensured by an unprecedented use of military technology that could certainly be described as preventative, if not unambiguously preemptive, in character. As the war in the Pacific proceeded through its final months in the spring and summer of 1945, it became increasing apparent to the Harry S. Truman administration that the Japanese were not likely to surrender without organizing and staging a stalwart defense of their home islands. More pointedly, US military leaders viewed Tokyo's defense of Okinawa from April-June 1945, in the context of which 100,000 Japanese and 7,000 Americans perished, as a preview of what they anticipated would be a considerably more brutal struggle for the home islands.[11] At least in part as a result of that assessment, Truman elected to force the Japanese into submission by dropping atomic bombs on Hiroshima and Nagasaki on 6 and 9 August, respectively, which led to Tokyo's decision to surrender on 10 August. While those bombings killed nearly 200,000 civilians, they also rendered unnecessary a conventional invasion that would likely have produced the deaths of millions of Americans and Japanese. In that sense, the bombings were preemptive to the extent that they prevented an extraordinary loss of life that would, in all probability, otherwise have occurred. As American historian Victor Davis Hanson notes, the "plan of homeland defense (*ketsu-go*) was predicated on the idea that every

Japanese civilian and soldier alike would kill as many Americans as possible—resulting in either a fitting genocide for a still unconquered and unoccupied people or such mayhem for the enemy that the Americans, not the Japanese would seek negotiations. So the holocaust on Okinawa led to the dropping of the bombs, which led to a surrender rather than greater carnage for both sides."[12]

Cold War Era

During the course of the Cold War, American presidents used a variety of preemptive military and non-military means to further US interests relative to those of the Soviet Union. Examinations of the preventative efforts of the administrations headed by two particularly charismatic leaders—John F. Kennedy and Ronald Reagan—will prove especially useful in illustrating that point. The firm yet prudential management of the Cuban Missile Crisis in October 1962 by the former and the rollback of Soviet global influence by the latter were each demonstrative of the utility of the employment of proactive rather than strictly reactive policymaking tools in eliminating threats to the United States posed by a dangerous adversary.

The stiffest test Kennedy faced during his presidency came in October 1962 when American reconnaissance photos revealed an ongoing Soviet initiative to install nuclear-tipped missiles on the island of Cuba with the acquiescence, if not at the behest of, Communist dictator Fidel Castro. After considering a range of options that included a preemptive military invasion of Cuba to remove those missiles that had already arrived, Kennedy decided to impose a naval blockade of the island, which could technically be deemed an act of war under international law. Ultimately, Soviet leader Nikita Khrushchev backed down and removed the missiles from Cuba.[13] At its core, Kennedy's action was preemptive in that it prevented the Soviet Union from increasing markedly the threats it already posed to the continental United States and did so before the missiles were fully operational and the potential for their use was *imminent*. It was also illustrative of the fact that any administration typically has a range of preventative means at its disposal when required to deal with the escalation of an existing threat to its interests or the sudden emergence of a new one.

Similar to Kennedy, Reagan took a proactive stance in US-Soviet relations and he did so in the aftermath of Moscow's most aggressive foreign policy initiative since the 1962 episode in Cuba—its invasion of Afghanistan on the eve of the start of the 1980 presidential race in December 1979. After defeating President Jimmy Carter in the ensuing election, Reagan crafted and implemented a strategy that sought to confront the Soviet Union and "roll back" its global influence through two means. First, the Reagan administration engaged in a massive military buildup that included the proposed development of a Strategic Defense Initiative to safeguard the United States against the threat of Soviet intercontinental missiles via space-based lasers. Second, it challenged Moscow by supporting insurgencies fighting Soviet-backed regimes in developing world states ranging from Afghanistan to Nicaragua and spent much less money than the Soviet Union in the process. Collectively, these initiatives helped to convince Gorbachev the Soviets could no longer compete with the United States in terms of either economic vitality—and related conventional military reach—or political influence. As a result, Moscow gradually reduced its control over the Warsaw Pact, which led to the proverbial closing act of the Cold War, one that was managed by the George H.W. Bush administration from 1989-1992 and left the Clinton administration facing a new set of threats over the balance of the 1990s.[14]

Put simply, Reagan recognized that he could prevent unnecessary American—and, for that matter, Central and Eastern European—sacrifices, whether in terms of military outlays or the limitation of economic opportunity and political freedom over the long term through the implementation of a range of proactive (and, to some extent, preemptive) policies in the short term. As Max Boot, a senior fellow at the Council on Foreign Relations, asserts, "Ronald Reagan waged political, economic, and moral warfare on the 'evil empire,' and even sponsored proxy wars, but he prudently refrained from direct military attacks. His is a preemptive strategy we can and should apply around the world today."[15]

Post-Cold War Era

As argued in Chapter 1, the Clinton administration did not effectively reduce, let alone eliminate, the threats posed to American interests at home and abroad by either Al Qaeda or Iraq. However, it did learn a valuable lesson with respect to the utility of preemptive action in the region of the world upon which it focused most of its foreign policy attention—the Balkans. After standing by as Bosnian Serb leaders Radovan Karadzic and Ratko Mladic (both of whom have been charged with war crimes by the International Criminal Tribunal for the Former Yugoslavia (ICTY) but remained at large as of March 2004) presided over the slaughter of thousands of Muslim and Croat civilians during the 1992-95 civil war in Bosnia-Herzegovina, Clinton chose to act when a similar threat of genocide emerged in Kosovo in 1999. Instead, Clinton acted preemptively to prevent then Serbian President Slobodan Milosevic from eliminating the ethnic Albanian minority in Kosovo, pressing successfully for NATO intervention without a UN Security Mandate.[16]

For their part, the Western Europeans (France and Germany included) accepted Clinton's leadership and, by association, the preemptive use of military force wholeheartedly. Consequently, Milosevic was left with no choice but to cease his ethnic cleansing campaign and is presently being tried for war crimes and crimes against humanity by the ICTY in The Hague. In short, preemption worked for the Clinton administration long before its formal articulation as US policy by Bush in the 2002 NSS. As Gen. Wesley Clark, who served as NATO's Supreme Allied Commander in Europe during its operations against Serbia and subsequently conducted an unsuccessful run for the Democratic Presidential Nomination in 2003-04, has written, "Nations and alliances should move early to deal with crises while they are still ambiguous and can be dealt with more easily, for delay raises both the costs and risks. Early action is the objective to which statesmen and military leaders should resort."[17]

Post-9/11 Era

Regrettably, neither Clinton nor George W. Bush acted either early or proactively enough to prevent the occurrence of the events of 9/11. The attacks on the World Trade Center and Pentagon did, however, impress upon the Bush administration and the American public at large that the United States was not nearly so invulnerable to the sudden infliction of massive civilian casualties by an external adversary as was previously believed. That realization led correctly to a fundamental re-evaluation not only of American national security strategy but also of the way in which it should be articulated publicly. To treat the attacks as a criminal matter and leave the subsequent investigation and response to the Justice Department—Clinton's method choice after the February 1993 bombing of the garage of the North Tower of the World Trade Center—would have been inconceivable morally as well as politically. Yet, drafting and issuing a new NSS in the short term, would have been equally impractical and thus imprudent.

Instead, the Bush administration began by defining the fundamental challenges the United States would face in waging a war against terrorism of indeterminate length, one generally comparable in its global scope, if not in the monolithic nature of the adversary, to the five decade long Cold War that had defined American foreign policy over the latter half of the previous century. It then planned and conducted Operation Enduring Freedom against Al Qaeda and its Taliban sponsors in Afghanistan from October-December 2001 as a means both to weaken bin Laden's network and serve notice to those regimes that chose to support terrorist groups that their actions would entail serious consequences. Next, it used much of 2002 to identify and issue overt warnings to those states it perceived as the most stalwart and, consequently, the most threatening, pursuers of WMD and sponsors of terrorism—most notably Iraq, Iran and North Korea. Lastly, it incorporated a range of military and non-military preemptive and preventative means to safeguard US interests at home and abroad into the NSS that Bush promulgated that September.

Overview of Bush Administration's National Security Strategy

American presidents have employed a variety of means in conducting foreign policy throughout US history. The particulars of their approaches were in the past and are presently conditioned by the contemporary circumstances and events to which they have had to respond. Yet, irrespective of the temporal context, three rules have always proven indispensable to effective presidential policymaking and decision taking. It is first necessary to determine and prioritize the nation's interests, second to assess the capabilities at one's disposal to use in safeguarding those interests and third to formulate and implement national security policy and strategy accordingly. Above all, given those rules, the Bush administration's NSS is demonstrative of a keen understanding of the need to consider the interconnected relationship between interests, commitments and capabilities in responding to unanticipated changes in the international security environment.

Most indispensably, Bush's NSS recognizes the increased vulnerability of the United States to attacks by transnational terrorist organizations and their supporters (whether state or non-state actors) as was so clearly—and tragically—demonstrated by the events of 9/11. In particular, the document defines three fundamental national interests—the defense, preservation and extension of the peace through collaboration with the world's great powers at the expense of its terrorists and tyrants—on behalf of which Bush promises to utilize America's unparalleled economic, military and political assets. However, it cleverly frames those interest-based objectives in principled rhetoric, noting that the United States seeks to promote a "balance of power that favors ... political and economic freedom, peaceful relations with other states and respect for human dignity" and also stressing that "today, the international community has the best chance since the rise of the nation-state in the seventeenth century to build a world where great powers compete in peace instead of continually preparing for war. Today, the world's great powers find ourselves on the same side."[18]

Domestic and foreign opponents of the Bush administration, along with some of America's European allies (France and Germany in particular), have derided its NSS as one based all but exclusively on the preemptive use of military force, whether employed unilaterally or multilaterally. But even a cursory reading of the document reveals such criticism to be misguided. It is 40 pages in length and the discussion of preemption encompasses just two sentences in one of its eight sections. Granted, Bush and his advisors placed an emphasis on the use of preemptive measures in light of the dire threats posed by terrorist groups and their state sponsors and heightened public sensitivities to those dangers as a result of the 9/11 attacks, but when taken as a whole, the NSS represents a considerably more wide ranging strategy. As Secretary of State Colin Powell has pointed out,

> The NSS made the concept of preemption explicit in the heady aftermath of September 11, and it did so for obvious reasons. One reason was to reassure the American people that the government possessed common sense. As President Bush has said—and as any sensible person understands—if you recognize a clear and present threat that is undeterrable by the means you have at hand, then you must deal with it. You do not wait for it to strike; you do not allow future attacks to happen before you take action. A second reason for including the notion of preemption in the NSS was to convey to our adversaries that they were in big trouble. ... Sensible as these reasons were, some observers have exaggerated both the scope of preemption in foreign policy and the centrality of preemption in US strategy as a whole.[19]

Justifiably, Bush cedes primacy to hard-core security issues over the low politics of the environment favored by his immediate predecessor in the White House (President Bill Clinton) and his opponent in the 2000 Presidential Election (Albert Gore). However, Bush does so by laying out the White House's strategy in terms of the proactive pursuit of eight separate goals, five of which relate directly to hard-core security issues and three more than pertain to efforts to foster economic growth and the construction of enduring democratic institutions in the developing world in general and across the Greater Middle East in particular. Specifically, the administration pledges that the United States will:

- Champion aspirations for human dignity.
- Strengthen alliances to defeat global terrorism and work to prevent attacks against us and our friends.
- Work with others to defuse regional conflicts.
- Prevent our enemies from threatening us, our allies, and our friends, with weapons of mass destruction.
- Ignite a new era of global economic growth through free markets and free trade.
- Expand the circle of development by opening societies and building the infrastructure of democracy.
- Develop agendas for cooperative action with other main centers of global power.
- Transform America's national security institutions to meet the challenges and opportunities of the twenty-first century.[20]

When one considers the range of preemptive, preventive and preventative measures discussed in the previous section, Bush's strategy appears not as a rash reaction to the 9/11 assaults, but as a comprehensive blueprint that takes into account the successes and failures of his predecessors in the White House over the past half-century. One of the means the United States used to weaken the Soviet Union's grip over its Warsaw Pact satellites over the long term, for instance, was by "opening societies and building the infrastructure of democracy" throughout Central and Eastern Europe. Most significantly, Reagan's willingness to push the Soviets to loosen and then release their control over the Warsaw Pact once the arms buildup of the early 1980s put Washington in a position of relative strength vis-à-vis Moscow, triggered the subsequent collapse of Communist regimes from Bucharest to East Berlin in the fall and winter of 1989-90. The Bush NSS is designed to eventually produce a similar democratization of the Islamic world. In that sense, it is both flexible and visionary rather than ill conceived and illogical. As Powell concludes, "Together, [its eight] parts add up to a strategy that is broad and deep, far ranging and forward looking, attuned as much to opportunities for the United States as to the dangers it faces."[21]

What is most instructive about the Bush administration's NSS is the extent to which it takes an assertive but multilateral stance in discussing the economic, political and military means the United States is prepared to use to preempt threats to American security at home and abroad.[22] The NSS suggests that such threats—most notably the acquisition, production and proliferation of WMD by dictatorial regimes—are best mitigated and eventually eliminated multilaterally through the organization of "coalitions—as broad as practicable—of states able and willing to promote a balance of power that favors freedom."[23] Furthermore, it renders critics' characterizations of the Bush administration's supposed aversion to working with the UN under any circumstances considerably less credible by justifying its doctrine of preemption in globally acceptable legal terms pertaining to a state's right to defend itself.[24]

Much of the criticism of Bush's foreign policy before, as well as during and after, the conduct of the Second Iraq War, rests primarily on the premise that he has acted unilaterally more often than not. Responding effectively to that criticism is relatively easy so long as one defines the term unilateralism first. The narrowest definition of the term would suggest that a given state is acting alone—that is, without the support, of any allies whatsoever, let alone the blessing of the UN Security Council or wider international community. A broader definition, by contrast, might indicate a coalition of less than 10 states acting without the authority of a formal Security Council resolution. Yet, neither of these definitions applies to US action in the contexts of either Operation Enduring Freedom or Operation Iraqi Freedom. In each case, the United States acted with the direct or indirect military, logistical and political support of no less than 50 states. In addition, the Security Council acceded to the former, albeit not to the latter. As Powell explains, "Partnership is the watchword of US strategy in this administration. Partnership is not about deferring to others; it is about working with them."[25]

Moving beyond its general and specific characterizations of the potential security threats the United States must confront (most notably the arming of terrorist organizations with WMD by tyrannical regimes) and the means to use in preempting those threats (collective diplomacy if possible; the multilateral or unilateral use of force if necessary), the NSS also prioritizes American interests regionally. Not unexpectedly, that prioritization places an emphasis on Greater Middle Eastern and South Asian security affairs generally and such long-standing imbroglios as the Israeli-Palestinian conflict and troubled Indian-Pakistani relationship in particular. Significantly, in addressing each of these contentious relationships, the NSS acknowledges the need for the United States to strike a balance between the interests of the disparate ethnic and religious groups involved.[26] It does so in large part in order to avoid deepening the anti-American sentiments that have in the past—and continue at present—to make members of the lower classes of the Islamic world susceptible to the recruitment efforts of regional and global terrorist organizations. Rice, for example, has pointed out, that the Bush administration "rejects the condescending view that freedom will not grow in the soil of the Middle East—or that Muslims somehow do not share in the desire to be free."[27]

Bush's NSS appears especially innovative when compared with the Clinton administration's final NSS, which it issued in December 1999. Clinton's NSS set three goals that—while related to Bush's aims—were not presented in nearly as proactive a manner: first, "to enhance America's security"; second, "to bolster America's economic prosperity"; and third, "to promote democracy and human rights abroad."[28] As Yale University historian John Lewis Gaddis, perhaps the most authoritative scholar of American national security policy over the past half-century, has pointed out, the differences between the Bush NSS and the 1999 Clinton NSS "are revealing. The Bush objectives speak of defending, preserving, and extending the peace; the Clinton statement seems simply to assume peace. ... Even in these first few lines, then, the Bush NSS comes across as more forceful, more carefully crafted, and—unexpectedly—more multilateral than its immediate predecessor."[29]

Strengths of Bush Administration's NSS

As is true of any NSS, Bush's has both strengths and weaknesses. However, in the Bush administration's case, the former overshadow the latter markedly. It has six fundamental strengths, each of which is examined in detail in the balance of this section.

First, it articulates an innovative strategic vision in an incisive manner, one that avoids the myriad diplomatic ambiguities of the 1999 Clinton NSS and is thus intelligible to a considerably broader American audience. The principal differences between the two documents relate primarily to focus—both in defining and prioritizing US national security interests and devising an approach that identifies and eliminates threats to those interests before such threats become imminent. While advocates of the Clinton blueprint suggest that its subtlety was necessary because of the lack of one overarching foreign policy challenge with which to deal during the late 1990s, Al Qaeda did present precisely that type of unambiguous threat at that juncture. Yet, rather than place an emphasis on confronting terrorists and their state sponsors, Clinton elected to pursue a wide range of objectives that were not linked in a cohesive manner. The result was a dearth of clarity in his NSS, particularly when compared to that of the Bush administration. The latter document, by contrast, leaves no doubt that the war on terrorism is central to American national security, but specifies a range of interconnected economic, military and political tools it intends to use in waging that conflict over the short, medium and long terms.

Second, Bush's NSS emphasizes that the United States will act to preempt threats to its interests rather than react to such dangers after the fact. This is an extraordinarily necessary adjustment in light of the events of 9/11. To deem the attacks a law enforcement matter, conduct an investigation and try those perpetrators eventually captured in a domestic court as the Clinton administration did following the February 1993 World Trade Center bombing would have been politically untenable and practically counterproductive after the 2001 strikes. Such a process would have done little to weaken Al Qaeda's capacity to plan and carry out an equally, if not more, devastating attack in the future. In addition, the concurrent development and proliferation of WMD, and possibility that Al Qaeda—or, for that matter, any other terrorist group—could obtain such munitions demanded that the United States use all necessary military and non-military measures at its disposal to prevent that outcome from transpiring. Furthermore, taking that stance required that Bush characterize terrorist organizations, as well as those states that choose to continue to support them to any degree whatsoever, as equally threatening and to do so publicly and unambiguously. Ultimately, it was the repeated public identification of states like Iraq, Iran and North Korea as presenting clear threats to American interests at home and abroad through the development of WMD and sponsorship of terrorism that gave the

Bush's NSS teeth. It also opened the administration to international criticism of its rhetorical classification of that trio as an "axis of evil" endangering the peace of the world, which was a necessary and by no means unacceptable political cost of the nascent strategy.

Third, Bush's NSS expresses the administration's prudential willingness to strike a balance between multilateral and unilateral action in confronting terrorists and their state sponsors. In particular, Bush notes pledges in the NSS that the United States will act multilaterally whenever possible and unilaterally only if absolutely necessary. With respect to the variable definitions of the term "unilateral" presented in the previous section, the Bush administration has yet to act in an unambiguously unilateral manner in conducting the war on terrorism generally or in any stage of ongoing operations in Iraq specifically. In its efforts to limit—and eventually eliminate—the threats posed to American interests by Al Qaeda, the United States has received support from its European, Middle Eastern and Central, South and Far East Asian allies that includes intelligence sharing, law enforcement cooperation, the deployment of military forces and leadership of nation-building operations in states ranging geographically from Iraq to the Philippines. In addition, although the Bush administration did not secure a clear UN mandate to eliminate Saddam's regime through the conduct of the Second Iraq War, it attempted to acquire Security Council support repeatedly and lobbied successfully for the passage of Resolution 1441. That measure warned Saddam explicitly that any further non-compliance with past or present UN resolutions would result in "serious consequences," which could certainly have been interpreted as an eventual use of force against Iraq.[30]

Fourth, Bush's NSS addresses soft as well as hard security issues and justifies its doctrine of preemption in accordance with established international legal norms. It explains, for example, that "for centuries, international law recognized that nations need not suffer an attack before they can lawfully take action to defend themselves against forces that present an imminent danger of attack." It then adds a necessary caveat that relates to the changing nature of the dangers presented by non-state actors in the 2000s, arguing that "the greater the threat, the greater is the risk of inaction—and the more compelling the case for taking anticipatory action to defend ourselves, even if uncertainty remains as to the time and place of the enemy's attack."[31] Yet, it also acknowledges that such action need not always involve the use of force, stressing instead the importance of incorporating economic, environmental and healthcare initiatives designed to ameliorate living standards in the developing world into the struggle against transnational terrorist organizations. The rationale for that argument is instructive, especially when one takes a long-term view. Terrorist groups typically find fertile recruiting ground within states where desperation and bitterness is prevalent among the populace, which is usually the case in developing states presided over by autocratic regimes. By providing economic aid to improve living standards in "failing" and "failed" states ranging regionally from Sub-Saharan Africa and the Middle East to Central and South Asia, the United States can eventually reduce the number of places with the potential to serve as bases of operation for Al Qaeda and mitigate the discontent that drives individuals to join bin Laden's organization.

Fifth, Bush's NSS prioritizes American security interests geographically, placing an emphasis on the Greater Middle East relative to other regions of the world—one that parallels America's commitment to the war on terrorist groups and their state sponsors broadly, and Iraqi and broader Greater Middle Eastern stabilization and democratization in particular. That commitment is evident in initiatives including, but not limited to, ongoing reconstruction operations in Afghanistan and Iraq as well as the promulgation of a "Road Map" designed to achieve the eventual resolution of the Israeli-Palestinian conflict. What is perhaps most significant of each of these initiatives is their multilateral nature. The United States, for example, has successfully lobbied its NATO allies to take the lead in the reconstruction of Afghanistan while it continues to focus on the search for bin Laden and liquidation of Al Qaeda and Taliban loyalists who remain entrenched in the hinterlands of that state. Similarly, it has received assistance from more than 60 coalition partners in ongoing nation-building endeavors in Iraq. The "Road Map," for its part, was drafted by a state/institutional quartet composed of the United States, Russia, the UN and the EU. While progress remains glacial vis-à-vis peace between the Israelis and Palestinians, the very promulgation of that plan was illustrative of Washington's willingness to work multilaterally whenever possible.

Sixth, Bush's NSS touches on the need for political reforms that would favor lower-class Muslims at the expense of the repressive regimes—some aligned with the United States—that are the rule rather than the exception across the Islamic world. More pointedly, since releasing its strategy, the Bush administration has asserted consistently that the Islamic world is both suitable for, and deserving of, the development of institutions based on free market economic and liberal democratic political principles. In an address just under a month prior to the commencement of Operation Iraqi Freedom, for example, Bush himself noted that:

> The world has a clear interest in the spread of democratic values, because stable and free nations do not breed the ideologies of murder. They encourage the peaceful pursuit of a better life. And there are hopeful signs of a desire for freedom in the Middle East. Arab intellectuals have called on Arab governments to address the "freedom gap" so their peoples can fully share in the progress of our times. Leaders in the region speak of a new Arab charter that champions internal reform, greater [political] participation, economic openness and free trade. And from Morocco to Bahrain and beyond, nations are taking steps toward [political] reform. A new regime in Iraq would serve as a dramatic and inspiring example of freedom for other nations in the region. It is presumptuous and insulting to suggest that a whole region of the world—or the one-fifth of humanity that is Muslim—is somehow untouched by the most basic aspirations of life. Human cultures can be vastly different. Yet the human race desires the same good things, everywhere on earth. In our desire to be safe from brutal and bullying oppression, human beings are the same. In our desire to care for our children and give them a better life, we are the same. For these fundamental reasons, freedom and democracy will always and everywhere have greater appeal than the slogans of hatred and the tactics of terror.[32]

Bush's comments, which were delivered at the American Enterprise Institute in Washington, paralleled the vision expressed in the NSS itself. Any overarching strategy must start somewhere. In the case of the democratization of the Greater Middle East, the point of departure was Iraq. If successful, it will serve as an example to Muslims within and beyond the Persian Gulf that economic prosperity and political freedom are realistic goals rather than outlandish dreams. Consequently, it will demonstrate to autocratic regimes throughout the Islamic world what may await them should they continue to deny their people an opportunity for gradual democratic change.

Weaknesses of Bush Administration's NSS

Notwithstanding its many strengths, Bush's NSS also has two significant weaknesses. First, it appears to make a somewhat ethnocentric—and not necessarily accurate— assumption that its allies (whether in Europe or the Greater Middle East) will acquiesce in if not welcome the Bush administration's attempts to defend, preserve and extend peace under American auspices. That assumption proved to be at least somewhat, albeit not wholly, inaccurate in each of those regions, as evidenced by the difficulty Bush had in building a diverse coalition to confront Saddam via the conduct of the Second Iraq War.

There are two fundamental reasons why. First, the end of the Cold War left the United States in a hegemonic position as the world's sole remaining superpower. Its predominance in terms of collective economic, military and political power and influence, along with the concurrent global proliferation of American popular culture have left many in Europe and the Middle East—leaders as well as the citizens they govern—bitter over their own inadequacies. Second, in addition to a sense of angst over their inability to prevent the United States from taking whatever action it deems appropriate to safeguard its national interests, those very interests, in some cases, conflict with the aims of American allies and adversaries alike. In the Middle East, for example, it should have come as less of a surprise to the Bush administration than was the case that authoritarian leaders in places such as Saudi Arabia and Egypt would frown on a vision of long-term democratization that would ultimately reduce their own power at best and cause their regimes to fall at worst. Put simply, they were less fearful of an Iraq that had not threatened its neighbors with direct military invasion since the end of the Persian Gulf War in 1991 than they were of the democratic empowerment of restive populations.

Second, Bush's NSS does not fully acknowledge the extent to which concomitantly de-emphasizing the low politics of the environment (still a high-priority issue in many Western European capitals) and pressing for the forcible disarmament of states such as Iraq, Iran and North Korea will foster serious discord in transatlantic relations in the short term and, perhaps, over the long term as well. In short, the Bush administration did not strike a particularly conciliatory tone in the transatlantic relationship broadly or in Franco-American and German-American relations specifically during the months leading up to the events of 9/11. Rather than acknowledge and then attempt to de-emphasis foreign policy differences between Washington and Western European capitals—most notably over the latter's support for and the former's rejection of the International Criminal Court and Kyoto Protocol on Global Warming, respectively—Bush publicized them. In addition, he imposed tariffs on European steel, an imprudent example of protectionism that belied the Republican Party's long-standing promotion of free trade and one he was forced to rescind following a ruling to that effect by the World Trade Organization in 2003.

The 9/11 attacks and subsequent conduct of Operation Enduring Freedom restored a measure of solidarity in the transatlantic relationship (notwithstanding a bit of European bitterness over the marginalization of their military contributions to the war against Al Qaeda and the Taliban). However, that goodwill quickly dissipated in the wake of Bush's unveiling of the NSS, and the subsequent run-up to the Second Iraq War deepened existing divisions across the Atlantic and opened new ones within Europe between the anti-war French and Germans on one hand and the pro-war British, Spanish, Italian and Polish governments on the other. Many of those differences would still have existed even had the Bush administration struck a more conciliatory tone with the French and Germans among others over the first eight months of 2001. However, that course of action may have muted their public expression to an extent during the diplomatic encounters that preceded the US-led invasion of Iraq in March 2003.

Application of NSS to the Case of Iraq

As touched on previously, the timing of the release of the Bush administration's NSS was by no means coincidental. It came just days after the President's UN address regarding the threats posed to American security, Middle Eastern stability and Security Council credibility, a speech that itself marked the one-year anniversary of Al Qaeda's attacks on the World Trade Center and Pentagon. The construction of a coalition, albeit one lacking unequivocal UN support, and subsequent planning and conduct of the Second Iraq War served as a practical test of the doctrine of preemption articulated in the NSS. The purpose of this final main section of the chapter, in turn, is to review the process through which the United States applied Bush's NSS to the case of Iraq between the President's address to the UN General Assembly in September 2002 and the invasion of Iraq by coalition forces under American and British leadership in March 2003. It is not intended to be comprehensive in scope as the balance of the monograph addresses the diplomacy associated with the buildup to the conflict, the conduct of Operation Iraqi Freedom and subsequent nation-building operations in Iraq in depth. Instead, it assesses the general utility of the application of the NSS to the case of Iraq.

In the contexts of UN Security Council Resolution 687 and 16 subsequent Security Council resolutions since 1991—the last of which (Resolution 4112) was passed unanimously on 8 November 2002—the UN demanded that Iraq make a range of behavioral modifications to ensure its re-acceptance as a productive member of the international community.[33] Saddam's regime failed to comply fully with each one of these resolutions. In particular, Iraq defied UN mandates by declining to: (a) eliminate its biological, chemical and nuclear WMD developmental programs in a verifiable manner; (b) cease its attempts to acquire ballistic missiles with ranges greater than 150 kilometers; (c) renounce all terrorist organizations and refuse to harbor any members of such groups within its borders; (d) return all foreign prisoners seized during its 1990 invasion of Kuwait and subsequent Persian Gulf War; and (e) refrain from repressing its domestic population.[34]

Ultimately, the Bush administration applied a variety of economic, diplomatic and politico-military tools in the context of a four-stage approach to the disarmament of Iraq and liquidation of Saddam's regime. The first stage was rhetorical in nature. It commenced with Bush's address to the UN General Assembly in September 2002 and continued with his nationally televised speech to the American people from Cincinnati a month later.[35] In each case, the President issued stern demands for Iraq to disarm in order to impress upon Saddam and the international community how seriously Washington viewed the matter. However, Bush was also careful to express his willingness to afford the UN an opportunity to achieve that objective peacefully before the United States would consider either the multilateral or unilateral use of military force against Iraq. Furthermore, key members of the administration's national security team—most notably Rice, Powell and Secretary of Defense Donald Rumsfeld—and also British Prime Minister Tony Blair struck similar tones in reiterating the administration's demands between September 2002 and March 2003.

The political stage focused on the development of American and international legal measures to justify diplomatic and military action against Iraq. Domestically, Bush worked diligently to secure Congressional authorization of the use of force to disarm Iraq should such action become necessary, which he achieved through the resounding passage of a joint resolution to that end by the House and Senate in October 2002.[36] Internationally, Powell collaborated with his British, French, Russian and Chinese counterparts on the Security Council to fashion Resolution 4112, which called for Saddam to readmit and cooperate unconditionally with weapons inspectors under the auspices of the UN Monitoring, Verification and Inspection Commission (UNMOVIC) or face "serious consequences."[37] The resolution passed by a 15-0 vote in the Security Council on 8 November 2002 and was agreed to by Iraq six days later.

Ultimately, the Bush administration used its policy toward Iraq as a test case for the practical implementation of the NSS. It did so through a three-part strategy that has unfolded between September 2002 and the present. First, Bush attempted to use diplomatic measures to ensure Iraqi disarmament, most notably by securing the return of UN weapons inspectors to Iraq under the auspices of Security Council Resolution 4112.[38] Second, when Saddam refused to comply fully with the weapons inspectors, the United States collaborated with the United Kingdom—and, to a lesser degree, a range of other allies including Australia and several Eastern and Central European states—to forcibly remove the Iraqi regime from power in orchestrating a campaign that lasted just over one month between mid-March and mid-April 2003. Third, the Americans and British are currently leading a coalition of the willing to build a democratic system in Iraq over the long term.

During the initial stage of the above process, French President Jacques Chirac was the most vociferous of several foreign leaders to express their unambiguous opposition to the use of military force to disarm Iraq and employed all diplomatic measures at his disposal to block that course of action. For example, although France voted for Resolution 4112, it did so only because that measure did not explicitly sanction the use of force against Iraq. Ultimately, when the United States, the United Kingdom and Spain indicated they would seek a second resolution condoning military action to disarm Saddam's regime, Chirac responded that "whatever the circumstances, France will vote no," ensuring that the campaign for any such resolution was stillborn.[39]

Chirac's behavior raised one overarching question: Why was he so insistent that the United States not remove Saddam from power? In short, there were three reasons, each of which included both domestic and international components. First, France had close public and private economic ties with Saddam's regime, which it was understandably eager to preserve. Second, France plays host to a growing Muslim population, one whose members were unequivocally opposed to US military action against Iraq and by no means averse to expressing their opposition in violent—and thus socially destabilizing—ways. Third, Chirac perceived the Iraq crisis as an opportunity to revitalize flagging French prestige—both within and outside of Europe—in opposition to American predominance in the post-Cold War international system.

In the process of opposing the use of force to remove Saddam from power, Chirac sparked divisions within both NATO and the European Union (EU). Most significantly, Germany elected to join France in obstructing US attempts to forge consensus within NATO on Washington's policy toward Iraq, resulting in a de facto division of the European continent into wings favoring and opposed to the Bush administration's doctrine of preemption. These divisions, in turn, had spillover effects in the context of the EU. With respect to transatlantic community broadly defined, France, Germany—and a number of less influential states including Belgium and Luxembourg—entrenched themselves on one side of the debate over Iraq, while the United Kingdom, Spain, Italy, Portugal and the vast majority of prospective EU and NATO members from Eastern and Central Europe aligned themselves with the United States on the other side. Such divisions represent an inopportune—and unnecessary—complication to the scheduled enlargement of NATO and the EU to include several Central and Eastern European states that have staked out positions in opposition to two of the three most politically influential states in Europe.

Ultimately, the United States, France—and, albeit to a lesser degree, Germany—are each at least partially responsible for the predicament in which the transatlantic community finds itself on the eve of the dual enlargement processes slated to move forward in 2004. Bush, for example, could have done a better job accommodating Western European concerns over issues ranging from global warming to the imposition of American steel tariffs in 2001. Chirac, on the other hand, could have been more understanding of US worries over Iraq's development of WMD and sponsorship of terrorist groups, particularly in light of the tragic events of 9/11. The fact that neither did so at the time is now confined to the past. As to the present and future, it is clear that the Bush administration will continue to employ the range of tools it articulated in the NSS to eliminate threats to American interests—and, to the degree possible—the interests of US allies from Europe to the Greater Middle East. The extent to which those sets of interests coincide will depend on the judgments of allies—some old and some new—situated in capitals ranging from Paris to Baghdad.

Conclusions

At its core, this chapter was designed to address five fundamental issues, all of which were associated at least to some extent with the Bush administration's doctrine of preemption as articulated in the context of the NSS it released in September 2002. First, it examined a series of historical precedents for the use of preemptive action, whether military or non-military in character, placing an emphasis on the twentieth century. Second, it reviewed the central tenets of that strategy, those related to preemptive and preventative action over both the short and long terms. Third, it assessed the strengths of Bush's NSS. Fourth, it assessed the weaknesses of Bush's NSS. Lastly, it discussed the application of the preemptive use of force to the case of Iraq in 2002-03.

Collectively, the evidence presented in the sections pertaining to each of those issues leads to several useful conclusions. First, any policy or strategy must be assessed on the basis of the rationality of its content and the utility of its practical application. Bush's NSS was designed to preempt threats to American security interests at home and abroad over both the short and long terms. The changing perception of dangers to the United States in the aftermath of the events of 9/11 prompted the Bush administration to consider the direct—and, if necessary, robust— use of military force to preempt threats posed by terrorist organizations and their state sponsors before such threats become imminent. That strategy was certainly rational in theory. In practice, it meant confronting Saddam over his refusal to desist from pursuing the acquisition of WMD and support for terrorist groups including Al Qaeda. While the diplomacy preceding Operation Iraqi Freedom was somewhat problematic, particularly given that it alienated traditional US allies such as France and Germany, the conduct of the operation itself resulted in the liquidation of Saddam's regime to the benefit of Americans, the Iraqi populace at large and the broader Middle Eastern and international communities.

Second, Bush's NSS relies on a variety of tools to enhance the security of the United States and its allies, many of which pertain to the medium and long terms and do not rely on the direct use of military force. Encouraging the growth of free market economies and democratic political institutions in the developing world, for example, is also a central component of the Bush administration's strategy. It has pursued the realization of that objective by participating in multilateral nation-building operations in Iraq and convincing its NATO allies to take the lead in a similar capacity in Afghanistan. Each of these cases demonstrates the flexibility of the doctrine of preemption. Preventing future terrorist threats can be achieved both by the use of force against bin Laden and his followers and also by improving the standards of living and availability of political freedom in regions in which Al Qaeda has found willing recruits in the past. And, while the most visible of these initiatives are presently unfolding in the Greater Middle East, they could, should and probably will eventually be expanded to include the broader developing world.

Third, any strategy should ultimately be judged on the totality of its costs and benefits over the short, medium and long terms. Similar to the Reagan Doctrine discussed in the first main section of this chapter, the Bush Doctrine (as supporters and critics have tagged the preemptive NSS) has produced mixed reviews since it was unveiled nearly two years ago. Reagan's opponents viewed his willingness to take a proactive approach in rolling back Soviet influence as needlessly reckless. Ultimately, they were wrong. Bush's critics have expressed comparable concerns that the threats posed by Al Qaeda and its state sponsors can be deterred or contained. That may be true. However, the possibility that bin Laden, Saddam and their compatriots in terror cannot be contained is simply an unacceptable risk to take in the post-9/11 world. Bush recognized that almost immediately after the 9/11 attacks and he is now correctly using the range of options articulated in the NSS to ensure that a tragedy on that scale does not occur again, whether in the next year, decade or century.

Notes

[1] John Lewis Gaddis, "A Grand Strategy of Transformation," *Foreign Policy* (November/December 2002): 53.

[2] Steve A. Yetiv, *The Persian Gulf Crisis* (Westport, CT: Greenwood Press, 1997), 184-85. These requirements are set forth explicitly in United Nations (UN) Security Council Resolution 687, which was approved on 3 April 1991.

[3] George W. Bush, "Remarks at the United Nations General Assembly," *White House Office of the Press Secretary*, 12 September 2002; National Security Council (NSC), "A Decade of Deception and Defiance: Saddam Hussein's Defiance of the United Nations," Background Paper for President Bush's UN Address, *White House Office of the Press Secretary* (12 September 2002): 4-7.

[4] Bush, "Remarks at the UN."

[5] Ibid.

[6] Ibid.

[7] George W. Bush, "National Security Strategy of the United States of America," *White House Office of the Press Secretary* (17 September 2002): i.

[8] Condoleezza Rice, "2002 Wriston Lecture at the Manhattan Institute," *White House Office of the Press Secretary* (1 October 2002).

[9] United States Congress, "Joint Resolution Granting Authorization for the Use of Military Force Against Iraq," *United States Congress* (10 October 2002).

[10] UN Security Council, "UN Security Council Resolution 1441," *United Nations Press Office* (8 November 2002).

[11] Victor Davis Hanson, *Ripples of Battle: How Wars of the Past Still Determine How we Fight, How we Live and How we Think* (New York: Doubleday, 2003), 44-45.

[12] Ibid., 56-57.

[13] For a detailed account of the crisis from one of those directly involved at the time, see Robert F. Kennedy, *Thirteen Days: A Memoir of the Cuban Missile Crisis* (New York: W.W. Norton & Company, 1969).

[14] For a detailed examination of the Reagan Doctrine, see Mark P. Lagon, *The Reagan Doctrine: The Sources of American Conduct in the Cold War's Last Chapter* (Westport, CT: Praeger, 1994).

[15] Max Boot, "The Bush Doctrine Lives," *The Weekly Standard* (16 February 2004), 25.

[16] For detailed examinations of NATO intervention in Kosovo in 1999, see Wesley K. Clark, *Waging Modern War: Bosnia, Kosovo and the Future of Combat* (New York: Public Affairs, 2001) and Ivo H. Daalder and Michael E. O'Hanlon, *Winning Ugly: NATO's War to Save Kosovo* (Washington, DC: Brookings Institution Press, 2000).

[17] Clark, *Waging Modern War*, xx.

[18] Bush, "National Security Strategy."

[19] Colin L. Powell, "A Strategy of Partnerships," *Foreign Affairs* (January/February 2004): 24.

[20] Bush, "National Security Strategy."

[21] Powell, "A Strategy of Partnerships," 23.

[22] Bush, "National Security Strategy," 8. In particular, the NSS states that "[w]e must be prepared to stop rogue states and their terrorist clients before they are able to threaten or use weapons of mass destruction against the United States and our allies and friends."

[23] Ibid., 15.

[24] Ibid., 9.

[25] Powell, "A Strategy of Partnerships," 25-26.

[26] Bush, "National Security Strategy," 5-9.

[27] Rice, "Wriston Lecture."

[28] William J. Clinton, "A National Security Strategy for a New Century," *White House Office of the Press Secretary* (December 1999): iii.

[29] Gaddis, "A Grand Strategy," 50-51.

[30] UN Security Council, "Security Council Resolution 1441."

[31] Bush, "National Security Strategy," 11.

[32] George W. Bush, "President's Speech to the American Enterprise Institute," 26 February 2003, excerpted in *We Will Prevail*, 227.

[33] NSC, "A Decade of Deception and Defiance," 4-7; UN Security Council, "Resolution 4112."

[34] NSC, "A Decade of Deception and Defiance," 4-7.

[35] Bush, "Remarks on Iraq at Cincinnati Museum Center," 7 October 2002, excerpted in *We Will Prevail*, 192-200; Bush, "Remarks at UN General Assembly."

[36] United States Congress, "Joint Resolution for the Use of Military Force Against Iraq." The House approved the resolution by a 296-133 vote on 10 October 2002; the Senate approved it by a 77-23 vote on 11 October 2002.

[37] UN Security Council, "Security Council Resolution 1441."

[38] "The Cold Calculation of War," *Economist* (3 April 2003).

[39] "It's Not Easy being French," *Economist* (3 April 2003).

Chapter 3

Diplomacy and Brinksmanship

Introduction

The first major test of the Bush administration's NSS was Iraq. The administration's efforts to remove Saddam Hussein from power were in line with policy inherited from the Clinton administration and reflected both immediate, practical security concerns and a deep concern over Saddam's long-range impact on the war on terror, especially the potential for increased Iraqi support for anti-US terrorist groups. Among the immediate security interests raised by the Iraqi regime were regional instability, the pursuit of WMDs and the short- and medium-range systems needed to deliver these weapons, and the continuing need to deploy American military forces in the area to enforce the no-fly zones over northern and southern Iraq.

While Bush's September 2002 UN speech marked the formal opening of the campaign to oust Saddam, the decision to force Iraq to comply with international norms and their manifestation in repeated UN resolutions, or face regime-change, was made early in the administration. Hence, a long-term American security goal, the transition of Iraq to a "normal" member state of the Persian Gulf political and security system, coincided with the development and articulation of a new security strategy for the implementation of US goals—the NSS.

In its pursuit of regime change in Iraq, the Bush administration was criticized on both domestic and international levels for engaging in foreign policy, marked not by the multilateralism of US policy during the Cold War and immediate post-Cold War eras, but by unilateralism and hegemonic tendencies. Conventional wisdom seemed to suggest that the administration was abandoning the main tenets of American diplomacy, and the carefully-crafted efforts to develop a world order based on American post-World War II preferences for multilateralism.[1] This chapter examines the main components of the Bush administration's foreign policy toward Iraq within the framework of existing models of diplomacy and coercive bargaining. Specifically, the chapter seeks to identify whether the Bush administration's diplomacy was aberrant in comparison with long-standing trends in the nation's interaction with world actors and whether the wranglings over Iraq marked the beginning of a new phase of American foreign policy marked by brinksmanship and unilateral action.

While a comprehensive examination of US foreign policy and American diplomacy is beyond the scope of this book, this chapter presents the core features of modern American foreign policy and the contemporary debates over the utility and practicality of each. The functionality of international institutions is presented as a means to measure their costs and benefits to America's Iraq policy in light of their broader importance to the nation's diplomacy. Ultimately, the analysis seeks to move beyond the isolationism versus engagement debate, as well as the divide between proponents of unilateralism versus multilateralism, in order to integrate interests, goals and policy implementation in the discussion of the Bush diplomatic effort toward regime change in Iraq.

American Diplomacy and the Presidency

American diplomacy in the post-World War II era has been marked by a strong preference for multilateralism. Nonetheless, this proclivity has been periodically constrained by national security and economic interests. One manner in which to conceptualize the constraints is through Robert Putnam's lens of two-level games. Using game-theory, Putnam asserts that leaders are forced to play a multi-level game and try to maximize winnings on both the domestic and international levels (although at different times, either domestic or international wins can be more important). Putnam summarized his model in the following manner:

> The politics of many international negotiations can usefully be conceived as a two level game. At the national level, domestic groups pursue their interests by pressuring the government to adopt favorable policies, and politicians seek power by constructing coalitions among those groups. At the international level, national governments seek to maximize their own ability to satisfy domestic pressures, while minimizing the adverse consequences of foreign developments. Neither of the two games can be ignored by central decision makers, so long as their countries remain interdependent, yet sovereign.[2]

Throughout most of the Cold War, the domestic constraints on US presidents were lessened by a bipartisan consensus in favor of containments at the political level and a domestic consensus in support of strong national defense. Stanley A. Renshon characterizes the trend as one in which "public expectations changed ... [D]uring the cold war, the public—at first reluctantly, but ultimately solidly—came to understand and support the necessity of giving the president leeway in that fight."[3] The "leeway" granted to presidents by the public in turn provided successive presidents with enhanced public approval as part of a "rally around the flag" impact which, in turn, provided those same presidents with a greater ability to influence Congress and implement their agendas.[4]

The result of the deference granted to presidents in diplomatic issues and the bipartisan consensus on containment of the Soviet Union was that presidents were able to overcome divided government and work with Congresses of the opposing party to maintain what James K. Oliver described as a "fragile strategic coherence."[5] This coherence was reinforced by the organization of the American government and by institutional arrangements which tended to bolster the power of the presidency in regards to foreign policy.

The US preference for multilateralism reflects both domestic and international pressures on the US. In presidential studies, Aaron Wildavsky's "two presidency" theory holds that the office of the president is best conceptualized as being two distinct entities: a domestic presidency; and a foreign policy presidency.[6] Because the Constitution grants the president greater latitude in foreign affairs, the nation's chief executives often tend to concentrate in this area as a way to achieve tangible results without the constraints inherent in domestic policy.[7] Wildavsky noted that presidents "had much greater success in controlling the nation's defense and foreign policies than in dominating its domestic policies."[8] He also pointed out that the grave importance attached to foreign policy decisions: "[f]ew failures in domestic policy, Presidents soon realize, could have as disastrous consequences as any one of dozens of mistakes in the international arena."[9]

Simon Serfaty traces a trend in foreign policy which demonstrates how the pressures of the institutions of the US government tended to reinforce coherence in American diplomacy and security strategy during the Cold War. Writing in 1988, Serfaty noted that successive US presidents came into office with promise of developing new directions in foreign policy: "Since 1952 every newly elected President has pledged a new beginning in US foreign policy ... . The temptation to start anew has been all the more irresistible as each election has usually coincided with, or closely followed, an international crisis that left the country with a sense of danger or a taste of failure."[10] Incoming presidents sought to operationalize their campaign rhetoric, which was always based on efforts to distinguish differences in foreign policy between the current administration and its newly-elected successor. These "new directions" in foreign policy were articulated in inaugural speeches, often to great fanfare; hence Dwight Eisenhower's call for rollback and aggressive confrontation with the Soviet Union or John F. Kennedy's request for Americans to "pay any price, bear any burden, and face any foe to defend freedom," or Jimmy Carter's call for a new morality and emphasis on human rights in US policy.[11] Subsequently, however, events demonstrated new beginnings ... proved to be false starts, as their hyperbolic rhetoric exaggerated the range of options available to the nation's foreign policy" and, instead,

> [w]ithin a few months each new President's attempts to stamp his imprint on foreign policy began to sink under the weight of a legacy that refused to go away: a war in Asia for Eisenhower, an ill-advised invasion in the Caribbean for Kennedy, another war in Asia for Nixon, and a self-defeating effort to transform the arms control structure for Carter.[12]

This pattern continued in the aftermath of the Cold War. The first President Bush (1989-1993) sought to develop a "new world order," only to have his foreign policy vision blunted by the twin pressures of domestic concerns and the raise of ethnic violence which undermined his diplomatic plans for increased cooperation and international security. Candidate Clinton sought to distinguish himself from incumbent Bush by promising a more assertive foreign policy in regards to the Balkans and Somalia only to ultimately continue his predecessor's Balkan strategy and accept an ignominious retreat from Somalia, all the while maintaining the Bush containment strategy toward Iraq. Candidate George W. Bush was perceived as a neo-isolationist president, uninterested in foreign policy, however, the terrorist attacks of 11 September forced his administration to engage in a range of diplomatic initiatives and foreign military operations and develop policies that mirrored the broad-based efforts of the Cold War as his administration sought to contain and rollback global terrorism in much the same way as successive Cold War administrations engaged in the bipolar confrontation. Nonetheless, while the Bush administration has adopted a range of strategies and tactics that mirror those employed in the Cold War struggle, the US faces a dramatically changed international system in the post-11 September world.

Presidents and Brinksmanship

Modern American diplomacy has often been characterized by the personal intervention of the president. For instance, at the beginning of the twentieth century, the entrance of the US onto the world stage was personified by Teddy Roosevelt.[13] Roosevelt became both the symbol and embodiment of a new and assertive American style of diplomacy.[14] Roosevelt was the first president to travel outside of the US and one of his last acts as president was to dispatch an American naval force, the "Great White Fleet" around the world as a demonstration of the power of the nation. [15] Roosevelt also arranged for a revolt in Panama in order to secure the rights to build the Panama Canal. When criticized for his actions, Roosevelt declared:

> I confidently maintain that the recognition of the Republic of Panama was an act justified by the interests of collective civilization. If ever a government could be said to have received a mandate from civilization to affect an object of accomplishment of which was demanded in the interest of mankind, the United States holds that position with regard to the inter-oceanic canal.[16]

This theme of American exceptionalism would mark Roosevelt's tenure as president. In a different diplomatic context, Roosevelt won the Nobel Prize for his successful efforts to negotiate an end to the Russo-Japanese War. The next Roosevelt, Franklin Delano, also personified American diplomacy as he attended a succession of summits with the leaders of the Allied nations of World War II. Indeed, the post-World War II diplomacy of the US has been marked by "summit diplomacy" as various presidents have sought to capitalize on foreign policy successes through positive publicity and as the role of the secretary of state has declined in the aftermath of the 1947 National Security Act which "relegated the secretary to be one voice among a group of presidential advisors that include figures such as the National Security Advisor, the Secretary of Defense, and the Chairman of the Joint Chiefs of Staff."[17]

Even as American diplomacy has become increasingly personalized and concentrated in the hands of the president, there has been a corresponding rise in the tactics of brinkmanship in US foreign policy. First used extensively during the Eisenhower administration, the basis for brinksmanship was the perception that by forcing adversaries right up to the point of military conflict, American diplomats could gain maximum concessions from their opponents. Brinksmanship involves extensive use of harsh or threatening rhetoric, combined with provocative actions, including military deployments. The policy was, and remains, usually associated with hawkish or aggressive foreign policy. Many scholars have compared brinksmanship with psychological warfare and noted its potential negative consequences. For instance, the historian John Lewis Gaddis describes the record of brinksmanship during the Eisenhower administration in the following terms:

> The record of the Eisenhower years is littered with memorable examples of Dulles's penchant for overstatement (or reporters' abridgement of them— "massive retaliation," "liberation," "agonizing reappraisal," the "immorality" of neutrality, "brinksmanship" all of which conveyed in more forceful and dramatic terms than reality warranted what the administration was trying to do. The result was to confuse the public, alarm allies, and no doubt thoroughly bewilder adversaries.[18]

Nonetheless, successive presidents have utilized brinksmanship as a means to gain concessions in foreign policy. Kennedy made great use of the tactic during the Cuban Missile Crisis and was able to craft a compromise that provided greater advantage to the US than to the USSR.[19]

The administration of George W. Bush has also embraced the main tenets of brinksmanship. One result has been increased charges of unilateralism by Bush's critics. Brinksmanship is a tactic, unilateralism remains a policy preference. Throughout post-World War II American foreign policy, the nation has consistently pursued "selective" multilateralism. As Stewart Patrick contends, "The United States often engages in 'forum shopping,' choosing among the UN, regional entities, and informal coalitions to expand its influence and limit its obligations. As a rule, the United States prefers narrower collectivities … to diverse bodies with universal membership."[20] Bush's foreign policy has been from the outset merely a continuation of this selective multilateralism, combined with old-fashioned brinksmanship. For instance, during his presidential campaign in 2000, Bush's national security advisor, Condoleezza Rice, accused the Clinton administration of surrendering American national security interests to "the interests of an illusionary international community" because the administration mistakenly believed that "the support of many states—or even better, of institutions like the United Nations—is essential to the legitimate exercise of power."[21] Rice went on to declare that "multilateral agreements and institutions should not be ends in themselves."[22] Instead, the Bush administration sought from its very beginning to reassert the supremacy of national security interests over multilateralism as a specific interest. The then State Department Director of

Policy Planning, Richard Haass asserted that the incoming Bush administration would examine each potential multilateral involvement within the context of the broader goals of American foreign policy and national security interests through cost-benefit analysis.[23] Still, the Bush administration was confronted, both before and after the attacks of 11 September, with the legacy of US Cold War policy.

Diplomatic Questions and the End of the Cold War

The end of the Cold War did initiate a steady erosion of the Cold War consensus in US foreign policy and ushered a range of questions over the role of the United States in international affairs. These questions are varied and complex, but they are the main determinants of a nation's foreign policy strategy. For instance, Patrick Callahan has developed a useful rubric that called for strategy examined along a range of seven "dimensions."[24] First, what is the appropriate "level of engagement"—how deeply engaged should the US be in world affairs? Specifically, what commitments should be avoided or what self-limitations should be placed on US actions?[25] Second, what are the priorities of the US? Third, what is the "geographic scope" of American policy? Should Washington endeavor to be engaged on a global level or should US engagement be limited to key regions or even key states? Fourth, how, or even should, the US attempt to exercise leadership? Should it follow a unilateral or a multilateral path and what is the appropriate relationship between the US and key international institutions? Fifth, what role should "military might" and power play in American diplomacy.[26] Sixth, should the US be "interventionist" or "noninterventionist"— should Washington try to influence or craft the internal institutions and both political and economic systems of other states or other regions? Seventh, and finally, how should Washington address the issue of globalization? Should the US embrace free trade and the global economy or should it seek to tie its economic policies to broader questions of political or human rights or environmental issues?[27]

The range and breadth of these questions are sufficiently daunting, but within each major question group there are a considerable number of sub-questions. In their introduction to a section of their book on the use of force, Robert J. Art and Kenneth N. Waltz point out that there are at least four major questions about the use of military force and the utility of military power:

> First, should the United States, the world's premier military power, continue to use its might for its own interests and for those of other states as well, and if so, how should its military might be employed? Second, how much of a danger is the spread of nuclear weapons, and how can the danger be dealt with? Third, can outside powers intervene effectively in the internal conflicts of other states, and if they do intervene, what tactics will be most effective? Fourth, how has terrorism changed over the past thirty years, and what can be done to counter it?[28]

These questions are addressed on several levels in the Bush NSS, yet their very nature is so broad, and concurrently fundamental, that they extend beyond the NSS and continue to be grappled with at several levels. Those questions over the appropriateness of the use of military force and power are the legacy of the Cold War, specifically, America's experience in Vietnam.

The Vietnam Legacy

No other foreign policy event exercises a greater impact on contemporary policy formulation than Vietnam. Vietnam undermined the public confidence in the presidency to a degree not seen by any other event during the Cold War. It also resulted in both overt and tacit restrictions on future presidents over the use of military force. For instance, the 1973 War Powers Act (a law that no president has accepted as constitutional) restricts the ability of a president to deploy military forces without congressional consent. The act was designed to prevent future long, drawn-out conflicts in which Congress had little ability to control events once the initial decision to deploy troops was made.[29] At the same time, there developed a widely-held belief among politicians and career bureaucrats that Americans were adverse to battlefield casualties and unwilling to accept significant military loses.

The legacy of Vietnam strikes to the heart of the age-old diplomatic debate between assertive and reactive foreign policy (or between appeasement and the Clausewitzian maxims on the use of military force to achieve diplomatic objectives). Diplomacy and force are often intertwined as states pursue foreign policy interests. As James A. Nathan points out "for most of history, force has been diplomacy's twin and its nemesis: the sun and symbol of diplomacy's failure."[30] Because of the lessons of World War II, appeasement was seen as a failed and dangerous policy. Writing in the 1960s, Hans Morgenthau summarized the perception of appeasement by most international relations scholars during the Cold War: "One might say that appeasement is a corrupted policy of compromise, made erroneous by mistaking a policy of imperialism for a policy of status quo."[31] Frederick Hartmann is even more damning in his denunciation: "It is precisely when the vital interests are bartered in return for minor concessions, or none at all, that appeasement has taken place. Appeasement may result from weakness or ignorance, either from an inability to fight or a misconception of the effects on vital interests."[32] The result was the "Munich analogy" in which perceived weakness or vacillation in foreign policy was held to be equal to Neville Chamberlain's appeasement of Hitler on the eve of World War II.[33]

Yet even as appeasement faced scholarly scorn in the 1950s and 1960s, the use of force was increasingly questioned as a result of America's involvement in Vietnam. That the United States continued its military efforts in Vietnam for too long reflected the fear of successive administrations of being labeled proponents of appeasement and of encouraging Soviet aggression by not taking strong action. American officials feared that the failure to support South Vietnam would undermine US military guarantees to other states. Secretary of State Dean Rusk wrote in 1965 of the US pledge to defend South Vietnam: "[i]f that commitment becomes unreliable, the communist world would draw conclusions that would lead to our ruin and almost certainly to a catastrophic war."[34] Nathan contends that

> Dulles, Kennedy, Johnson, and Nixon persisted in Vietnam not for the South Vietnamese, nor because there was a winning strategy at hand; but because it was feared that an erosion in the appearance of steadfastness and power would injure American alliances and embolden American enemies. Indecision in Vietnam could, it was feared, precipitate the kind of test by aggressors that would necessitate larger wars for greater stakes, on the one hand, or risk either nuclear war or capitulation on the other.[35]

The result was that both the US and the USSR "both regarded each other as essentially aggressive entities that only understood the language of strength" and "each power feared that any action—or failure to act—that allowed the other side improve its position would be regarded as an expression of weakness and encourage further aggression."[36] Consequently, the Cold War was viewed very much as a zero-sum game in which one side's progress only came at the expense of its opponent.[37] Just as Munich indicated the limits of appeasement and the potential disastrous consequences of giving into coercive diplomacy, the lessons of Vietnam reaffirmed the terrible results of over-reliance on military power without a concurrent emphasis on possible diplomatic solutions. Nathan concludes that Vietnam represented "a failure to use diplomacy when it was relevant."[38] Vietnam led to a major reassessment of containment and convinced American leaders that the nation could not pursue global containment based purely on military power, but had to use statecraft and diplomacy to supplement its security guarantees.[39]

Carter, Reagan and the End of Appeasement

With the election of Carter in 1976, there was a short-lived effort to ease the superpower struggle and insert a new morality in US foreign policy. For instance, Carter ended support for anti-communist regimes in Iran and Nicaragua because of their human rights records and he demonstrated a willingness to tolerate aggressive Soviet policies in exchange for arms control agreements such as the Strategic Arms Limitation Talks (SALT) II.[40] Carter's presidency marked the twilight of a brief period of appeasement in US foreign policy. The Soviet invasion of Afghanistan undermined his efforts at détente and led to a renewal of intensity in the Cold War. The historian John Lewis Gaddis notes that Carter had the "misfortune to come to power at a time when the Soviet Union was launching a new series of challenges to the global balance of power" and the US faced a "general decline in super-power authority."[41] In addition, Gaddis writes that "effects of the post-Vietnam conviction" limited the option of the "use of force" as a means to provide credibility to assertive responses to Soviet action.[42] Carter was forced to return to aggressive containment with the Carter Doctrine which was promulgated during the State of the Union Address on 23 January 1980. In the address, Carter declared that: "An attempt by any outside force to gain control of the Persian Gulf Region will be regarded as an assault on the vital interests of the United States of America, and such an assault will be repelled by any means necessary, including military force."[43] Carter further stated that "verbal condemnation is not enough. The Soviet Union must pay for its aggression" in Afghanistan and other areas.[44]

The Carter Doctrine signaled the end of the last significant effort at global appeasement and the height of the constraints of the Vietnam legacy, it marked the formal commitment of the United States to defense of the status quo in the Persian Gulf region. This commitment would be endorsed by each of Carter's successors both formally and informally. Meanwhile, Carter's immediate successor, Reagan, continued the erosion of the Vietnam legacy through military deployments and a renewed rollback policy toward the Soviet Union. Reagan's policies were codified in the Reagan Doctrine.[45] The Doctrine pledged US support and aid for "those risking their lives on every continent from Afghanistan to Nicaragua to defy Soviet-supported aggression."[46] After the 1983 US invasion of Grenada to displace a Cuban- and Soviet-backed regime that had taken power, then-Secretary of State George Schultz commented that the action was a sign to the Soviets that "Western democracies were again ready to use the military strength they harbored and built up over the years in defense of their principles and interests."[47] Finally, as detailed in this book's introduction, George H. W. Bush adopted an assertive series of policies to counter Saddam Hussein's invasion of Kuwait, thereby maintaining both the general trend away from appeasement in foreign policy and continuing the policy of his predecessor of viewing any threat to regional stability in the Persian Gulf as a major threat to US interests.

The Need for New Enemies and Iraq

During the Cold War, the Soviet Union was a constant enemy for the US and the superpower struggle dictated the main element of American diplomacy: the containment of communism. As Samuel P. Huntington notes, the US may have enacted various specific policies during the bipolar conflict, but "its one overriding national purpose was to contain and defeat communism. When other goals and interests clashed with this purpose, they were usually subordinated to it."[48] With the end of the Cold War, Bush was confronted with a range of new villains and opponents of US foreign policy interests, including notably Manuel Noriega and Saddam Hussein.

For Clinton, Slobodan Milosevic provided a ready-made opponent and, of course, Saddam Hussein remained a constant potential threat to both regional stability in the Persian Gulf and to broader US security interests. More significantly, even though it was initially an ephemeral and not easily quantifiable threat, was the danger of Islamic terrorism. The first bombing of the World Trade Center occurred just 37 days after Clinton took office. Over time and after a succession of terrorist attacks, Al Qaeda would emerge as one of the principal challenges to US security and foreign policy.

The emergence of a variety of new threat perceptions in the post-Cold War exemplified both changes in the international system and the traditional tendency for Americans to view foreign actors in black and white terms, and to define themselves in opposition to outside interests. Shoon Kathleen Murray and Jason Meyers comment that "it is an old adage that people need foreign enemies and, by implication, that if they lose one enemy, then another will soon be found to replace it."[49] Other authors have noted that "[i]t seems that we [the US] have always needed enemies and scapegoats; it they have not been readily available, we have created them."[50] In the post Cold War era, the main "new" enemy of the US was Saddam Hussein. Psychologist Sam Keen writes that "Hussein is a marvelous enemy ... . We were getting desperate in our search for new enemy."[51] Before the events of 11 September, the Bush administration came into office with the belief that Saddam Hussein represented the greatest threat to US interests and that Iraq was the globe's most dangerous rogue state.[52]

The US perception of Saddam Hussein as a major threat to international peace and stability contrasted significantly with the view point common in many allied states that Iraq could be contained and that Saddam was mainly a threat to the people of Iraq. A range of states, including the main European allies of the US, Russia, and China offered lukewarm support for the US containment policy through the 1990s, but France and Russia increasingly agitated for an end to economic sanctions against Iraq in order to pursue lucrative oil contracts in existence since before the 1991 war.[53] They also sought an end to direct military containment. For instance, when the US used air and missile strikes against Iraq in 1996 following the Iraqi occupation of Irbil, France not only opted out of the military effort but French President Jacques Chirac asserted that the attacks were only election-year bravado on the part of the Clinton administration while another French official noted that Iraq "was acting entirely on its own soil."[54]

During the 1998 missile strikes which followed Saddam's forced removal of UN weapons inspectors, Moscow even recalled its ambassadors from Washington and London (the first such diplomatic action since 1971).[55] China and France coordinated an official protest and a range of US allies in the Persian Gulf also denounced the strikes. Even formerly reliable allies such as Saudi Arabia demonstrated displeasure at the US action by constraining the ability of US forces to launch attacks from Saudi bases and Riyadh even denied overflight permissions for their territory.[56] Following the US-led strikes, there was a widespread perception that Saddam had won the contest with the US by splintering the anti-Iraq coalition and proving his willingness to stand-up to American pressure. A former commander of British military forces in the Persian Gulf opined that the most probable long-term result of the attacks would be "to strengthen Saddam in his position," and a diplomat in Baghdad echoed these comments with the proclamation that "anytime Saddam Hussein is still alive or in power, he is a winner."[57]

By the end of the 1990s there was growing sentiment that Iraq could be contained without the UN sanctions regime, but with the continued explicit threat of US military action if the regime misbehaved. In an essay on containing Saddam, noted international relations scholars John J. Mearsheimer and Stephen M. Walt remind their readers that

> History provides at least two pieces of evidence demonstrating that Saddam is deterrable. First although he did launch conventionally-armed SCUD missiles at Saudi Arabia and Israel during the Gulf War, he did not launch chemical or biological weapons at the coalition forces that were decimating the Iraqi military. Moreover, senior Iraqi officials ... have testified that Iraq refrained form using its chemical weapons because the Bush administration had made ambiguous but unmistakable threats to retaliate with nuclear weapons if Iraq used WMD. Second, in 1994, Iraq mobilized the remnants of its army on the Kuwaiti border ... . But when the UN issued a new warning and the United States reinforced its forces in Kuwait, Iraq quickly backed down.[58]

John Mueller and Karl Mueller summarized the containment argument in the following manner:

> If the specter of retaliation successfully deterred Iraq from launching chemical attacks during that conflict [the first Iraq War], as many argue, it can do so again. Instead of exaggerating the threat posed by Iraq's biological and chemical arsenal, the United States and Britain should simply explain that if Iraq uses these weapons it will face cataclysmic punishment—including, potentially, an invasion—that would strike at Saddam directly and not just his long-suffering subjects. US and allied forces can be kept at the ready in the neighborhood. Is some Iraqi opposition groups show real and credible promise of being able to overthrow the dictator, they might be given support.[59]

The attacks of 11 September changed the strategic calculus for the Bush administration. With the issuance of the NSS, the Bush administration gave formal notice that it intended to abandon containment and that it had no interest in appeasement. Instead the administration would engage in broad preemptive security policies in order to forestall future attacks on the US. The Bush administration therefore sought to move from reactive diplomacy to proactive, preventative policies.

For the Bush administration, the war on terror was never just about toppling the Taliban regime in Afghanistan, instead Operation Enduring Freedom was viewed as one part of a larger and longer-term effort to combat international terrorism and to specifically undermine and eliminate existing radical Islamic fundamentalist terrorist networks. In his first major speech following the 11 September attacks, Bush declared that "Our war on terror begins with Al Qaeda, but it does not end there. It will not end until every terrorist group of global reach has been found, stopped and defeated."[60] Bush went on to describe his vision of a campaign with truly global reach:

> Our response involves far more than instant retaliation and isolated strikes. Americans should not expect one battle, but a lengthy campaign, unlike

any other we have ever seen. It may include dramatic strikes, visible on TV, and covert operations, secret even in success. We will starve terrorists of funding, turn them one against another, drive them from place to place, until there is no refuge or no rest. And we will pursue nations that provide aid or safe haven to terrorism. Every nation, in every region, now has a decision to make. Either you are with us, or you are with the terrorists. From this day forward, any nation that continues to harbor or support terrorism will be regarded by the United States as a hostile regime.[61]

In this regard, the military campaign in Afghanistan was simply "Phase One" of the war on terror and after the fall of the Taliban, the administration began casting about for the most significant targets for "Phase Two."[62]

Many of America's allies in the Afghan campaign, however, did not expect the war on terror to continue in robust fashion after the fall of the Taliban. A range of West European governments expected the military campaign to cease and that the US would concentrate on law-enforcement and intelligence activities that would constrain future terrorist attacks and damage terrorist networks.[63] Most attributed the rhetoric of the Bush administration to brinksmanship. The consensus among many leaders was that the US had been attacked and that it had justly exercised its right of self defense. The political philosopher Patrick Hayden notes that "owing to the previous unresponsiveness of the Taliban regime and the time-sensitive nature of attempting to apprehend Al Qaeda operatives and eliminate their camps, the United States at least had an excuse, and probably a justification, for launching the military campaign in Afghanistan when it did."[64]

In the end, however, global leaders perceived that the "Afghanistan-first strategy was an Afghanistan-only strategy."[65] Hence, nations across the globe were ready to join the US when Bush declared that "This is not, however, just America's fight. And what is at stake is not just America's freedom. This is the world's fight. This is civilization's fight. This is the fight of all who believe in progress and pluralism, tolerance and freedom. We ask every nation to join us."[66] In reality, Bush meant every word of his speech and fully intended that the campaign in Afghanistan would only be the opening front in the war on terror. This misunderstanding of intention would be one of the main factors which would complicate the diplomacy surrounding the Bush administration's second phase in the war on terror—the campaign against Iraq.

Coercive Diplomacy and Iraq

With the labeling of Iraq as part of the axis of evil in the 2002 State of the Union address, Bush formally launched the diplomatic campaign against the Hussein regime. As early as 1998, Congress had voted to endorse regime change in Iraq as a component of the Iraq Liberation Act. The law specifically stated that "it should be the policy of the United States to support efforts to remove the regime headed by

Saddam Hussein from power in Iraq and to promote the emergence of a democratic government to replace that regime."[67] The act went on to detail the regime's crimes and cited Iraqi noncompliance with UN inspections as a key factor necessitating regime change. The law called on then-President Clinton "to call upon the United Nations to establish an international criminal tribunal for the purpose of indicting, prosecuting, and imprisoning Saddam Hussein and other Iraqi officials who are responsible for crimes against humanity, genocide, and other criminal violations of international law."[68]

As noted, Clinton preferred a containment policy toward Iraq. His secretary of state, Madeleine Albright often noted that Saddam was "in a box."[69] Clinton did try to reformulate the sanctions regime, but his efforts were rebuffed by the French and Russians. By 2000, France was Iraq's "largest trading partner" and Russia was the nation's "largest creditor"; consequently, both states preferred to end the sanctions entirely, rather than recalculate them.[70]

In addition, in the aftermath of the 11 September attacks there was considerable public support in the United States for further military action. Such support was, however, not directly tied to the 11 September attacks. For instance, in February 2001, a poll revealed that a majority of Americans (some 52 percent) "favored sending American ground troops to the Persian Gulf in an attempt to remove Saddam Hussein from power in Iraq."[71] By November, following the terrorist attacks, public support for military action against Saddam Hussein, including the use of ground forces, had risen to 74 percent, but such sentiment declined throughout the summer months of 2002, until it stabilized at around 57 percent in September.[72] Significantly, such support remained firm even without major efforts on the part of the Bush administration to rally domestic support.

> Where Iraq probably does help Republicans is by keeping congressional Democrats focused on debating the merits of an attack, rather than on pushing the domestic issues on which they have an advantage, and by keeping national security and military matters on the table, allowing Republicans to capitalize on their own advantages on this front, and potentially play up Democrats' past "anti-military" votes.[73]

The Bush administration launched a two-prong effort to garner support for a military campaign against: one prong involved rallying domestic support; and the second prong revolved around diplomatic efforts to build an anti-Saddam coalition and gain support from international organizations. Bush sought wins on both the domestic and international level and endeavored to link the two versions of the negotiating "game" together. Hence, the Bush administration believed that broad domestic support was the key to gaining international backing for action against Iraq since public sentiment and congressional endorsement of a military operation would both enhance the credibility of the administration's policy and provide incentives for other states to bandwagon with the US if it appeared that America would act because of domestic demand. The Bush administration also wanted strong domestic backing as a way to pressure the UN into endorsing US action.

On the domestic front, the public support for military action against Iraq combined with Bush's high poll numbers brought considerable pressure on Congress to support the administration. With Republican support assured, Bush was also able to gain the endorsement of Tom Daschle the Democratic leader in the Senate, and Dick Gephardt the Democratic leader in the House. The leadership of both parties promised Bush that they would vote on a resolution authorizing the use of force before the November 2002 congressional elections.[74] On 11 October 2002, the House of Representatives voted 296-133, and the Senate voted 77-23, in favor of a resolution giving Bush the authority to go to war with Iraq.

The UN Effort

The centerpiece of the Bush administration's initial public diplomatic effort on Iraq was the President's 12 September 2002 speech to the UN. In the address, Bush highlighted Iraq's human rights violations. He described how Iraq had violated a succession of UN Security Council Resolutions and that the UN had concluded as recently as 1998 that Iraq continued to possess stockpiles of WMDs, in continuing disregard for previous agreements and resolutions. Bush also noted that Saddam "accepted a series of commitments" but had "proven instead only his contempt for the United Nations, and for all his pledges. By breaking every pledge—by his deceptions, and by his cruelties—Saddam Hussein has made the case against himself."[75] Bush described the ineffectiveness of the contemporary sanctions regime and its manipulation by the Saddam regime. In some of the more forceful areas of the speech, Bush declared that " the conduct of the Iraqi regime is a threat to the authority of the United Nations, and a threat to peace. Iraq has answered a decade of U.N. demands with a decade of defiance. All the world now faces a test, and the United Nations a difficult and defining moment."[76]   He further asked whether "Security Council resolutions to be honored and enforced, or cast aside without consequence? Will the United Nations serve the purpose of its founding, or will it be irrelevant."[77] Bush warned that if the UN did not act, the US would. He concluded his speech with a warning of the potential results if the Iraqi regime where to provide WMDs to terrorist organizations and called upon the world body to undertake strong action.[78]

Domestically, the speech met with great approval and provided impetus for the congressional resolution authorizing the use of force. Daschle voiced his approval of the speech and stated "[e]very time the president continues to speak out, he strengthens his case."[79] Democratic Senator Joe Biden of Delaware even described Bush's speech as "brilliant" and provided a tepid endorsement for unilateral action: "The worst option is going it alone, but it is an option."[80]

The international response was also generally positive. Many countries openly signaled their approval of Bush's tactic of going before the UN in an effort to lobby the world organization. The step also seemed to dilute increasing criticism of US unilateralism. Accompanying the speech was a US request for a new Security Council

Resolution that would provide an ultimatum of sorts for Saddam: Allow unfettered weapons inspections and turn-over all banned weaponry and arms or face military action. France officially applauded the speech. The French Foreign Minister Dominique de Villepin declared that "the status quo is unacceptable," and that France "cannot agree to violations of any Security Council resolutions."[81] Chirac proposed a two-stage proposal that would include an initial resolution along the lines of Bush's proposal, followed by a second one to authorize force if Iraq did not comply. Even Iraq's longtime patron, Russia, signaled its support for renewed inspections and Moscow pledged not to oppose the use of force if such action had international backing.[82] UN Secretary General Kofi Annan warned against unilateral action by the US, but he also declared that the "Security Council must face its responsibilities."[83] The strongest and most vocal support for Bush's speech came form Great Britain and talks began between the two allies over the wording of a resolution which, it was agreed, would be proposed by Britain.

The October congressional vote added pressure on the UN Security Council to adopt a resolution reinstating the inspections regime in Iraq. The result was UN Security Council Resolution (UNSCR) 1441 which was unanimously adopted on 8 November 2002. The resolution declared that Iraq was in material beach of previous UN measures. It also provided for an enhanced inspections regime and clear deadlines for Iraqi compliance. UNSCR 1441 demanded unimpeded access to all Iraqi sites and required a detailed report from Baghdad on its WMD programs. Finally, the resolution warned Iraq of "serious consequence" if it did not comply with the UN mandate.[84]

The unanimous vote on UNSCR 1441 disguised a number of continuing differences among the Security Council members, particularly between a US-led faction, including Great Britain and Bulgaria, and a faction led by France, including Germany and Russia. The central point of contention was over whether or not Iraq would face automatic punishment if the Security Council deemed the country in continued violation of UN resolutions. Fred Kaplan described the result thus: "The United States gets to declare Iraq in material breach and to threaten its leaders with war if they don't take this final chance to comply. At the same time, France (which, after all, has veto power) retains the right to keep any move toward war bottled up inside the Security Council as long as its diplomats can manage."[85] Hence, American officials perceived that UNSCR 1441 was a stepping stone for more serous action against Iraq, while French leaders perceived the Resolution as another in a long line of Security Council dictates, and certainly not the beginning of the end of the process. It would be this basic dichotomy that would lead to the diplomatic implosion at the UN.

Brinksmanship and the UN

As it became apparent through the winter of 2002-2003 that Saddam had reverted to his cheat and retreat strategy from the 1990s.[86] The Iraqi regime produced a 12,000-page report on their WMD programs (which, it turned out, contained no new evidence or documentation). There were also a variety of tactics employed to frustrate the work of the UN inspectors which entered Iraq on 27 November. Meanwhile, the US began laying the groundwork for a second resolution. The second resolution had now become a key component of administration strategy since a range of states, including traditional US allies France, Germany and Canada. Concurrently, the US worked to assure bilateral cooperation from key states such as Turkey, Saudi Arabia, Kuwait and other Gulf countries.

Meanwhile there were a number of trends which ran counter to US efforts and threatened American strategy. First, Saddam was no longer viewed as the threat that he had been at the time of his invasion of Kuwait. In fact his status among Arab states had improved considerably. For instance, Saddam had adopted a "return to Islam" strategy designed to improve his image among radicals. In one manifestation of this trend, the Iraqi regime began paying the families of Palestinian suicide bombers a $10,000 bounty. The regime also pledged $881 million for the Palestinian Authority.[87]

Second, Iraq's importance as a trading partner to several key members of the previous anti-Saddam coalition had grown steadily during the 1990s. In addition to a range of contracts for oil with France and Russia, Moscow had become increasingly keen on recouping its share of Iraqi debt. Furthermore, by 2001, Iraq's main trading partners were, France, Russia, China and Egypt, in that order. Early in 2002, Iraq and Russia developed a $40 billion mutual economic package.[88]

Third, even among those states that bitterly opposed the Saddam regime and sought an end to his regime, there was widespread concern over the long-term ramifications of the Iraqi leader's removal. The ethnic and religious differences within Iraq led many in the Gulf region to fear that the fall of Saddam could lead to the break-up of Iraq and usher in regional instability. Former US ambassador to Turkey, Mark Parris argued before the war that the removal of Saddam would led to open war between Turkey and Iraq's Kurds, while Geoffrey Kemp of the Nixon Center pointed out that Iran was concerned that conflict in Iraq could unleash a flood of Iraqi refugees.[89] A US-led war in Iraq was also seen as likely to destabilize Jordan. Perhaps the most significant negative outcome of US military action against Saddam would be what the Brookings Institute's Michael O'Hanlon described as the "al-Jezeera effect": the potential that as millions of Arabs watched and listened to news reports about the war, there would be widespread anger against the US and a rise in recruits for anti-American radical Islamic terrorist organizations.[90]

Fourth, in Germany, national elections at the end of September 2002 doomed efforts to gain German support for military action. Incumbent Chancellor Gerhard Schröder adopted an anti-war platform which resonated with voters after months of losing ground to his center-right rival, Edmund Stoiber, because of the country's poor economic performance. The campaign became very heated as the right accused Schröder's party of risking the nation's close ties with Washington for short-term political gain. Tensions did escalate as Germany's Justice Minister, Herta Däubler-Gmelin, compared Bush's policies to those of Adolf Hitler and asserted that if Bush was not currently president, he would be in jail for business ethics violations.[91] In return, US Secretary of Defense Donald Rumsfield refused to meet privately with German Foreign Minister Joschka Fischer at a NATO meeting in Warsaw. Schröder's strategy in this two-level game was to ensure his domestic win, even if it meant sacrificing Germany's position in the international system. His gamble paid-off in that his party was narrowly reelected.

Fifth, and finally, Schröder's actions in Germany attested to a growing anti-war movement in Europe and Canada. While US public opinion supported military action against Iraq, European opinion tended to support military action only in the context of another UN Security Council Resolution and many European states faced a public who opposed military strikes even with UN endorsement. For instance, even in pro-US states such as Great Britain or the Netherlands, a majority of people surveyed in January 2003 opposed military intervention in Iraq (68 percent were opposed in Great Britain and 80 percent opposed in the Netherlands). However, if there was a new UN resolution, opposition dropped to 15 percent in Great Britain and 28 percent in the Netherlands. On the other hand, even with a fresh UN resolution, a majority of respondents opposed military action in states such as Germany (52 percent), Austria (72 percent) and Greece (71 percent).[92]

Public opinion in Europe also became increasingly opposed to US foreign policy in general during the Iraq crisis. A poll taken during the summer of 2002 revealed that while 53 percent of Americans ranked the Bush administration's foreign policy as "excellent or good," 56 percent of Europeans ranked it as "fair to poor."[93] This gap remained on specific issues as well. Among Americans, 55 percent ranked the administration's management of the Afghan campaign as excellent to good, while 60 percent of Europeans rated the administration as fair to poor. Craig Kennedy of the German Marshall Fund of the US, which cosponsored the poll, commented that he did not perceive the results "as criticism of the US so much as it reflects the European view that America really is the superpower and what it does affects everything."[94]

In spite of the range of opposition to US policy toward Iraq, the Bush administration sought to press on with military preparations and efforts to garner official support. Iraq was phase two of the war on terror and the administration received increasing intelligence signals that Saddam might ally with Al Qaeda. This was particularly troubling in light of Saddam's historical pursuit of WMDs. The Iraqi regime would not have to enter into any formal alliance to allow it to disseminate information about the development of chemical or biological weapons, instead it need only act as an incubator for terrorist WMD efforts to inflict great damage on US interests. There was also growing sentiment in the administration and Congress that containment and deterrence were no longer practical when the nation's main security threat was terrorism. Virginia Senator John Warner, a ranking Republican, characterized the impotence of deterrence when applied to terrorism in the following manner: "The concept of deterrence that served us well in the twentieth century has changed. ... Those who would commit suicide in their assaults on the free world are not rational and are not deterred by rational concepts of deterrence."[95] There was also legitimate concern that Iraq could not be allowed to continue acting as a rogue or pariah state and opening violating UN resolutions—especially since there were lingering questions about the nation's WMD capabilities and intelligence that Saddam was continuing to pursue WMDs. Finally, the administration perceived that the removal of the Saddam regime would provide an opportunity to attempt to foster democracy in the Middle East. Because of the level of secularism throughout much of the country, many planners contended that Iraq was the optimum state to develop democratic and pluralistic institutions.

Throughout the winter of 2002/2003, one of the main signals from Washington was that the US was prepared to take unilateral action if other states did not bandwagon with American policy. The midterm congressional elections in November 2002 had resulted in Republican gains in both houses of Congress as the Bush administration was able to cast the vote as a referendum on his management of the war on terror and on his popularity. The results bucked historical trends whereby the party of incumbent presidents tended to lose seats. Instead the Republicans gained 2 seats in the Senate (which gave them control of the chamber) and they added to their majority in the House. The elections strengthened Bush's hand domestically, and many in the administration perceived that the vote also sent a signal internationally that the US public supported Bush's Iraq policy. There were also practical military considerations: Rumsfield and the Defense Department planners wished to avoid any military action during the Iraqi summer and contended that the US would have to either strike during the spring or wait until the next fall or winter.

The administration engaged in both tacit and overt brinksmanship. Hardliners within the administration, led by Cheney and Rumsfeld, employed increasingly harsh rhetoric against both Iraq and those American allies, such as France and Germany, which questioned the build-up to war. In response, the anti-war nations became increasingly intransigent toward compromise. One concrete manifestation of the transatlantic tensions was the most significant crisis in German-US relations since the Second World War. While the administration blamed the crisis on Germany's unwillingness to negotiate, the German government blamed US unilateralism. For instance, Schröder referred to a speech by Cheney and asserted that "it just isn't good enough to learn from the American press about a speech which clearly states 'we are going to do it, no matter what the world or our allies think'."[96] Albright characterized the tensions as the result of "European unease with American pretensions, coupled with American doubts about European resolve," and asserted that the diplomatic conflict "created the potential for a long-term and dangerous rift."[97]

Powell led the moderates within the administration who sought to craft a compromise that would ensure broad international support, but would still move forward with phase two of the war on terror—the military campaign against Iraq. Powell was particularly interested in gaining a second UN resolution which he perceived as key to gaining more members of the anti-Saddam coalition and in legitimating US actions. A second resolution would also allow governments, such as that of Tony Blair, to participate in a military coalition by providing a mechanism to counter domestic opposition. Meanwhile, the hardliners increasingly insisted that a second resolution was not needed since UNSCR 1441 had already threatened action in the face of Iraqi noncompliance. The months immediately preceding the outbreak of the war were marked by intense diplomacy as the US sought to build a series of coalitions, including a diplomatic grouping in the UN and a more formal military coalition, and to rally world opinion. Concurrently, Germany and France emerged as the leaders of an anti-US coalition which sought to prevent the passage of a second UN resolution on Iraq and to prevent states from joining with the US-led military effort.

Diplomatic Complications and the UN

In the midst of the Bush administration's lobbying efforts, the ongoing inspections in Iraq complicated US diplomatic efforts. In March 2000, Hans Blix, a Swede, was appointed to oversee a new inspections regime for Iraq, the UN Monitoring, Verification and Inspection Commission (UNMOVIC). UNMOVIC was placed in charge of the new inspections required by UNSCR 1441. On 13 November 2002, Iraq formerly accepted the conditions of UNSCR 1441, and five days later, UN inspectors returned to Iraq.

In a series of reports to the UN Security Council and in remarks to the public and press during the key months of January and February 2003, Blix provided rhetorical ammunition for both sides of the debate. In his report of 9 January, Blix condemned Iraq for not having a real commitment to disarmament and for impeding the progress of inspectors. He also noted that Iraq's 12,000-page report on its weapons programs was incomplete and misleading. However, he also noted, that "we have been there for some two months and been covering the country in ever wider sweeps and we haven't found any smoking guns."[98]

In response, the US began to assert that no "smoking gun" was needed and instead, Iraqi non-compliance was enough to justify military action. White House Spokesman Ari Fleischer noted that "The problem with guns that are hidden is you can't see their smoke," and that the US knew "for a fact that there are weapons there."[99] Powell commented that "If the international community sees that Saddam Hussein is not cooperating in a way that would not allow you to determine the truth of the matter, then he is in violation of the UN Resolution (1441). ... You don't really have to have a smoking gun."[100] The US pointed out that Iraq was not allowing the inspectors to have private interviews with Iraqi WMD scientists as was required and that Baghdad continued to forbid the use of surveillance aircraft through January.

Meanwhile, the anti-war coalition utilized Blix's reports as evidence that the inspections needed more time and that military action was premature. But with the new year, American military preparations were well under way and the Bush administration had launched a new initiative to develop a coalition of the willing, one that could operate with or without UN endorsement of military action. While the administration did not abandon its UN diplomacy, by January, it had already begun to engage in a new round of diplomacy based more on bilateralism than multilateralism.

Notes

[1] For an overview of US efforts to develop a multilateral world order in the post-World War II era, see John G. Ruggie, ed., *Multilateralism Matters: The Theory and Praxis of an Institutional Form* (New York: Columbia University, 1993); and John G. Ruggie, Winning the Peace: America and World Order in the New Era (New York: Columbia University, 1996).

[2] Robert Putnam, "Diplomacy and Domestic Politics: The Logic of Two-Level Games," *International Organization*, 42 (Summer 1988), 434.

[3] Stanley A. Renshon, "The World According to George W. Bush," Stanley A. Renshon and Deborah Welch Larson, eds., *Good Judgment in Foreign Policy: Theory and Application* (New York: Rowman & Littlefield, 2003), 275.

[4] William W. Lammers, "Strategies for Presidential Leadership in the Post-Cold War Era," Anthony J. Eksterowicz and Glenn P. Hastedt, eds., *The Post-Cold War Presidency* (New York: Rowman & Littlefield, 1999), 8. For a more thorough examination of the ability of presidents to use public opinion to secure their agendas in Congress, see Richard Brody, *Assessing the Presidency: The Media, Elite Opinion, and Public Support* (Stanford: Stanford University Press, 1991).

[5] James K. Oliver, "The Foreign Policy Presidency After the Cold War: New Uncertainty and Old Problems," Eksterowicz and Hastedt, 26.

[6] Aaron Wildavsky, "The Two Presidencies," S. Z. Theodoulou and M. A. Cahn, eds., *Public Policy: The Essential Readings* (Englewood Cliffs, NJ: Prentice Hall): 237-50. See also, Steven Shull, ed., *The Two Presidencies* (Chicago: Nelson Hall, 1991).

[7] Such constraints exist on an institutional level, including Congress or the Supreme Court. These constraints also exist on the level of public opinion.

[8] Wildavsky, 237.

[9] Ibid., 239.

[10] Simon Serfaty, *After Reagan: False Starts, Missed Opportunities & New Beginnings* (Washington, D.C.: Johns Hopkins University School of Advanced International Studies, 1988), 4.

[11] Ibid., 5-6.

[12] Ibid., 7-8.

[13] See H. W. Brands, *TR: The Last Romantic* (New York: Basic Books, 1997); or Frederick W. Marks, III, *Velvet on Iron: The Diplomacy of Theodore Roosevelt* (Lincoln: University of Nebraska Press, 1979); or Edward J. Marola, ed., *Theodore Roosevelt, the US Navy, and the Spanish American War* (New York: Palgrave, 2001).

[14] For a more thorough exploration of this theme, see David Burton, *Theodore Roosevelt: Confident Imperialist* (Philadelphia: University of Pennsylvania Press, 1968).

[15] On the Great White Fleet, see James R. Reckner, *Teddy Roosevelt's Great White Fleet* (Annapolis: Naval Institute Press, 1988).

[16] Theodore Roosevelt, "The Panama Canal," in James A. Richardson, ed., *A Compilation of the Messages and Papers of the Presidents*, vol. 10 (Washington, D.C.: GPO, 1908), 701.

[17] Tom Lansford, *The Lords of Foggy Bottom: American Secretaries of State and the World They Shaped* (New York: International Encyclopedia Society, 2001), 2.

[18] John Lewis Gaddis, *Strategies of Containment: A Critical Appraisal of Postwar American National Security Policy* (New York: Oxford University Press, 1982), 162.

[19] See Raymond L. Garthoff, *Reflections on the Cuban Missile Crisis* (Washington, D.C.: Brookings Institute, 1987).

[20] Stewart Patrick, "Multilateralism and Its Discontents: The Causes and Consequences of US Ambivalence," Stewart Patrick and Shepard Foreman, eds., *Multilateralism & US Foreign Policy: Ambivalent Engagement* (Boulder: Lynne Rienner, 2002), 12.

[21] Condoleeza Rice quoted in ibid., 13.

[22] Condoleeza Rice quoted in ibid.

[23] Ibid., 14.

[24] Patrick Callahan, *Logics of American Foreign Policy: Theories of America's World Role* (New York: Longman, 2004), 5-6.

[25] Ibid., 5.

[26] Callahan specifically asks "to what extent and in what ways does foreign policy depend on military might?," ibid.

[27] Ibid., 6.

[28] Robert J. Art and Kenneth N. Waltz, "Current Military Issues," in Robert J. Art and Kenneth N. Waltz, eds., *The Use of Force: Military Power and International Politics*, 6th ed. (New York: Rowman and Littlefield, 2004), 281.

[29] The law requires the president to notify Congress within 48 hours of deploying troops. Congress then has 60 days to approve the deployment, otherwise, the president has only an additional 30 days to remove the troops. The law was vetoed by President Richard Nixon, but Congress overrode the veto. For a more detailed overview of the act, see Eliot A. Cohen, "Constraints on America's Conduct of Small Wars," *International Security*, 9/2 (Fall 1984): 151-81; or Michael Rubner, "The Reagan Administration, the 1973 War Powers Act, and the Invasion of Grenada," *Political Science Quarterly* 100/4 (Winter 1985-1986): 627-647.

[30] James A. Nathan, *Soldiers, Statecraft, and History: Coercive Diplomacy and International Order* (Westport: Praeger, 2002), 135.

[31] Hans J. Morgenthau, *Politics Among Nations: The Struggle for Power and Peace*, 4th ed. (New York: Knopf, 1967), 61.

[32] Frederick Hartmann, *The Relations of Nations*, 3rd ed. (New York: Macmillan, 1967), 96.

[33] For an overview of appeasement and its place in international relations theory, see Ralph B. A. Dimuccio, "The Study of Appeasement in International Relations: Polemics, Paradigms, and Problems," *Journal of Peace Research* 35/2 (March 1998): 245-59.

[34] Quoted in John Lewis Gaddis, "Implementing Flexible Response: Vietnam as a Test Case," Art and Waltz, 223.

[35] Nathan, 147.

[36] James G. Richter, "Perpetuating the Cold War: Domestic Sources of International Patterns of Behavior," *Political Science Quarterly* 107/2 (Summer 1992), 271.

[37] Ibid.; see also Paul Huth and Bruce Russett, "Deterrence Failure and Crisis Escalation," *International Studies Quarterly* 32/1 (March 1988): 29-45; and Robert Jervis, "Deterrence and Perception," *International Security* 14/1 (Summer 1989): 5-49.

[38] Nathan, 147.

[39] William H. Meyer, *Security, Economics and Morality in American Foreign Policy: Contemporary Issues in Historical Context* (Upper Saddle River, NJ: Pearson Prentice Hall, 2004), 29.

[40] Seyom Brown, *Faces of Power: United States Foreign Policy From Truman to Clinton* (New York: Columbia University Press, 1994), 319.

[41] Gaddis, 350-51.

[42] Ibid., 351-52.

[43] US, White House, "The President's State of the Union Address," Press Release (23 January 1980).

[44] Ibid.

[45] For an examination of the Reagan Doctrine, see Mark P. Lagon, *The Reagan Doctrine: The Sources of American Conduct in the Cold War's Last Chapter* (Westport, CT: Praeger, 1994); Peter Rodman, *More Precious Than Peace: The Cold War Struggle for the Third World* (New York: Charles Scribner's Sons, 1994); Coral Bell, *The Reagan Paradox: American Foreign Policy in the 1980s* (New Brunswick: Rutgers University Press, 1989); or Daniel Spikes, *Angola and the Politics of Intervention* (Jefferson, NC: McFarland and Company, Inc., Publishers, 1993).

[46] Ronald Reagan, quoted in Charles Krauthammer, "The Reagan Doctrine," *The New Republic* (17 February 1986).

[47] George Shultz, *Turmoil and Triumph: Diplomacy, Power and the Victory of the American Ideal* (New York: Charles Scribner's Sons, 1993), 340.

[48] Samuel P. Huntington, "The Erosion of American National Interests," *Foreign Affairs* 76/5 (September/October 1997), 30.

[49] Shoon Kathleen Murray and Jason Meyers, "Do People Need Foreign Enemies: American Leaders' Beliefs After the Soviet Union," *Journal of Conflict Resolution* 43/5 (October 1999), 555.

[50] David Finaly, Ole Hosti and Richard Fagen, *Enemies in Politics* (Chicago: Rand McNally, 1967), 7.

[51] Sam Keen quoted in Don Lattin, "The Enemies We Love to Hate," *San Francisco Chronicle* (30 August 1990), B3, cited in Murray and Meyers, 555.

[52] On this theme, see Bob Woodward, *Bush at War* (New York: Simon and Schuster, 2002).

[53] F. Gregory Gause, III, "Getting It Backwards on Iraq," *Foreign Affairs* 78/3 (May/June 1999), 62.

[54] Edward Mortimer, "Saddam Defiant After US Strikes," *Financial Times* (4 September 1996), 1.

[55] "Russian MPs Brand Clinton 'Sex Maniac'," *BBC* (18 December 1998).

[56] Douglas Jehl, "US Fighters in Saudi Arabia Grounded," *The New York Times* (19 December 1998).

[57] Scott Peterson, "Iraq Hurt by Bombs, But Can US Topple Saddam?," *The Christian Science Monitor* (21 December 1998), 1.

[58] John J. Mearsheimer and Stephen M. Walt, "Can Saddam Be Contained? History Says Yes," *Occasional Paper*, Belfer Center for Science and International Affairs Security Program (12 November 2002), online at http://www.comw.org/qdr/fulltext/mearsheimerwalt.pdf.

[59] John Mueller and Karl Mueller, "Sanctions of Mass Destruction," *Foreign Affairs* 78/3 (May/June 1999), 53.

[60] George W. Bush, "Address to a Joint Session of Congress and the American People," Washington, D.C. White House Press Release (20 September 2001), online at http://www.whitehouse.gov/news/releases/2001/09/20010920-8.html.

[61] Ibid.

[62] Ivo H. Daalder and James M. Lindsay, *America Unbound: The Bush Revolution in Foreign Policy* (Washington, D.C.: The Brookings Institute, 2003), 117.

[63] Ibid.

[64] Hayden also notes that "US policy with respect to the war's justification and objectives was largely informed by and sensitive to the normative constraints of the just war tradition," Patrick Hayden, "The War on Terrorism and the Just Use of Military Force," Patrick Hayden, Tom Lansford and Robert P. Watson, *America's War on Terror* (Aldershot: Ashgate, 2003), 115.

[65] Ibid.

[66] Bush, "Address" (20 September 2001).

[67] Quoted in Steve LaRoque, "Congress First Voted to Back Regime Change in Iraq in 1998," US, Department of State, International Information Programs (19 September 2002), online at http://usinfo.state.gov/regional/nea/iraq/text/0919cngr.htm.

[68] Ibid.

[69] David Frum and Richard Perle, *An End to Evil: How to Win the War on Terror* (New York: Random House, 2003), 22.

[70] Ibid., 23.

[71] CNN/USA Poll (21 February 2001) cited in "Conflict With Iraq," *Americans and the World: Public Opinion and International Affairs* (Program on International Policy Attitudes), online at http://www.americans-world.org/digest/regional_issues/Conflict_Iraq/mil_action.cfm.

[72] Ibid.

[73] In addition, conventional wisdom held that the lackluster economy would be the main focus of voters in the 2002 elections, leading to Republican losses in Congress; Mark Halperin, Elizabeth Wilner and Marc Ambinder, "ABC 2002: Midterm Elections Outlook," *ABC News*, online at http://abcnews.go.com/sections/politics/DailyNews/2002_outlook.html.

[74] Tom Raum, "Iraq Action Sought Before UN Vote," *Associated Press* (18 September 2002).

[75] George W. Bush, "President's Remarks at the United Nations General Assembly," New York (12 September 2002), White House Press Release, online at http://www.whitehouse.gov/news/releases/2002/09/20020912-1.html.

[76] Ibid.

[77] Ibid.

[78] Ibid.

[79] Jim Abrams, "Democrats Praise Bush For UN Speech," *Associated Press* (13 September 2002).

[80] Ibid.

[81] "Bush: US Will Move on Iraq if UN Won't," *CNN.com* (13 September 2002), online at http://www.cnn.com/2002/US/09/12/bush.speech.un/.

[82] Ibid.

[83] Ibid.

[84] UN, *Security Council Resolution 1441*, S/2002/1198 (8 November 2002) online at http://www.un.int/usa/sres-iraq.htm.

[85] Fred Kaplan, "Resolution Dissolution: How the US and France Botched UN Resolution 1441," *Slate* (6 March 2003), online at http://slate.msn.com/id/2079746.

[86] During the 1990s, Saddam had confounded UN inspectors and the US by consistently taking his country to brink of war and then backing down as a way to constantly test the cohesion of the coalition. His brinksmanship elevated his status in the Arab world and undermined American leadership. By surviving successive American strikes, he also gained hero status among anti-American or anti-Western groups; Daniel Byman and Matthew Waxman, *Confronting Iraq: U.S. Policy and the Use of Force Since the Gulf War* (Santa Monica: Rand 2000), 64.

[87] Jerrold M. Post and Amatzia Baram, "Saddam is Iraq: Iraq is Saddam," *Counterproliferation Papers: Future Warfare Series*, no. 17 (November 2002), 57.

[88] Ibid., 45.

[89] David Von Drehle, "Debate Over Iraq Focuses on Out come: Multiple Scenarios Drive Questions About War," *The Washington Post* (7 October 2002), 1.

[90] Ibid.

[91] Kate Connolly, "Bush Suffers Nazi Jibe From Germans," *The Guardian* (20 September 2002).

[92] EOS-Gallup Poll (January 2003), cited in "European War Views," *BBC* (6 February 2003).

[93] Glenn Frankel, "In Public Opinion, US, Europe More United Than Apart," *The Washington Post* (4 September 2002), A1.

[94] Ibid.

[95] Von Drehle, A1.

[96] Gerhard Schröder, quoted in James P. Rubin, "Stumbling into War," *Foreign Affairs* 82/5 (September/October 2003), 49.

[97] Madeleine Albright, "Bridges, Bombs, or Bluster?" *Foreign Affairs* 82/5 (September/October 2003), 7.

[98] Hans Blix, quoted in Edith M. Lederer, "Blix Says no Smoking Guns Found in Iraq," *Associated Press* (9 January 2003).

[99] "UN Keeps up Hunt for Smoking Gun in Iraq, US Says None Needed," *Agence-France Presse* (10 January 2003).

[100] Ibid.

Chapter 4

A Coalition of the Willing

Introduction

In the post-World War II era, one of the main components of American foreign policy has been multilateralism. However, as noted, US multilateralism has often been selective and issue-oriented. The US has used formal and informal multilateral configurations in order to pursue its specific national interests. Consequently, successive administrations have viewed international institutions and multinational coalitions as a way to enhance, or preserve, American power in the post-World War II era.[1] Throughout the Cold War, the United States paid considerable attention to these multilateral forums since they were necessary to balance against the Soviet bloc. In the post-Cold War era, the importance of multilateral institutions to the US has lessened concurrently with divergence of interest between the US and the leading memberstates of these organizations. Without the threat of a common enemy, the ties which bound the US and its allies have loosened, though not dissipated. The states of the transatlantic region still have a range of common interests in security, economic and political issues. However, as the diplomatic wranglings over Iraq demonstrated, the potential for deep and public disagreement over specific policies will likely only accelerate in the future.

The diplomatic offensive by the United States in the lead-up to the Iraq war contrasted several competing, though not necessarily different, visions of world governance. The United States claimed that it was acting to reaffirm the power and prestige of the UN because the world body had been unable or unwilling to enforce its own resolutions in regards to Iraq. US officials pointed to the words of former UN Secretary General Boutros Boutros-Ghali speaking in the aftermath of the first Gulf War with Iraq: "the search for improved mechanisms and techniques will be of little significance unless this new spirit of commonality is propelled by the will to take the hard decisions demanded by this time of opportunity."[2] France maintained that it sought to establish the supremacy of the UN and weaken the unilateral power of individual states during the Iraq debates, yet Paris has consistently utilized the UN and the EU as a means to magnify its own national power and enhance its capabilities as a nationstate.[3]

In the end, the United States relied on a narrow coalition of willing countries to conduct the military operations against Iraq and a slightly larger coalition to handle the aftermath of the campaign. The preponderance of American military power has significantly weakened the need for troops and other allied assets to bolster US capabilities during missions, and negative experiences during a variety of coalition actions in the 1990s have reinforced preferences among American defense planners which rely on US assets. This combination of factors eroded any enthusiasm that the Bush administration might have had for a broader coalition, even though a more inclusive group would have elevated the legitimacy of the campaign among the international community. This chapter traces the coalition efforts by the US and the parallel efforts by the main anti-war states, Germany and France, to prevent the development of any multilateral grouping more substantial than a limited coalition of the willing.

Reluctant Sheriff?

The promulgation of the Bush NSS with its preemption doctrine revised debate over the appropriate role of the US as the world's lone superpower. Writing in 1997, Richard Haass, who joined the Bush administration as the State Department's Director of Policy Planning after having also served in the first Bush administration, expressed that there was a need for an "international sheriff" to organize "coalitions or posses of states and others" ("others" being defined as regional or international organizations) because of this "age of deregulation" in the international system.[4] Haass argues that the breakdown of the bipolar Cold War system left the world without clear structure and undermined the accepted "rules" of the international system. One result is the rise of new security threats, including substate actors. As with the traditional, or mythic, John Waynesque sheriff of the Old American West, there are times when the lawman has to ride alone in order to accomplish his duty, while at times, he must form the aforementioned posse. Also, as with the sheriff of "High Noon" fame, there are times when doing what is right means taking action even if the rest of the town either fails to back you or is even openly hostile. The analogy, though crude, can be applied to the US actions toward Iraq. Officials within the Bush administration were convinced that action had to be taken against Iraq in order to forestall the spread of WMD technology to terrorist groups. They were likewise convinced that their erstwhile allies, including France and Germany, were unwilling to take strong action because of a lack of resolve and a predilection for appeasement policies.

It should be noted that European unease with America's superpower status is not something new or unique to the Bush administration. Before the 2000 elections, Jeffrey Gedman asserted that everywhere in Europe you bump into the thesis that America is the 'rogue superpower'.[5] During the succession of humanitarian crises of the 1990s, Europeans increasingly complained that the US had abrogated its traditional leadership role. Furthermore, the failure of the US to pay its UN dues during the Clinton administration created widespread hostility as "Diplomats, including Americans, say that anger toward the United States is beginning to erode support on issues vital to Washington."[6] Most significantly, increasing disapproval of US policies threatened to undermine the nation's predominance in "soft power."[7] This trend was especially troublesome since America's soft power had traditionally been one of the country's most powerful agents of change in the international arena. American soft power also reinforced global preferences for US leadership on a range of economic and political issues.[8]

Tony Smith combines Nye's notions of soft power with traditional Wilsonian idealism and asserts that "given the vital American security interests served by the expansion of democracy worldwide, Wilsonianism will continue to serve as a principal guide for policy."[9] Fareed Zakaria suggests that Bush's foreign policy contains significant Wilsonian influences. For instance, Zakaria argues that Bush's statement that "America has, and intends to keep, military strengths beyond challenge, thereby making the destabilizing arms races of other eras pointless, and limiting rivalries to trade and other pursuits of peace" is "the most Wilsonian statement any President has made since Wilson himself, echoing his pledge to use American power to create a "universal dominion of right."[10] Zakaria also declares that

> Many of Bush's recent proclamations are Wilsonian. He advocates democracy in Palestine and wants to build a modern, democratic state in Iraq as part of a wider effort to democratize the Arab world. Last month, at the United Nations, in explaining why Iraq was a threat to world peace, he said that 'open societies do not threaten the world with mass murder.' But while he adopts some of Wilson's loftiest ideals, Bush is also following some of his most fatal practices. Wilson's means were often highly unilateral.[11]

For the Europeans, the cowboy motif was appealing as a way to explain Bush's foreign policy—far more appealing than comparisons with Wilsonian internationalism. What the Bush administration believed was resolve and steadfastness, others perceived as unilateralism and manifestations of the worst aspects of American hegemonic tendencies. Whereas officials in European capitals spoke publicly about being able to recognize the nuances and "grays" of international issues, they accused Bush of seeing matters in stark black and white and of being overtly confrontational. Bush's personal style reinforced these perceptions. In promoting a conference on "God and Foreign Policy," the Pew Forum on Religion and Public life summarized some of the stark differences in perception as presented by the EU's foreign policy chief, Javier Solana. Solana characterized the difference in outlook between the US and many European states as a "'cultural phenomenon'—the distinctly American tendency to view international events through a strict religious lens of morality. In a recent interview with the *Financial Times*, he contrasted the United States' 'binary model' with the more nuanced worldview of Europeans, stating that for Americans, 'It is all or nothing. For us Europeans, it is difficult to deal with because we are so secular. We do not see the world in such black and white terms'."[12] One result of these differences has been a "growing divergence between the United States' self-perception as the moral and political leader of the West and European perceptions of the United States as a flawed superpower."[13]

Hans-Ulrich Klose, vice chair of the German Parliament's foreign relations committee, stated that "Much of it is the way he [Bush] talks, this provocative manner, the jabbing of his finger at you. ... It's Texas, a culture that is unfamiliar to Germans. And it's the religious tenor of his arguments."[14] A story in *The New York Times* quoted an unnamed American diplomat as pointing out the similarities between Bush and another "cowboy president"—Ronald Reagan: "much of it is the way he [Bush] talks, the rhetoric, the religiosity. ... It reminds them of what drove them crazy about Reagan. It reminds them of what they miss about Clinton. All the stereotypes we thought we had banished for good after September 11—the cowboy imagery, in particular—it's all back."[15]

Deputies

As with any good sheriff, Bush did have a number of loyal "deputies" among foreign leaders. While Bush's style and mannerisms were distasteful to a number of European politicians, including Chirac and Schröder, others formed close relationships with Bush, especially in the aftermath of the 11 September attacks. However, the split among European leaders reaffirmed the lack of a clear and coherent foreign policy of the EU and a lack of coordination by individual EU states. William Wallace points out that "Henry Kissinger is said to have remarked that the problem with 'Europe' is that nobody in Washington knew the telephone number to call in event of crisis. The contrast in images he presented was between an efficient, strategically oriented, US government and an incoherent, slow-moving European caucus."[16] One concrete result of this has been an often-repeated strategy by the United States to engage in bilateral efforts with European states to either enhance multilateral efforts or to overcome or diminish multilateral opposition. This strategy was used by the Bush administration as part of its campaign to develop a coalition of the willing.

Great Britain has long been America's closest ally in Europe and the leader of the pro-American coalition in Europe during the Iraq crisis was Tony Blair. Blair emerged during the aftermath of 11 September as one of the staunchest allies of the US. He was present at Bush's address to a joint session of Congress and received a standing ovation after Bush thanked the British for their support and singled-out Blair with the phrase "thanks friend." Of all of the European leaders, Blair has had the most impact on US policy. He participated in the administration's planning of the Afghan campaign and worked to position Great Britain as a bridge between the US and Europe in the war on terror.[17] Blair also played a major role in convincing Bush to delay an expansion of military action against Iraq and other targets during Operation Enduring Freedom.[18] In return, Bush continued diplomatic efforts at the UN, long after he had lost patience with the organization in an effort to help Blair with his domestic audience.

In addition to Great Britain, a range of other states backed US policy from Afghanistan through Iraq. These countries included the traditional Atlanticist states of Europe, such as the Netherlands and Denmark, as well as Australia and Japan. Italy and Spain also emerged as key allies of the US. The conservative governments in both states readily backed the US campaign in Afghanistan and extended their support during the UN negotiations over Iraq. Spain was particularly important as an ally, since it was one of the rotating members of the Security Council. In addition, Bush and Spain's contemporary Prime Minister, Jose Maria Aznar, developed a close-working relationship. At one point during the Iraq situation, aides noted that Aznar "probably talks to Mr Bush more frequently than any other European leader."[19] The Eastern European states which were either new members of NATO or sought NATO and EU membership also supported the US position. Poland's President Aleksander Kwasniewski was a particularly enthusiastic US supporter and at one point declared in reference to Iraq that "if it is President Bush's vision, it is mine."[20]

Coalition Efforts and Counter Efforts

The military and political success of the Bush administration's coalition of the willing during Operation Enduring Freedom set the tone for military plans toward Iraq. Rumsfeld and the Joint Chiefs of Staff emphasized the advantages of relying on US assets to conduct the major operations. Operation Enduring Freedom confirmed the utility of a US-military-centric strategy. One of the main lessons from Afghanistan that was touted was that "a military hub-and-spoke command operation has worked far better for Washington than the consensus decision-making on which it had to rely during the NATO air campaign over Kosovo and Serbia in 1999, which left many in the US Defense Department deeply frustrated."[21]

Participation by British or Australian troops was also welcome since there was a long history of cooperation between the militaries of these states and a general sense that the Anglo-Australian forces could be "trusted" not to become bogged down by political interference or command and control issues. In addition, there was a clear recognition that any campaign in Iraq would vary greatly from Afghanistan on one key point: there was no effective Iraqi resistance which had the potential of the Northern Alliance to provide the bulk of the ground forces. Unlike Afghanistan, the US would not be able to rely on the combination of precision weaponry and indigenous allies which comprised the "Afghan Model."[22] Instead, there was little military incentive for the Bush administration to seek substantial troop contributions for the initial combat phase of any attack on Iraq. Instead, there would have to be large numbers of US ground forces committed to the campaign and there were real doubts about the potential quality and capability of potential allied forces, with the aforementioned exception of the British and Australian forces, and about the potential for political interference to compromise military operations. The Pentagon far preferred that US forces have almost unfettered lines of command and decision-making.

Militarily, the main objectives of Bush's coalition diplomacy were to gain the necessary base and transit permissions which would allow US forces to deploy easily and quickly. A secondary consideration was for the State Department to line-up the necessary forces to undertake the stabilization and nation-building operations that would follow the fall of Saddam and his regime. American military planners endorsed the utility of one aspect of the Afghan Model whereby the US undertook the majority of the combat operations and coalition forces moved in during the aftermath to provide the range of security missions that they had demonstrated significant capability for through missions in the Balkans and ongoing operations in Afghanistan.

Consequently, the main thrust of coalition diplomacy on the military front would be threefold. First, the US had to secure base and transit permissions from those countries opposed to the war. This would be especially important in the case of Germany since the main European bases of the US military were in that country. Second, the US would need to ensure that the European allies, including those anti-Iraq war states, were willing to backfill existing missions. The US needed its nominal allies not participating in any potential Iraqi conflict to provide forces to existing operations in the Balkans and Afghanistan. Third, and finally, the Bush administration wanted basing rights in Turkey and a range of states in the Persian Gulf in order to launch attacks, including both air and ground assaults. Turkey, Kuwait and Saudi Arabia were particularly important. Turkey was seen as the potential launching site of a "second front" against Iraq. Kuwait would logically serve as the main point of attack, while Saudi Arabia contained the main US command center in the region.

UNMOVIC and the Impact of Inspections

As US diplomats and defense planners worked to secure the necessary military arrangements for an invasion of Iraq, the main drama continued to be at the UN as the US sought to develop a political or diplomatic coalition. Blix's January 2003 report on inspections was critical of the Iraqi regime's efforts to disarm or cooperate with UNMOVIC. Blix stated that "Iraq appears not to have come to a genuine acceptance, not even today, of the disarmament which was demanded of it."[23] He specifically cited Iraqi harassment of inspectors and the refusal of the regime to accept monitoring overflights and efforts to interview Iraqi WMD scientists.

Blix also cited a range of specific unresolved problems and issues concerning Iraq's WMD programs. He noted that there were questions about Iraq's production of the nerve gas VX: "there are questions to be answered concerning the fate of the VX precursor chemicals, which Iraq states were lost during bombing in the Gulf War or were unilaterally destroyed by Iraq."[24] In addition, there were some 6,500 chemical bombs unaccounted for, with combined chemical warheads on the order of 1,000 tons. Iraq had also not satisfactorily explained the discovery of 122 mm chemical mortar "warheads" at a new bunker southwest of Baghdad, an issue which Blix declared "could also be the tip of a submerged iceberg. The discovery of a few rockets does not resolve but rather points to the issue of several thousands of chemical rockets that are unaccounted for."[25] Blix further cited Iraq's failure to declare the importation of 650 biological growth cultures which had the "potential ... to produce about 5,000 liters of concentrated anthrax."[26] Furthermore, the head of UNMOVIC described the discovery of the Al Samoud 2 and Al Fatah missiles which violated range restrictions on missiles imposed by previous UN Security Council resolutions.

This created a window of opportunity for the Bush administration to press for strong action. Just four days after Blix's statement to the Security Council, Blair was in Washington meeting with Bush. The British Prime Minister pressed his American counterpart for an immediate introduction of a second resolution to authorize the use of force. Bush refused Blair's request.[27] While Blair argued that there was now support for the resolution, Bush argued that Blix's report was the forerunner of future, more damning, statements and that UNMOVIC was likely to discover a "smoking gun" which would assure passage of a second resolution.

Indeed, even France had begun to signal a willingness to consider the use of force. In early January, even before Blix's report, Rice met with Chirac's main foreign policy advisor Maurice Gourdault-Montagne, and informed him that war was inevitable.[28] One result was that Chirac and his advisors began to formulate strategies to ensure that France would not be marginalized or left out of the decision-making processes surrounding Iraq, even if that meant supporting or contributing to a military option. Growing anti-French sentiment in the US was also clearly troubling to Chirac. The French ambassador to the US, Jean-David Levitte was dispatched to a range of venues in an effort to reassure Americans that France was "a loyal ally grateful for American help in the world wars of the last century."[29]

Although the official line from Paris was that the French supported the continuation of inspections, Chirac's government undertook a range of steps that indicated it was reconciled to war and did not want to be "cut off from the Americans."[30] In addition, domestic elites in France exerted pressure on Chirac to not limit France's options. The BBC noted that "by publicly standing shoulder to shoulder with the pacifist Germans, he [Chirac] has—according to many observers—painted himself into a corner."[31] Thus, de Villepin called for continued inspections, but also offered French Mirage fighters if combat broke out as he noted that France had not ruled out the use of force. Chirac even dispatched a French aircraft carrier battlegroup to the region in case conflict broke-out.

Momentum Swings—The Old Europe/New Europe Debate

Bush's gamble proved to be a "mistake" as the Iraqi regime, sensitive to the gathering war clouds, began to cooperate more fully with UNMOVIC, including destroying its stockpiles of Al Samoud 2 and Al Fatah missiles.[32] The Iraqis also began easing their harassment of UNMOVIC and the regime turned over a range of requested documents and other evidence. Meanwhile, the anti-war movement in Europe and the United States gained its own momentum through a series of large demonstrations. While these episodes had little impact on US public or congressional opinion, they added pressure on other governments to adopt anti-Iraq war platforms.

In the midst of the rising unease between the US and its key European allies, Rumsfeld made a series of comments which added to the heightened tensions and hardened the resolve of both sides of the issue. Speaking at a press conference on 22 January 2003, Rumsfeld offered a conceptualization of the debate which simply reflected the traditional split between the Atlanticist and the Europeanist states within Europe. However, his word choice offended many and further alienated those governments opposed to US policy. Rumsfeld sought to characterize the administration's efforts to form a coalition of the willing by noting the cooperation

Washington had received from many European states, while acknowledging the problems the US had encountered with other countries. In response to a question about the problems the US had met from some European states, the Secretary of Defense stated

> Now, you're thinking of Europe as Germany and France. I don't. I think that's old Europe. If you look at the entire NATO Europe today, the center of gravity is shifting to the east. And there are a lot of new members. And if you just take the list of all the members of NATO and all of those who have been invited in recently—what is it? Twenty-six, something like that?—you're right. Germany has been a problem, and France has been a problem.[33]

In many ways, Rumsfeld merely expressed the main viewpoints of many in the administration. [34] Germany and France remained committed to a policy of containment which the US had decided to abandon because of its impracticality toward terrorism. Instead, through the Bush doctrine and the NSS, the US was prepared to adopt a preemptive strategy designed to forestall future threats before they had the capability to exert harm to the US or to American interests. To Rumsfeld, and many in the administration, the "Old" Europeans simply did not understand that with the attacks of 11 September, terrorism had ceased to be a law enforcement issue and had instead became a national security priority for the US.

For the anti-Iraq war Europeans, Rumsfeld's comments were suggestive of the worst excesses of US foreign policy. They implied that the US could ignore the priorities of "Old" Europe as it built a coalition of the willing from the traditional Atlanticist states and the Eastern states of "New" Europe. During the Cold War, the Soviet threat, which prompted a need for alliance cohesion, meant that the US had to take into account the policy preferences of European states. With the end of the Cold War and the subsequent unparalleled dominance of the US, the impetus for cooperation was weakened and the temptation for unilateral primacy could potentially relegate the major powers of Europe to the occasional coalition of the willing—when the US needed or wanted their cooperation for its own reasons.

Rumsfeld also touched a political nerve by publicly stating what everyone already knew: European governments did not have a common foreign and security policy. In spite of repeated efforts, the Iraq crisis demonstrated that when confronted with serious international issues, many European governments first sought to pursue their national interests before they even sought cooperation or coordination on foreign policy matters. In this regard, the French and Germans were as guilty as the states that supported the US for both nations were pursuing anti-Iraq war policies based on particular self-interests, domestic politics in the case of Germany and efforts to maintain its international power and prestige for France. For France, the loss of empire has reduced the nation to medium-power status, but its seat on the UN Security Council and its role in the EU both provide it with influence in the international system that is not proportional to its economic and military power potentials. In contrast, Edward C. Luck points out that "[g]iven its singular power, the United States has been more prone than most countries to question the legitimacy and fairness of institutions whose rules and procedures do not take into account the distribution of power in the real world outside."[35]

One result of France's contemporary foreign policy is that Paris naturally prefers to enhance the structures that magnify its power, while seeking to constrain any individual superpower such as the United States. Even before the debate over Iraq, a French member of the National Assembly noted that "it is appropriate to be downright anti-American."[36] The noted international relations scholar Stanley Hoffman characterized European attitudes toward the US in the following manner: "The United States is perceived as a bully ready to use all means, including overwhelming force, against those who resist it: Hence, Hiroshima, the horrors of Vietnam, the rage against Iraq, the war on Afghanistan."[37]

During the Iraq crisis, Chirac sought to reaffirm France as the leader of Europe. For instance, Philippe Moreau Defarges of the French Institute for International Relations has noted that Chirac believed that the anti-war public sentiment in Europe would allow him to assert that only he can "speak in the name of these people. I am the true leader of Europe."[38] Rumsfeld's conceptualization of the divide between a pro-US "New" Europe which supported the US war on terror and an anti-US "Old" Europe which sought to constrain US primacy undermined Chirac's leadership bid and efforts to present a united Europe. The split between the old and new Europe would only grow as the prelude to war with Iraq continued. Ultimately, the split would not only undermine loose efforts at European unity, it would create visible fissures in the main institutions that have marked the post-World War II era, including the UN, NATO and the EU.

The Renewed Political Battle

Sensing its political momentum slipping away, the Bush administration sent Powell to the UN on 5 February to make the US case before the world body. The Secretary of State was long perceived as the leader of the moderates within the administration and most observers credited Powell with being the main influence behind Bush's original appeal to the UN that resulted in UNSCR 1441. However, by January, even Powell had become increasingly hawkish on Iraq.

Powell's transformation was based on two main factors. The first was France's open break with the US and the second was Powell's sentiment that the administration needed to present a "united front."[39] Through conversations with de Villepin, Powell was convinced that he had gained a commitment from the French which would allow the inspections to continue, with the promise of support for military authorization if the inspections seemed to be dragging-on. By January, Powell came to the conclusion that the French were being duplicitous. Powell noted that his impression of conversations with French officials was that "they said … we should let this process continue," however, "it's not clear to me how long they want it to continue or whether they're serious about bringing it to a conclusion at some time."[40] Instead, Powell realized that

France seemed to desire to stretch the inspections on indefinitely, no matter what the findings were. After going to great lengths, and laying his credibility on the line, to convince Bush to take the UN route, the French actions, in the words of Patrick Clawson of the Washington Institute for Near Eat Policy, "cut him [Powell] off at the knees. It must have been terribly discouraging to him."[41]

In addition, Bush's determination to seek a military solution to Iraq, combined with the diplomatic tensions, led Powell to conclude that US officials needed to unite in order to pressure both Iraq and the Europeans. Powell hoped that a strong signal from Washington could prompt a diplomatic break-through between the transatlantic partners. In order to increase the pressure on the Europeans and to strengthen the US case for military action, Powell agreed to go before the UN and present the administration's case.

Consequently, at the UN, Powell delivered a powerful and stinging indictment of the Iraqi regime. Powell declared that:

> Resolution 1441 was not dealing with an innocent party, but a regime this Council has repeatedly convicted over the years. Resolution 1441 gave Iraq one last chance, one last chance to come into compliance or to face serious consequences. No Council member present and voting on that day had any illusions about the nature and intent of the resolution or what serious consequences meant if Iraq did not comply.[42]

Powell also presented a range of evidence, including tape recordings of Iraqi intelligence officers discussing methods to prevent UNMOVIC inspectors from carrying out their duties. The Secretary of State noted that Iraq still possessed 8,500 liters of anthrax and that Iraq was still endeavoring to purchase and acquire materials for a nuclear-weapons program. He also presented satellite photos of suspected Iraqi mobile WMD laboratories and evidence of the movement and transshipment of items at sites just prior to their inspection by UNMOVIC. There was documentary evidence of orders by the Iraqi leadership to destroy documents and other forms of evidence. Finally, Powell listed specific Iraqi violations of UNSCR 1441 in terms of the resolutions call for cooperation across a range of areas in the inspection process. Powell closed his remarks with an intelligence assessment that highlighted links between Saddam's regime and Al Qaeda and other Islamic terrorist organizations and declared:

> Today, Iraq still poses a threat and Iraq still remains in material breach. Indeed, by its failure to seize on its one last opportunity to come clean and disarm, Iraq has put itself in deeper material breach and closer to the day when it will face serious consequences for its continue defiance of this Council.
>
> My colleagues, we have an obligation to our citizens. We have an obligation to this body to see that our resolutions are complied with. We wrote 1441 not in order to go to war. We wrote 1441 to try to preserve the peace. We wrote 1441 to give Iraq one last chance.

Iraq is not, so far, taking that one last chance.

We must not shrink from whatever is ahead of us. We must not fail in our duty and our responsibility to the citizens of the countries that are represented by this body.[43]

Within days of Powell's presentation, two states, Slovenia and Romania, offered additional evidence to support the Secretary's assertions. The Slovenian government reported that Iraq had tried to purchase equipment that could be used to enrich uranium to weapons-grade in contradiction of standing UN sanctions. Iraqi agents approached private companies in Slovenia in 1999 and 2000 but the country's Foreign Minister Dimitrij Rupel asserted that "There were attempts [by Iraq] of commercial dealings, but we were quick in preventing them."[44] Romanian officials also confirmed that Iraq had endeavored to buy nuclear-enrichment equipment and technologies in 1995, 1996 and 1999. The sales were prevented through intelligence cooperation between the US and the Romania.[45]

Meanwhile, on 10 February, on the eve of Blix's next report, Iraq also approved the use of American, French and Russian spy planes to monitor suspected WMD sites. UNMOVIC's chief inspector on the ground in Iraq even reported that he perceived a "good beginning" and a new "positive attitude" on the part of the Iraqi regime.[46] In his second report of the new year, Blix reported progress in destroying chemical weapons, including mustard gas, that were at sites identified and sealed by the previous inspections regime.[47] He also noted improvements in Iraqi cooperation and pleaded for the inspections to be given more time. The head of UNMOVIC also cast doubts on some aspects of Powell's presentation, including contentions that Iraq had attempted to purchase nuclear technologies from states in Africa.

Blix pleaded for more time for the inspections and contended that, with increased Iraqi cooperation, UNMOVIC could complete its work in a matter of months, rather than years. He argued that: "Today, three months after the adoption of resolution 1441 (2002), the period of disarmament through inspection could still be short, if 'immediate, active and unconditional cooperation' with UNMOVIC and the IAEA were to be forthcoming."[48] Significantly, for the Bush administration, Blix's February report had "no sound bite" which could be used to promote military action and as the BBC reported, "from that point on, somehow the momentum slipped away from the Americans."[49]

Following Blix's February statement, the anti-Iraq war states renewed their efforts to forestall any American military action toward Iraq. On 14 February, the UN Security Council was the scene of speeches by foreign ministers of the sitting council members. French Foreign Minister de Villepin used the occasion to argue strongly for a continuation of inspections and declared that "there is an alternative to war, disarming Iraq through inspections"—de Villepin's speech was greeted with applause, a rarity in the Security Council chamber.[50] The French minister's speech was followed by addresses from Igor Ivanov, Russia's foreign minister, which was also meet with applause, and Germany's Fischer. Both supported their German colleague and spoke in favor of continued inspections. The British Foreign Minister, Jack Straw and

Spanish Foreign Minister Ana Palacio, argued that the UN needed to fulfill its obligations and stand firm in the face of continuing Iraqi noncompliance, even if minor progress was being made. Meanwhile in Europe, Schröder and Swedish Prime Minister Goeran Persson reaffirmed their opposition to military action. Furthermore, Austria announced that without a second UN Security Council resolution specifically authorizing the use of force, it would not allow American troops or military equipment to be transported across its territory.[51]

NATO's Woes

A political battle also raged in the corridors of NATO. In early February, NATO member Turkey tried to invoke Article 4 of the transatlantic alliance's founding treaty which states that: "The Parties will consult together whenever, in the opinion of any of them, the territorial integrity, political independence or security of any of the Parties is threatened."[52] In its application, the Turkish government emphasized the "importance of showing that there could not be any problems in defense mechanism of NATO" and that "such a stance would not mean inciting a war in Iraq but it would have a deterring effect."[53] The action created one of the worst divisions in the history of the North Atlantic alliance. Germany, France and Belgium united to veto the request. Germany and France saw the veto as a way to impede the US diplomatic effort for war, while in Belgium, national elections frightened the ruling coalition into believing that if it consented to the Turkish request, the nation's strong anti-war sentiment could cause them to lose at the polls.[54]

Then-NATO Secretary General Lord Robertson initially tried to minimize the dispute and declared that "there is complete agreement among NATO countries about their commitment to defend Turkey, and on the substance of the planning measures;" and that "there has been a disagreement is over when to formally task this military planning. Not whether to plan but when to plan."[55] Nonetheless, It quickly emerged that the nineteen-member alliance had divided into sixteen versus three, and significantly, that three, or possibly fewer, states could block NATO action on any given issue. The leaders of the three states began to come under widespread pressure to not allow Iraq to destroy NATO, especially in the face of increasing American criticism that the triumvirate was allowing "petty politics" to damage the most important component of European security.[56] In France Jacques Barrot, a prominent member of Chirac's coalition noted that "Saddam Hussein must not manage to break this Atlantic alliance, which is a guarantee of peace in the world."[57]

The US, supported by Robertson, engaged in some artful maneuvering to break the impasse. First, the discussions over Turkey's request were moved to the Defense Planning Committee (DPC). Following France's withdrawal from NATO in 1966, France has not been a member of the DPC and was thus shut-out of the ongoing talks. Second, with their numbers reduced to two, Germany and Belgium faced intense pressure from the US and other NATO members. Germany gave in first, and then isolated-Belgium followed after the DPC agreed to consider several amendments. The DPC agreed to consider Turkey's request and then endorsed a range of options which included the preventative deployment of AWACs, counter-WMD systems and theater missile defense assets.[58] Lord Robertson declared that "Alliance solidarity has prevailed. NATO nations have assumed their collective responsibility towards Turkey, a nation at the moment under threat."[59] US NATO Ambassador Nicholas Burns expressed the pleasure of the Bush administration: "we have a clear NATO decision to plan for the support for Turkey. ... And within several days, we have a clear commitment by all 18 allies [the NATO members minus France] that we will deploy AWACs and Patriot systems to Turkey."[60] In summarizing the incident, Lord Robertson stated: "I am happy to announce that we have been able—collectively—to overcome the impasse we have faced for the past few days. We agree on substance, we agree on timing and we agree on how to integrate our collective solidarity with Turkey in the wider context.[61]

Gains and Losses for the Coalition

The NATO decision was particularly important for the Bush administration. It needed Turkish assent to launch its planned second front against Iraq from the North. NATO's action had also isolated France just prior to a major EU summit on Iraq. In addition, the administration planned to introduce a second resolution into the UN to declare Iraq in violation of UNSCR 1441. The resolution would be cosponsored by the US, Great Britain and Spain. The administration signaled a willingness to add language to the resolution to establish timelines for the inspections and specific tests of Iraqi compliance.[62] Nonetheless, as James Rubin points out, most European leaders now perceived that "force had become an object in itself, and that Washington was using diplomacy simply to smooth the way for an invasion."[63] This was true even of the states that supported US military action.

The Bush administration had also received some multilateral endorsements from Europe and hoped these would help turn the tide of official policy and of public opinion in Europe. In a clear rebuff to assertions by France and Germany that those two nations were speaking for "Europe," on 30 January 2003, eight European NATO members issued an open letter of support for US policy toward Iraq. The Eight included Great Britain, the Czech Republic, Hungary, Italy, the Netherlands, Poland, Portugal, and Spain. The letter affirmed European thanks for previous US actions and pledged support for the future. It also reflected the main sentiments of the Bush administration, including its Wilsonian proclivities, and greatly pleased the President. The letter declared that:

We in Europe have a relationship with the US which has stood the test of time. Thanks in large part to American bravery, generosity and farsightedness, Europe was set free from the two forms of tyranny that devastated our continent in the 20th century: Nazism and communism. Thanks, too, to the continued cooperation between Europe and the US we have managed to guarantee peace and freedom on our continent. The trans-Atlantic relationship must not become a casualty of the current Iraqi regime's persistent attempts to threaten world security. In today's world, more than ever before, it is vital that we preserve that unity and cohesion.

We know that success in the day-to-day battle against terrorism and the proliferation of weapons of mass destruction demands unwavering determination and firm international cohesion on the part of all countries for whom freedom is precious.[64]

The letter from the NATO-Eight was followed by another endorsement from aspiring NATO members of Eastern Europe (known as the Vilnius 10—a group created to help aspiring NATO applicants). The letter from the Vilnius Group was from seven members: Albania, Bulgaria, Estonia, Croatia, Latvia, Lithuania, Macedonia, Romania, Slovakia, and Slovenia. In their open letter of 5 February, the Vilnius Group stated: "Our countries understand the dangers posed by tyranny and the special responsibility of democracies to defend our shared values. The trans-Atlantic community, of which we are a part, must stand together to face the threat posed by the nexus of terrorism and dictators with weapons of mass destruction."[65]

The actions of the Vilnius Group reflected the greater support that the former communist states of Eastern Europe have demonstrated for the US, partly in appreciation for American support during the Cold War and their independence efforts during the 1980s and 1990s.[66] The endorsement also reflected the desire of Eastern European governments to establish closer ties with Washington in order to prevent domination by the major powers of Europe, mainly France and Germany, and to increase economic and security ties with the US. For instance, Slovak Prime Minister Mikulas Dzurinda declared that his country's "decision was not only about Iraq, but also about Slovakia's future direction and about its chances to become a part of the democratic world."[67] With the rising tensions between the US and Germany, officials in several of the East European states, including NATO-members Poland, Hungary and the Czech Republic, saw an potential opportunity to acquire any bases or military assets that might be shifted from Germany. As the prelude to war continued, Washington tacitly encouraged these aspirations and began to negotiate over rewards and inducements.

By late January and early February, the growing coalition of the willing began to offer specific support for the US. Since the US did not seek significant troop deployments, many governments found it easy to offer a range of aid and support. Bulgaria offered the use of airfields and airspace and dispatched a small contingent (150 soldiers) of troops trained to deal with WMD warfare to be placed on standby in the Persian Gulf region. Slovakia also deployed 75 troops to join a 360-man Czech anti-chemical-and-biological-warfare unit that was deployed in Kuwait. Romania announced that it would allow the US and its allies the use of bases and airspace and would dispatch troops if needed. Meanwhile, Hungary not only allowed the use of Hungarian airspace and bases, the government agreed to the US desire to establish a training facility for Iraqi exiles who would accompany US troops during any ground operation.[68] Finally, Poland offered the use of special operations forces, and a small Polish contingent would serve during the invasion with allied troops.

While many members of the coalition, such as Great Britain and Australia, supported the US from principal, others sought concrete or specific rewards from Washington. For instance, in exchange for being used as a base for the northern or second front, Turkey sought some $30 billion in US aid and debt relief. Egypt and Jordan also asked for increased economic aid in return for support. On the other hand, Kuwait, which was ravaged by Iraq a decade earlier, eagerly endorsed military action and offered a range of assistance to the US, including staging areas. Likewise, when Saudi Arabia proved reluctant to allow the US to use bases in the kingdom, Qatar built new runways and other military facilities which would allow the Americans to command the war from the tiny sheikdom (the US did in fact shift the regional headquarters of Central Command, the US command overseeing the invasion, from Saudi Arabia to Doha, Qatar).

Japan demonstrated its backing for the US in an unusual diplomatic offensive. While Japan usually avoids confrontational issues at the UN, the Japanese government launched a diplomatic effort to persuade "undecided" members of the Security Council to back the Anglo-US-Spanish resolution. Tokyo even warned the French in an official statement that "[i]f the international community divides, it will not only benefit Iraq, but also place in doubt the authority and effectiveness of the United Nations."[69] Japan also offered financial assistance to states bordering Iraq and in the broader Middle East, including $1.3 billion to Egypt, Syria, Turkey and Jordan.[70]

The Dutch announced that, under the auspices of Article 4 of the NATO Treaty, they would dispatch Patriot missile batteries to Turkey in case of war. Because of continuing opposition from France and Germany, the deployment would not be a formal NATO mission, but instead a bilateral arrangement between the Dutch and Turkish governments. France and Germany did protest the move. French Foreign Ministry spokesman Bernard Valero argued that the deployment sent the wrong signal, that war was inevitable. He publicly confirmed the French position that the alliance should not take any steps that could be perceived as gearing-up for war: "In this context nothing would justify that the alliance associates itself with preparation for an eventual military operation."[71] Nonetheless, the DPC approved the deployment of AWACs to Turkey and on 24 February, the first NATO aircraft departed for duty in Turkey from Germany.[72]

Ultimately, US hopes for a second front from Turkey were dashed. The Bush administration was unwilling to provide the requested $30 billion in aid for Turkey. Instead the administration sought a smaller figure. On 1 March 2003, the Turkish Parliament voted to deny US forces access to bases in the country. The vote was the result of three main factors. First, public opinion in Turkey was strongly against the war. Second, many parliamentarians perceived the vote as a means to raise the stakes with Washington in order to increase the Bush administration's aid offer. Third, and finally, because of Turkey's longstanding internal conflict with its Kurdish minority, many lawmakers were fearful that the removal of the Iraqi regime might lead to the break-up of Iraq and the establishment of an independent Kurdish state which would then support the Kurdish independence movement in Turkey.

The vote shocked the administration and the US military both of which had long considered Turkey one of the most reliable allies of the US. The vote forced a recalculation of US military plans and the decision to proceed with only one major front. The decision surprised many in the Turkish government who believed that Washington would continue its negotiations. Instead, Turkey became marginalized in the strategic planning for the region and the Kurds ultimately gained the protection of US forces. Alan Cowell, writing in *The New York Times* aptly summarized the result after the war: "Without firing a single shot, Turkey's military has had an expensive war. Its commanders have not only lost a special bond with the United States that had endured for half a century, but it also forfeited a chance to secure a strategic bridgehead in Kurdish northern Iraq."[73]

In describing the mix of motivations to support the US, former US NATO ambassador Robert Hunter called the pro-US state "a coalition of the convinced, the concerned and the co-opted."[74] The coalition that was arrayed against Saddam in 2003 would be a very different one than the grand coalition that was assembled in the aftermath of the invasion of Kuwait. However, the US-dominated group matched Pentagon priorities. The US military preferred to rely on American troops, with support from British, Australian and Polish forces. Nonetheless, the Bush administration still sought to expand the official and tacit support, and thereby the size, of the coalition, even if countries only offered moral encouragement. Unlike the first US-led war against Saddam, there would not be large contingents of Muslim troops, nor would there be financial donors ready to cover the costs of the conflict. These differences undermined international perceptions of the coalition, even if the military power and capability of the new grouping was more potent.

France and Germany

The Franco-German reaction to East European support for the US matched any of the anti-"Old" Europe rhetoric coming from Washington. Chirac warned the aspiring EU and NATO members from East Europe that their support for the US was "dangerous" and "reckless" and declared that the countries "would have done better to shut up" than to issue the letters in support of the US.[75] Chirac went on to warn the countries that their positions would harm their chances of entering the EU. He declared that "If they had tried to decrease their chances for getting in Europe, they couldn't have done a better job" and that their actions "can only reinforce an attitude of hostility" from the other EU members."[76]

In terms of concrete action, France and Germany were able to pressure Greece, which held the rotating presidency of the EU, to withdraw invitations that had been extended to the potential new memberstates for an EU summit on Iraq. The East European states reacted defiantly and issued their own rhetorical firebombs. For instance, the Czech Foreign Minister Cyril Svoboda compared contemporary attitudes toward Iraq and Saddam Hussein to the 1938 Munich Conference and the general European policy of appeasement towards Germany and Hitler. She also linked the current debate to inaction as the Soviet Union took over the states of Central and Eastern Europe. She noted dryly that "[w]e certainly have seen the results of appeasement. It's much easier to tolerate a dictator when he's dictating over somebody else's life and not your own."[77]

Poland's Prime Minister Leszek Miller declared that "[w]e are too big and too proud a country, with a rich history, tradition and a conviction about our importance in Europe, to keep quiet," and that Poland "will speak when we consider it appropriate and we will say what we consider appropriate."[78] An official spokesman for the Estonian government issued a statement which noted that "Every country has a right to its own opinion, and we don't regret ours."[79] The influential Slovak daily *Pravda* presented a scathing editorial which proclaimed the sentiment of the East European states: "Europe will have to be different from what it was like before our entry ... and listen more to the voice of small states."[80] The editorial also declared: "After the enlargement, the EU will be different. Less French or German, less Chirac's—and no worse for that."[81] The result was an obvious and open split both within the EU and between some members of the EU and the applicant countries which undermined claims of American unilateralism and bolstered the Bush administration's stance.

Meanwhile, relations between the US and France and Germany continued to deteriorate. Chirac's government led a very public campaign against the US effort to develop an anti-Saddam coalition. Meanwhile Germany, which held the rotating chair of the UN Security Council, publicly supported France and engaged in efforts behind the scenes at the UN to block the Anglo-US-Spanish resolution.[82] In early February, Rumsfeld again increased tensions during testimony before Congress when he cited Germany, along with Cuba and Libya as the main opponents to military action against Saddam. In response to a question about potential international support if a war commenced, Rumsfeld asserted that many countries that were publicly opposed to the war would support the US and then stated that "there are three or four countries that have said they won't do anything. I believe Libya, Cuba and Germany are the ones that I have indicated won't help in any respect."[83] The conservatives in Germany seized on the comments to attack the Schröder government. Michael Glos, the leader of one of the center-right opposition parties, the Christian Social Union exclaimed that "alarm bells should ring in Berlin when Germany is placed on the same level as countries like Cuba and Libya."[84] As the level of rhetoric continued to increase, the positions of the pro-US and anti-US states continued to harden.

Rumsfeld's congressional remarks were followed by further statements which roundly criticized the Franco-German position. Two days after putting Germany in the same category as Cuba and Libya, the Secretary of Defense stated that those who cautioned against war "could well make war more likely, not less, because delaying preparations sends a signal of uncertainty" and that "there is no chance" that Saddam will voluntarily disarm.[85] Significantly, Bush backed Rumsfeld's comments with a verbal broadside of his own and declared that Saddam "was given a final chance. He is throwing away that chance."[86] Members of the US Congress even began hearings and discussions on methods which could be employed to "punish" France and Germany for their actions, including sanctions or restrictions on specific imports such as wine or bottled water, as well as the withdrawal of American troops from bases in Germany.[87]

Russia also opposed US military action, but Moscow pointedly refrained from taking an overtly public anti-war leadership position on the lines of Paris or Berlin. Initially, Putin's government tried a delicate balancing act toward the US. For example, Moscow sent signals to the Bush administration that it clearly opposed military action, but would abstain rather than veto any war resolution in the UN. In addition, Putin and Bush had developed a strong personal and working relationship and many Russian officials wanted to maintain close ties with Washington. As an incentive for cooperation with the US, the Bush administration offered to repeal some remaining economic restrictions that had been in place since the Cold War.[88] Russia joined France and Germany on 11 February in a declaration calling for continued inspections, but still not ruling out the use of force (China issued a declaration of support of the statement from the triumvirate).[89]

On the other hand, Russia wanted to preserve its economic interests in Iraq where forty percent of the oil-for-food program (about $2 billion annually) was handled by Russian companies and the nation had almost $40 billion in unrealized oil contracts. In the short term, Russia also had a vested interest in limiting Iraq's oil exports as it continued to develop its own export capabilities. Putin also cited his concern for increased Islamic terrorism as a motive for opposing military action.

As the Franco-German position hardened, Moscow became more vocal in its opposition to war. By the end of February, Putin had decided to cast his lot with the French and Germans and publicly come-out in full opposition to the war. On 28 February, Ivanov announced that Russia would veto any new resolution which threatened the use of force against Iraq. Ivanov declared that "Russia has the right to a veto in the UN Security Council and will use it if it is necessary in the interests of international stability" and that "Russia will not be in favor of any new resolution which allows the use of military force directly or indirectly to solve the Iraqi issue."[90]

Countdown to War

On 7 March, Blix reported that Iraq had accelerated cooperation, but that further inspections were still needed and that there were still unresolved issues between UNMOVIC and the Iraqi regime. That day the British introduced a measure into the Security Council to amend the Anglo-US-Spanish declaration. The amendment stated that Iraq had "failed to take the final opportunity afforded by resolution 1441 unless, on or before 17 March 2003, the Council concludes that Iraq has demonstrated full, unconditional, immediate and active cooperation."[91] The coalition members on the Security Council, supported by Japan and other allies, engaged in an effort to convince the "swing" votes to support the coalition resolution.[92] However, these states consistently asked for the permanent members to develop a compromise in order to avoid alienating either side. In addition, since France and Russia had both already threatened to veto any resolution authorizing the use of force, most of the swing states perceived that it would be useless to commit themselves to either position. Russia responded with France and Germany in a joint statement which opposed military action. On 15 March the three issued a declaration, supported by China, which stated "that in the present circumstances nothing justifies abandoning the inspection process and resorting to the use of force."[93] Meanwhile, coalition troops continued their deployments and preparations for military action in their staging areas in Kuwait.

Bush met with the main leaders of the diplomatic effort, including Blair, Aznar and Portuguese Prime Minister Jose-Manuel Durão Barroso in the Azores. On 16 March, the three leaders held a press conference and made it clear that war was imminent. Blair summarized the main arguments of the coalition, including the notion that

Saddam was employing the same "cheat and retreat" tactics that had marked his relationship with the UN for the previous twelve years. Blair also noted that "there's not a single person on the Security Council that doubts the fact that he [Saddam] is not fully cooperating today."[94] The leaders also affirmed the importance of the transatlantic alliance and decried the fact that France and Germany were willing to undermine the security regime which had proved so successful in Europe. Most significantly, the four leaders contended that the diplomatic effort was drawing to a close and that neither side was close to agreement. The following day, Great Britain's ambassador to the UN withdrew the coalition resolution and Bush announced an ultimatum that gave Saddam 48 hours to leave Iraq or face armed attack by the coalition.

Notes

[1] Melvyn Leffler, "The American Conception of National Security Policy and the Beginnings of the Cold War," *American Historical Review* 89 (April 1984), 360.

[2] Boutros Boutros-Ghali, quoted in James S. Sutterlin, *The United Nations and the Maintenance of International Security: A Challenge to be Met*, 2nd ed. (Westport, Conn: Praeger, 2003), 10.

[3] For more on this theme, see Adrian Treacher, "Europe as a Power Multiplier for French Security Policy: Strategic Consistency, Tactical Adaptation," *European Security* 10/1 (Winter 2001/2002): 22-44.

[4] Richard N. Haass, *The Reluctant Sheriff: The United States After the Cold War* (New York: Council on Foreign Relations, 1997), 6.

[5] Jeffrey Gedman, "Our European Problem," *The Weekly Standard* (19 June 2000), 13.

[6] Barbara Crossette, "Darkest Hour at UN," *The New York Times* (21 September 1998), A6.

[7] Joseph S. Nye, Jr., *The Paradox of American Power: Why the World's Only Superpower Can't Go it Alone* (New York: Oxford University Press, 2002), 68. Nye defines soft power as "the ability to attract through cultural and ideological ideal," as opposed to hard power which is "a country's economic and military ability to buy and coerce," Joseph S. Nye, Jr., "Redefining the National Interest," *Foreign Affairs* 78/4 (July/August 1999), 24.

[8] See Joseph S. Nye, Jr., *Bound to Lead: The Changing Nature of American Power* (New York: Basic Books, 1991).

[9] Tony Smith, *America's Mission: The United States and the Worldwide Struggle for Democracy in the Twentieth Century* (Princeton: Princeton University Press, 1994), 345.

[10] Fareed Zakaria, "Our Way: The Trouble with Being the World's Only Superpower," *The New Yorker* (14 October 2002), online at http://www.fareedzakaria.com/articles/nyer/101402.html.

[11] Ibid.

[12] The Pew Forum on Religion and Public Life, "God and Foreign Policy: The Religious Divide Between the US and Europe," Conference Program, Washington, D.C. (10 July 2003), online at http://pewforum.org/events/index.php?EventID=49.

[13] William Wallace, "US Unilateralism: A European Perspective," Patrick and Forman, 156-57.

[14] David E. Sanger, "Alliances With Europe: Bush Redraws Map," *The New York Times* (24 January 2003).

[15] Ibid.

[16] Wallace, 158.

[17] See Tom Lansford, *All for One: Terrorism, NATO and the United States* (Aldershot: Ashgate, 2002).

[18] Martin Walker, "The Blare of Blair," *Europe*, 411 (November 2001), 2.

[19] Sanger, "Alliances with Europe."

[20] Ibid.

[21] David M. Malone, "When America Banged the Table and the Others Fell Silent," *International Herald Tribune* (11 December 2001).

[22] On the Afghan Model and its inapplicability to Iraq, see Stephen Biddle, "Afghanistan and the Future of Warfare," *Foreign Affairs* 82/2 (March/July 2003), especially 45-46.

[23] Hans Blix, "An Update on Inspection," Report of the Executive Chairman of UNMOVIC to the United Nations Security Council, New York (27 January 2003), online at http://www.un.org/Depts/unmovic/Bx27.htm.

[24] Ibid.

[25] The Iraqi regime claimed the warheads were left over from the 1991 Gulf War and had been "lost", but Blix notes that they were discovered in a relatively new bunker which was constructed long after the war; ibid.

[26] Ibid.

[27] Daalder and Lindsay, 143.

[28] Marc Champion, et al., "How the Iraq Confrontation Divided the Western Alliance," *Wall Street Journal* (27 March 2003), 1.

[29] Richard Bernstein, "US and Public Opinion Leave Europe in the Middle," *International Herald Tribune* (18 February 2003).

[30] Jamie Coomarasamy, "France Treads Carefully on Iraq," *BBC News* (6 February 2003).

[31] Ibid.; the BBC article also summarized Chirac's dilemma by describing a political cartoon in one of the French dailies: De Villepin declares to Chirac "'We're heading to war. We need to find a way out.' The president replies 'For Saddam Hussein or for us?'," ibid.

[32] Daalder and Lindsay, 143.

[33] Donald Rumsfeld, "News Transcript: Secretary Rumsfeld Briefs at Foreign Press Center," Department of Defense News Transcripts (22 January 2003).

[34] Amity Shlaes summarized the view of many Americans in an opinion in *The Financial Times* by noting that the "old" Europe

> insult is sticking for the same reason that many other insults tend to stick: it contains truth. The US defense secretary was right. After all, Mr Bush's foreign policy, after a bit of evolution, could now be summed up as "bring on the new", or even "provoke the new, or perish." Germany's motto, by contrast, is "preserve the old" or "prevent repeats of old mistakes."
> Consider, for a start, the context that generated Mr Rumsfeld's remark. The US looks at the Middle East with hope. It believes that it can, by means of tough pressure and, if necessary, sustained military action, improve the prospects of liberty, prosperity and stability in the Gulf region;

Amity Shlaes, "Rumsfeld is Right About Fearful Europe," *The Financial Times* (28 January 2003), 21.

[35] Edward C. Luck, "The United States, International Organizations and the Quest for Legitimacy," Patrick and Forman, 55.

[36] Suzanne Daley, "Europe's Dim View of the US is Evolving Into Frank Hostility," *The New York Times* (9 April 2000).

[37] Stanley Hoffman, "Why Don't They Like Us?" *The American Prospect* 12/20 (19 November 2001); reprinted as Stanley Hoffman, "Why Don't They Like Us?," Eugene R. Wittkopf and

James M. McCormick, eds., *The Domestic Sources of American Foreign Policy: Insights and Evidence*, 4th ed. (New York: Rowman and Littlefield, 2004), 38.

[38] Elaine Ganley, "French-US Relations Fray Over Iraq War," *Associated Press* (12 February 2003).

[39] Glenn Kessler, "Moderate Powell Turns Hawkish On War With Iraq," *The Washington Post* (23 January 2003).

[40] Ibid.

[41] Ibid.

[42] Colin Powell, "Remarks to the United Nations Security Council," New York, State Department Press Release (5 February 2003), online at http://www.state.gov/secretary/rm/2003/17300.htm.

[43] Ibid.

[44] "Slovenia Says Iraq Wanted Nuke Equipment," *Associated Press* (6 February 2003).

[45] Ibid.

[46] Dafna Linzer, "Iraq Approves Inspectors' Use of U-2 Surveillance Planes, Iraqi Ambassador Says," *Associated Press* (10 February 2003).

[47] This included 50 liters of mustard gas at Muthanna, as well as quantities of the chemical precursors to mustard gas; Hans Blix, "Briefing of the Security Council," Report of the Executive Chairman of UNMOVIC to the United Nations Security Council, New York (14 February 2003), online at http://www.un.org/Depts/unmovic/blix14Febasdel.htm.

[48] Ibid.

[49] Jon Leyne, "Tiptoeing Along the Tightrope," *BBC News* (15 February 2003).

[50] "France Stance on Iraq Hardens," *BBC News* (14 February 2003).

[51] This meant that US troops and assets in Germany would need to be moved to Italy before they could be deployed to the Persian Gulf; ibid.

[52] *The North Atlantic Treaty* ("The Washington Treaty"), Washington, D.C. (4 April 1949), online at http://www.nato.int/docu/basictxt/treaty.htm.

[53] "Turkey Applies to NATO to Make Article Four of North Atlantic Treaty Operational," Anadolu Agency, cited at Turkish Press.com (10 February 2003), online at http://www.turkishpress.com/turkishpress/news.asp?ID=9009.

[54] Bernstein, "US and Public Opinion Leave Europe in the Middle."

[55] Lord Robertson, "Statement by the Secretary General on the North Atlantic Council Meeting on 6 February 2003," NATO Press Release (6 February 2003).

[56] "Lawmakers Say Allies Jeopardizing NATO," *Associated Press* (12 February 2003).

[57] Ganley, "French-US Relations Fray Over Iraq War."

[58] NATO, "Decision Sheet of the Defense Planning Committee: NATO Support to Turkey Within the Framework of Article 4 of the North Atlantic Treaty," NATO Press Release (16 February 2003).

[59] Lord Robertson, "Statement by NATO Secretary General, Lord Robertson, After the NATO Defense Planning Committee Meeting on 16 February 2003," NATO Press Release (16 February 2003).

[60] Barry Renfrew, "NATO, Minus France, Ends Split on Iraq," *Associated Press* (16 February 2003).

[61] Lord Robertson, "Statement by NATO Secretary General" (16 February 2003).

[62] Daalder and Lindsay, 143.

[63] Rubin, 49.

[64] The letter also noted the commonalities of the transatlantic alliance and the importance of the US-European relationship:

The real bond between the US and Europe is the values we share: democracy, individual freedom, human rights and the rule of law. These values crossed the Atlantic with those who sailed from Europe to help create the United States of America. Today they are under greater threat than ever.

The attacks of Sept. 11 showed just how far terrorists—the enemies of our common values—are prepared to go to destroy them. Those outrages were an attack on all of us. In standing firm in defense of these principles, the governments and people of the US and Europe have amply demonstrated the strength of their convictions. Today more than ever, the trans-Atlantic bond is a guarantee of our freedom;

Jose Maria Aznar, Jose-Manuel Durão Barroso, Silvio Berlusconi, Tony Blair, Vaclav Havel, Peter Medgyessy, Leszek Miller and Anders Fogh Rasmussen, "United We Stand" (30 January 2003).

[65] Albania, Bulgaria, Estonia, Croatia, Latvia, Lithuania, Macedonia, Romania, Slovakia, and Slovenia, "Statement of the Vilnius Group Countries in Response to the Presentation by the United States Secretary of State to the United Nations Security Council Concerning Iraq," New York (5 February 2003).

[66] Kim Gamel, "Eastern European Countries Support US Bid to Enforce Disarmament of Iraq," *Associated Press* (5 February 2003).

[67] Anna Mudeva, "Ex-Communist Europeans Rush to Help US Over Iraq," *Associated Press* (6 February 2003).

[68] Ibid.

[69] Kenji Hall, "Japan Pushes for Support of War in Iraq," *Associated Press* (12 March 2003).

[70] Ibid.

[71] "Dutch to Send Missile System to Turkey," *Associated Press* (7 February 2003).

[72] The deployment was noted with the official statement that NATO was "authorizing the military authorities to implement, as a matter of urgency, defensive measures to assist Turkey," NATO, "NATO AWACs to Patrol Skies Over Turkey," SHAPE Press Release (21 February 2003); NATO, "NATO AWACS Deployment to Turkey," NATO Press Release (21 February 2003).

[73] Alan Cowell, "Turkey's Stand Against the War in Iraq Costs it Influence in Region," *The New York Times*; reprinted in *The International Herald Tribune* (19 April 2003).

[74] Barbara Slavin, "US Builds War Coalition With Favors – and Money," *USA Today* (25 February 2003).

[75] John Vinocur, "Chirac's Outburst Exposes Contradiction Within EU," *International Herald Tribune* (18 February 2003).

[76] Ibid.

[77] Ibid.

[78] William J. Kole, "Emerging European Democracies Sound Off," *Associated Press* (24 February 2003).

[79] Ibid.

[80] Ibid.

[81] Ibid.

[82] Melissa Eddy, "Report: Germany Aimed to Block U.S. on War," *Associated Press* (16 March 2003).

[83] Donald Rumsfeld quoted in Tony Czuczka, "Germany Rejects Latest Rumsfeld Criticism," *Associated Press* (6 February 2003).

[84] Ibid.

[85] Robert Burns, "Bush, Rumsfeld Warn Against Delay on Iraq," *Associated* Press (8 February 2003).

[86] Ibid.

[87] Among the most strident members of Congress in the effort to "punish" the French and Germans were House Speaker Dennis Hastert (Republican of Illinois) and Senator John McCain (Republican Arizona). House Majority Leader Tom DeLay vented his anger in an anecdote that he relayed to many: "I was at a celebration of India's Independence Day," he told reporters, "and a Frenchman came walking up to me and started talking to me about Iraq, and it was obvious we were not going to agree. And I said, 'Wait a minute. Do you speak German?' And he looked at me kind of funny and said, 'No, I don't speak German.' And I said, 'You're welcome,' turned around and walked off," Jim VandeHei, "US Lawmakers Weigh Actions to Punish France, Germany," *The Washington Post* (12 February 2003), A16.

[88] Anna Badkhen, "Russia Weighs Allies Amid Weak Economy," *San Francisco Chronicle* (11 March 2003).

[89] In terms of the use of force, the joint statement declared that "There is still an alternative to war. The use of force can only be considered as a last resort. Russia, Germany and France are determined to ensure that everything possible is done to disarm Iraq peacefully. … it is up to Iraq to actively cooperate with the IAEA and the UNMOVIC. Iraq must fully accept its responsibilities," Russia, France and Germany, "Russia, France Germany Declaration on Iraq," Russian Foreign Ministry Press Release 333-11-02-2003 (11 February 2003); China, "China Supports Joint Declaration by Russia, France and Germany on Iraq" (11 February 2003) online at http://www.chinaembassy.bg/eng/41469.html.

[90] "Russia Warns of Iraq War Resolution Veto," *Associated Press* (28 February 2003).

[91] United Kingdom, "Iraq Amendment," New York (7 March 2003) online at www.cnn.com/2003/us/03/07/sprj.irq.amendement/index.html.

[92] Of the fifteen members of the Security Council, the US, Great Britain, Spain and Bulgaria supported the resolution to use force. The "swing" votes included Angola, Cameroon, Chile, Guinea, Mexico and Pakistan. The members opposed to the resolution included China, France, Germany, Russia and Syria.

[93] France, Germany and Russia, "Declaration on Iraq," Agence France-Presse (15 March 2003).

[94] US, White House, "Press Availability with President Bush, Prime Minister Blair, President Aznar and Prime Minister Barroso," Press Release (16 March 2003) online at http://www.whitehouse.gov/news/releases/2003/03/print/2003316-3-html.

Chapter 5

Operation Iraqi Freedom

Introduction

The diplomatic battles which foreshadowed the US-led invasion, in many ways overshadowed the actual military phase of the campaign to oust the regime of Saddam Hussein. The US and coalition military build-up in the region was slow and deliberate. The slow pace of the diplomatic intercourse allowed the US and its allies to preposition troops, aircraft, ships and other military equipment. The only major hurdle faced in the deployment was the refusal of Turkey to allow the US to launch a northern front from its territory. This necessitated some last minute redeployments, but the main strategy and force arrangements were relatively unaffected by Turkey's decision.

Just as Bush allowed Powell considerable freedom of action in shaping US diplomacy during the prelude to the war, the President also allowed Rumsfeld and the Defense Department's senior officers wide latitude to formulate and implement their preferred strategy. Freed from the perceived constraints of a multilateral military coalition, and its implicit political complications, US military planners sought to deploy the full range of American assets and capabilities in a campaign that would both showcase US firepower and minimize casualties. The administration sought a swift military victory as a means to entice other states to participate in the stabilization and nation building missions that would follow the assumed fall of the regime. In this fashion, Bush and his senior aides hoped that the conflict would follow the Afghan model in which US forces undertook the majority of combat missions, but coalition members provided the bulk of the peacekeeping and stabilization forces.

Central to the military plans was the concept of rapid dominance (which came to be known as "shock and awe"). Rapid dominance involved the use of extensive firepower and advanced weaponry. Large amounts of precision-guided and advanced munitions would hit targets within minutes of each other or even simultaneously. It was meant to exert a tremendous psychological impact on the enemy and to demoralize and bewilder enemy troops into inaction or retreat or outright surrender. Rapid dominance was the logical extension of the Weinberger-Powell Doctrine and the legacy of Vietnam. The concept was designed to maximize the military and intelligence advantages of the United States and to ensure a quick and relatively painless victory. US forces could, therefore, prevent the grinding and bloody ground combat that the nation faced in Vietnam. The confidence of the Defense Department was such, that it decided to embed reporters with military units in order to provide firsthand accounts of operations so they could "live, work and travel as part of the units in which they are embedded in order to facilitate maximum, in-depth coverage of US forces in combat and related operations."[1]

Ultimately, the initial combat phase of the war went very well for the United States and its small military coalition. The operation marked a complete rebuke to the Vietnam Legacy and demonstrated the capacity of the US military to quickly change battlefield strategy as the Defense Department abandoned the Afghan Model's reliance on the combination of indigenous allies, special operations forces and overwhelming air power, to utilize a more traditional ground-based war-plan. Michael O'Hanlon of the Brookings Institute notes that

> Throughout most of the twentieth century, the US armed forces were seen as an overmuscled giant, able to win wars through brute strength but often lacking in daring and cleverness. This basic strategy worked during the two world wars, making the United States relatively tough to challenge. But it failed in Vietnam, produced mediocre results in Korea, and worked in the Persian Gulf War largely because the terrain was ideally suited to American strengths.[2]

The 2003 invasion of Iraq would again allow the US to flex its military "muscle" and engage in the sort of land warfare for which its ground troops were well-suited. In addition, advanced weapons systems and new capabilities allowed the US-led coalition to utilize the "daring and cleverness" which had made the Afghan campaign "a masterpiece of military creativity and finesse."[3]

Weinberger-Powell Doctrine

The US military developed a range of lessons from Vietnam. Many of these were practical and involved tactics and battlefield strategy, but others dealt more broadly with questions of policy. One result was a lingering reluctance among senior military officers to engage in conflict based on political calculations. There was likewise an aversion to lengthy missions without clearly defined goals and an articulated endstate or withdrawal timeline.

In response to the military's concern over the potential for future quagmires, in 1984, Secretary of Defense Casper Weinberger promulgated what became known as the Weinberger Doctrine. This strategic vision held that military forces should not be deployed without: 1) clear objectives (issued before the deployment); 2) a timeframe for the operation to avoid open-ended commitments such as Vietnam (commonly known now as an "exit strategy" which is used to avoid "mission creep"); and 3) a clear mandate from the public that domestic support would be forthcoming for the operation.[4] Weinberger specifically sought to avoid what he described as the "admixture of diplomacy and the military" which he claimed might lead the US to use force to promote "stability, or changes in government or support of governments or whatever else."[5] Later Colin Powell, as Chairman of the Joint Chiefs of Staff would further codify the doctrine. Powell's notion of what made successful operations was deceptively "simple: Match political expectations to military means."[6] To the Weinberger Doctrine, Powell added the concept of overwhelming force—the principle that American forces should only go into combat when they had a decided advantage in firepower and support.

Military Interventions and the War on Terror

The first Gulf War against Iraq was deemed to be a broad affirmation of the utility of the Weinberger-Powell Doctrine. Yet, throughout the 1990s, the Doctrine had its critics. Former Secretary of State, George Schultz, declared that the Doctrine was "the Vietnam syndrome in spades, carried to an absurd level, and a complete abdication of the duties of [global] leadership."[7] Another former cabinet official and noted historian, James Schlesinger, disapproved of the doctrine and announced that he objected to "the emerging belief that the United States must fight only popular, winnable wars. The role of the United States in the world is such that it must be prepared for, be prepared to threaten, and even be prepared to fight those intermediate conflicts that are likely to fare poorly on television."[8] A study by the Council on Foreign Relations found that the doctrine was not applicable to most of the military interventions of the 1990s, including the humanitarian and nation building missions in Somalia and the Balkans and that:

> the Weinberger/Powell doctrine is useful only as a checklist that policymakers can use to ensure that they have carefully thought through a decision for military intervention. Even if certain aspects are missing, such as public support or clear objectives, the tests can serve to remind leaders that they need to be particularly careful about taking action.[9]

Military analyst Jeffrey Record adroitly summed up the criticism of the doctrine when he wrote that the Weinberger-Powell "doctrine purports to be a warning against another Vietnam, it is almost certainly unnecessary. The very experience of the Vietnam War remains the greatest obstacle to its repetition."[10]

Indeed, the military operations of the 1990s demonstrated the limits of application of the Weinberger-Powell Doctrine, as American forces suffered from mission creep in Somalia and remained in the Balkans far past their original end dates. For instance, in Somalia, the original humanitarian mission to provide food and aid to a starving populace evolved into an effort to establish a stable government (nation building) which led to major military operations. The nation building effort commenced as the "UN's credibility was in taters" because of its inability to distribute aid as the growing boldness of militia groups forced the UN mission to pay "ransom" in order to conduct its efforts.[11] In response, the US led military operations to capture the main warlords responsible for interfering with the UN operations. During one mission in October 1993, 18 Americans were killed. The UN blamed the US for creating the conditions which led to the attack by "operating under a separate military command, and for launching raids inconsistent with basic tenets of UN peacekeeping."[12] However, the

American losses and the subsequent press coverage of the bodies of US troops being dragged through the streets of Mogadishu undermined US popular support for the Somalia mission and led Clinton to withdraw US forces.[13]   The US withdrawal reinforced global views that the American public was unwilling to accept military casualties.

It was this latter perception that initially encouraged Al Qaeda and other terrorist groups. In an interview with Jim Miller (as reported by Bernard Lewis in *The New Yorker*) before the 11 September attacks, Osama bin Laden declared that:

> We have seen in the last decade the decline of the American government and the weakness of the American soldier, who is ready to wage cold wars and unprepared to fight long wars. This was proven in Beirut when the Marines fled after two explosions. It also proves that they can run less than twenty-four hours, and this was also repeated in Somalia. ... The youth were surprised at the low morale of the American soldiers. ... After a few blows they ran in defeat. ... They forgot about being the world leader and the leader of the new world order.[14]

Although the terrorist attacks of 11 September 2001 lessened the impetus behind most of the main restrictions of the Weinberger-Powell Doctrine, the doctrine remained in place through Operation Enduring Freedom and would influence the planning of subsequent operations. For instance, the reliance of the US on the Northern Alliance forces to conduct the brunt of the ground combat in Afghanistan and the use of extensive air and missile strikes are demonstrative of the continuing hesitancy to expose American troops to the potential for heavy casualties.

The Military Planning

The NSS was partially designed to counter perceptions of American weakness and to ensure that potential enemies were aware that the Bush administration planned to pursue an assertive and aggressive security policy. Against this background was a longstanding belief among senior members of the administration that Iraq posed a major threat to the stability of the international system and that the regime of Saddam Hussein was likely to ally itself with anti-American Islamic fundamentalist terrorist organizations if these groups were able to continue to undertake significant attacks on the United States. As senior members of the Defense Department began to plan for the possibility of war with Iraq, they examined a range of options and plans for military action.

Among the congressional delegations, many contended that the US should employ the same type of surgical strikes that successive administrations had used against Saddam. In other words, the US should identify and attack specific targets, such as suspected WMD sites, command and control structures and leadership components. Mississippi Republican Senator Thad Cochrane suggested that the US attack individual targets over time since he believed that "[t]he most appropriate and safest thing from our country's standpoint is to attack that one weapon system. ... I see nothing wrong with that. In fact, I think it would be morally unacceptable for us not to take this action."[15] However, Rumsfeld made it clear at the end of the summer of 2002, that the Bush administration could not destroy potential WMD sites or other targets with air power and missile strikes alone. During congressional testimony, the Secretary of Defense noted that "[t]he idea that it's easy to simply go do what you suggested ought to be done from the air, the implication being from the air, is a misunderstanding of the situation. The Iraqis have a great deal of what they do deeply buried."[16] Instead, Rumsfeld asserted that the only way to ensure complete destruction of potential WMDs and other weapon systems was to have troops on the ground.[17]

As they discussed options, US defense officials quickly came to the conclusion that the Afghan model of using indigenous troops to bear the brunt of the fighting or to at least supplement US ground forces was unsuited to Iraq. While the Kurdish *pesh merga* (militias) were relatively well-armed and organized, they lacked heavy artillery and transport. In addition, the use of the pesh merga would likely prompt Iraqi Arabs to unite against the invading forces. Outside of the pesh merga, there were no organized, effective resistance forces in Iraq.

There was widespread dissatisfaction with the existing regime. US planners sought to capitalize on these sentiments and believed that, especially in the Shiite areas of southern Iraq, coalition forces were likely to receive a welcome reception. The US worked to utilize existing Iraqi exile groups, such as the Iraqi National Congress, for intelligence support and to identify both targets and likely collaborators.

In late-August and early-September of 2002, the US began prepositioning units and equipment in the Gulf for a possible preemptive strike against Iraq. These included tanks and transport vehicles and other large equipment that was cumbersome to transport (the Pentagon usually contracted their transport to large commercial vessels).[18] In October, the Pentagon ordered an Army corps and a Marine expeditionary force to deploy headquarters units in Kuwait. By November, the US had four aircraft carrier battle groups in the Persian Gulf, and a month later, there was a fifth and then a sixth in January. As the military build-up continued, the Bush administration assured the UN and coalition partners, that it intended no immediate military action. The administration specifically pledged that it would not attack before the November congressional elections in the US or during the Muslim holy month of Ramadan or while UNMOVIC continued operations in Iraq. Instead, the military deployments were designed to accomplish two goals: 1) to increase pressure on the Iraqi regime to comply with UNMOVIC and UNSCR 1441; and, 2) to ensure that the US had the necessary forces in place in case military action was needed.

Weather

The weather and climate of the region played a major role in determining the timing of military operations. During the Iraqi summer, temperatures could rise as high as 120 degrees Fahrenheit (48 degrees Celsius). Planners had to take into account the possibility that coalition troops would have to don nuclear, biological and chemical

(NBC) protection gear which, because it seals a person's body against the elements and air, is extremely hot and uncomfortable. During the summer months, soldiers would have a very difficult time engaging in extended operations while they were wearing NBC suits.

The first US-led war against Iraq began in January and took advantage of the cooler winter months from November through March. Temperatures during this season average about 75 degrees Fahrenheit or 23 degrees Celsius, although temperatures sometimes fall below the freezing mark in January. US officials were also aware of another constraint of the late-spring months, the wind. Usually beginning in April, a hot, dry wind from the southeast, known as sharqi, produces gusts of up to 80 kilometers-per-hour and creates extensive dust and sand storms. These storms create poor visibility and damage equipment. The storms would also create problems for the precision-guided weapons used by the US and impair the ability of coalition forces to conduct air sorties.

Intelligence

UN inspections in the aftermath of the first Iraq War demonstrated that there had been a number of significant intelligence failures and that military strikes by the coalition were far less effective than US military officials believed at the time. Allied intelligence sources failed to determine that Iraq had 70 chemical warheads which could be used on Scud missiles or that the Iraqi nuclear program was much further advanced than was thought at the time. For instance, US intelligence services believed that Iraq had two main nuclear-related facilities which needed to be targeted, but after the war, UN inspectors discovered that there were over 20 sites, including 16 major centers, capable of ultimately producing enough enriched uranium to build four nuclear bombs each year.[19]

US intelligence capabilities continued to be constrained by the legacy of past policies. During the 1990s, the Clinton administration sought to emphasize "signals intelligence" (SIGINT) over "human intelligence" (HUMINT). This shift was the result of sentiments within the administration that SIGINT was "cleaner" than HUMINT and less likely to lead the US into deals or arrangements with individuals and groups that had violated human rights standards. One manifestation was that "senior advisors in the Clinton administration displayed open hostility toward the IC [intelligence community], particularly toward HUMINT."[20] As the military planned for the invasion of Iraq, it was constrained by the lack of HUMINT in Iraq. While the US intelligence community had maintained contacts within the Kurdish regions of the north and some anti-Saddam Shiite groups, it had not had time to reestablish a viable intelligence network in the country.

In addition, the UN inspectors ascertained that in spite of the heavy aerial bombardment which preceded the war, the coalition had failed to destroy some 150,000 chemical weapons, including warheads, canisters and bombs.[21] Furthermore, the CIA estimated that the aerial strikes had destroyed almost half of Iraq's armored forces, but later estimates found that the figure was closer to one-third.[22] One of the main intelligence missions of the war was to seek-out and destroy Iraq's mobile Scud launchers. Besides various human and satellite intelligence, the coalition also used various sensors to detect launches. Because of the psychological impact of the Scud launches on Israel and coalition states such as Saudi Arabia, General Charles Horner noted that the coalition "certainly employed many, many more assets toward keeping the Scuds inhibited than we originally thought we'd have to."[23] In summarizing the coalition effort to stop the Scuds, Marolda and Schneller assert that "coalition air power did not stop the launches and destroyed at best a few of the mobile launchers because of the limited capability of allied airborne sensors and the effectiveness of Iraqi decoy tactics."[24]

The combination of the lack of HUMINT and the potential for faulty intelligence about WMDs, or other enemy capabilities, as the campaign progressed convinced US planners that any operation needed extraordinary speed in order to immobilize enemy forces and prevent the use of unforeseen weapons or assets. Speed was also seen as a means to minimize US casualties and lessen damage to the infrastructure of the country. This, in turn, would facilitate the post-Saddam rebuilding of Iraq.

Network-Centric Warfare

Rumsfeld also sought to incorporate new military doctrines into his planning in an effort to maximize SIGINT capabilities. In October 2001, Rumsfeld appointed retired admiral Arthur K. Cebrowski as Director of the newly-established Office of Force Transformation. Cebrowski was charged to oversee reforms in US force postures which would allow military assets to react more quickly to events and for military commanders to shift strategy as conditions changed. Ultimately, Rumsfeld sought a more flexible and more adaptable US military which was marked by high levels of cooperation and integration between the branches.[25]

Cebrowski specifically sought to implement a concept known as Network-Centric Warfare (NCW). NCW is

> an information superiority-enabled concept of operations that generates increased combat power by networking sensors, decision makers, and shooters, to achieve shared awareness, increased speed of command, higher tempo of operations, greater lethality, increased survivability, and a degree of self-synchronization. In essence, NCW translates information superiority into combat power by effectively linking knowledgeable entities in the battlespace.[26]

Hence, NCW seeks to take advantage of the main areas in which the US generally has clear military superiority, including firepower, communications, intelligence, mobility and flexibility. NCW also seeks to provide commanders in the field with the maximum amount of information and flexibility in order to make decisions and to react quickly to changing battlefield conditions. Finally, NCW provides a means to ensure that both the soldiers in the field and their commanders in the rear have not only the same information, but both elements have the utmost amount of information available in order to react more quickly than their enemies.[27] The integration of the various components of NCW results in the ability for the US to utilize a rapid dominance strategy, similar to the blitzkrieg of World War II.

Shock and Awe

Ultimately, the plan developed for the invasion of Iraq was compatible with the main tenets of the Weinberger-Powell Doctrine. The US attack was envisioned as a demonstration of overwhelming force against an inferior enemy with lesser capabilities. The majority of troops would be American, although there would be a sizeable British contingent and small numbers of special operations forces from other states. American strategy was to be a combination of the need for overwhelming force from the Weinberger-Powell Doctrine and the NCW.

At the core of the US strategy was the NCW concept expressed through an attempt to achieve rapid dominance on the battlefield.[28] The "rapid" component of the strategy refers to the ability to move forces and assets before an enemy can react. In order to achieve rapid dominance, the US has to be able to move and shift assets more quickly than the enemy at any point during a campaign, including the before- and after-action movements. "Dominance" refers to two strategic imperatives: 1) the power to destroy an enemy's ability to resist through massive and overwhelming firepower; and 2) the ability to destroy an enemy's will to resist. Dominance affects not only the enemy's frontline troops, but to be effective, it must also paralyze the command and control structures in the rear. In short, rapid dominance is based on the premise of an attack so powerful that it completely saps the enemy's will and ability to fight. The application of rapid dominance is known as "shock and awe." As the originators of the term explain:

> Shutting the [enemy] country down would entail both the physical destruction of appropriate infrastructure and the shut-down and control of the flow of all vital information and associated commerce so rapidly as to achieve a level of national shock akin to the affect that dropping nuclear weapons on Hiroshima and Nagasaki had on the Japanese.[29]

Ullman and Wade go on to explain the interplay between rapid dominance and shock and awe:

> The basis for Rapid Dominance rests in the ability to affect the will, perception, and understanding of the adversary through imposing sufficient Shock and Awe to achieve the necessary political, strategic, and operational goals of the conflict or crisis that led to the use of force. War, of course, in the broadest sense has been characterized by Clausewitz to include substantial elements of "fog, friction, and fear." In the Clausewitzian view, "shock and awe" were necessary effects arising from application of military power and were aimed at destroying the will of an

adversary to resist. Earlier and similar observations had been made by the great Chinese military writer Sun Tzu around 500 B.C. Sun Tzu observed that disarming an adversary before battle was joined was the most effective outcome a commander could achieve. Sun Tzu was well aware of the crucial importance of achieving Shock and Awe prior to, during, and in ending battle. He also observed that "war is deception," implying that Shock and Awe were greatly leveraged through clever, if not brilliant, employment of force.[30]

In order to achieve shock and awe, a military force needs to possess four basic features. First, the attacker must have "total knowledge" of the enemy and the environment.[31] Intelligence must be seamless, constantly updated and easily shared among troops. Second, there must be "brilliance in execution." The battlefield tactics of the attacker must be superior to the efforts of the defenders.[32] Third, the key to all other features of shock and awe is "rapidity." The attacking forces must be able to move with lightening speed and not only outpace the defenders, but be able to consistently employ the element of surprise.[33] Fourth, and finally, the attackers must be able to control the "environment."[34] In this case, environment does not refer to the physical features of the battlefield, but the electronic airwaves. The attackers must be able to control the flow of information and disrupt the enemy's communications and sensory capabilities.

Significantly, shock and awe is not limited to the use of bombs and weaponry. It can also involve the use of special operations forces to disrupt or destroy infrastructure or cut power lines or communications. Shock and awe may also involve efforts to destroy the enemy leadership. Ullman and Wade describe this as the "selective, instant decapitation of military or societal targets to achieve shock and awe."[35] For shock and awe to work in the Iraq campaign, Ullman argued that "if you can strike quickly at all elements of the power—political and military—simultaneously ... you can so shock the system that you impose a paralysis, and the enemy is incapable of responding. So when Saddam pulls the levers, they're not there."[36]

Military Constraints

For shock and awe to be effective, an enemy force has to be willing to surrender. Shock and awe unleashes massive firepower and disrupts communications and information so that once the enemy perceives that the situation seems hopeless, it gives up. If the enemy is ready to fight to the death, then the utility of shock and awe is severely constrained. One question on the eve of the US-led invasion was whether or not Iraqis with close ties to the regime would fight to the end. Many Iraqis associated with the regime had considerable reason to believe that if their control was weakened, the population, especially the Shiites, would rise in rebellion to extract vengeance on the Baathists. In an effort to encourage Iraqis to surrender, even before the war began, the US engaged in a wide-ranging psychological operation to assure key military and political figures that they would be safe even if Saddam was deposed.[37]

The coalition's initial plan for shock and awe was dealt a significant setback by Turkey's refusal to allow US troops to launch a northern offensive. The diplomatic interaction over the issue was widely publicized and Saddam was well aware that the main thrust of the US would have to come from the South. This allowed him to concentrate Iraqi forces and it forced the US to redeploy units that were on their way to Turkey to other staging areas.

Another hurdle faced by the coalition was that the Iraqis knew they were going to face a shock and awe campaign as before the military action began, various US defense officials discussed the severity of the coming attack. In response, Saddam took steps to try and protect his main weapons systems and to disperse troops. He also divided Iraq into different zones, each under the command of a trusted family member or loyal subordinate. That way, if the regime was "decapitated," or even if the US simply was able to disrupt communications, there would still be a regional command and control system in place to direct resistance.

Finally, through Bush's efforts to support British Prime Minister Tony Blair by gaining a second UN resolution, the timetable for military action had been pushed back into March. Had the campaign begun in January or February, the weather would have been much better for the coalition. Instead, the invading allies would face increasing heat as March wore into April and they were confronted with the sharqi. These winds blew sand and dust into motors and other equipment and slowed movement by obscuring visibility.

The Iraqi Military

Years of military and economic sanctions had seriously eroded the fighting capabilities of the Iraqi military. By 2003, the Iraqi military was about half the size it had been in 1991.[38] In addition, the impact of the 1991 Gulf War and the continuing no-fly zones meant that Iraq had no effective air force. In addition, years of cat-and-mouse games with allied aircraft patrolling the northern and southern no-fly zones had degraded Iraq's anti-aircraft capabilities and provided US intelligence with very precise evaluations of the country's capabilities. Iraq still had about 300 aircraft, although only about half of those were serviceable. There were also about 100 attack helicopters and about 275 transport or cargo helicopters.[39] The coalition would, by default, have almost unchallenged air superiority even before the actual military campaign began. The coalition also had little to fear from the tiny Iraqi Navy which fielded only six small patrol boats and some mine vessels.

The majority of Iraq's military equipment was older, Soviet-era weaponry. While Iraq did possess a considerable number of tanks (2,000-2,600) and artillery, only about 700 T-72 tanks were considered modern and a match for US armor.[40] Iraq was able to purchase small quantities of equipment and munitions through clandestine channels during the 1990s, but the majority of these purchases were to upgrade command and control and anti-air systems.[41] The Iraqis were able to purchase some advanced Kornet antitank missiles and Global Positioning System (GPS) jammers, but only in limited quantities. The morale and effectiveness of the Iraqi Army had been severely degraded during the 1990s by Saddam as he sought to ensure that military officers did not conduct a coup against him. As a result, the Iraqi leader deliberately had a centralized command system and did not allow meaningful communication between commanders in the field.[42] Saddam also tried to ensure the loyalty of certain units by giving them better equipment and supplies, a tactic which further eroded overall military morale.

The Iraqi Army that prepared to oppose the US-led coalition was essentially a force that was completely opposite of the coalition forces. Where the coalition would use the most sophisticated and modern equipment, including unmanned drones and stealth aircraft, the Iraqi weapons systems were a decade or more out-of-date. Where the coalition troops would be highly coordinated and flexible, with a decentralized command system, the Iraqi military was ill-prepared to coordinate movements or attacks and was hampered by a highly rigid and hierarchical command structure. Whereas defenders usually have an advantage over attackers, in this case, the highly sophisticated communications and intelligence capabilities of the coalition forces would give them the advantage in terms of terrain and the element of surprise. Finally, coalition forces had high morale and confidence in their abilities and their leadership, while the Iraqis were often demoralized and more fearful than confident in their leadership.

Operation Iraqi Freedom

As the diplomatic interaction wound-down, the coalition had about 300,000 troops. The majority of the coalition forces were American, but there were also 45,000 British troops and 2,000 Australians. In addition, Poland deployed about 200 special operations units and both Spain and Denmark supplied troops that were not used in combat. Opposing the coalition were 450,000 Iraqi troops. Although many of these were ill-equipped and led, the Republican Guard, Special Republican Guard and the paramilitary Fedayeen Saddam ("men of Sacrifice") were well-trained and equipped. While the coalition strategy called for shock and awe, the allied forces would be outnumbered. As Max Boot, the Olin Senior Fellow in National Security Studies at the Council on Foreign Relations, points out,

> Traditionally, war colleges have taught that to be sure of success, an attacking force must have a 3 to 1 advantage—a ratio that goes up to 6 to 1 in difficult terrain such as urban areas. Far from having a 3 to 1 advantage in Iraq, coalition ground forces (which never numbered more than 100,000) faced a 3 to 1 or 4 to 1 *disadvantage* [italics in the original].[43]

US commanders in the region suggested that the US should deploy more troops. General Tommy Franks, the commander of Central Command, and therefore the theater commander, argued for about 500,000 troops and a campaign similar to the first Iraq War which began with a lengthy aerial bombardment. However, Rumsfeld stuck with his original plans since he believed that the coalition shock and awe campaign could overcome Iraqi numerical superiority.

Following his ultimatum of 17 March, Bush ordered military operations to commence two days later. Special operations forces, many already in place in Iraq, initiated covert strikes on key targets and pre-sighted targets for the coming attack. On 19 March, the first major blow from the coalition occurred in the form of a limited attack on Baghdad, designed to eliminate Saddam and other elements of the Iraqi leadership through missile strikes. Intelligence reported that Saddam and senior regime figures were at Dora Farms, just outside of Baghdad. Bush met with his senior cabinet officials and after four hours of debate, gave Franks approval to launch the raid against Dora Farms. Two US stealth fighters dropped precision-guided bombs on the complex and the US fired 40 Tomahawk cruise missiles at the location. The attack destroyed the complex, but it failed to kill Saddam.[44]

The attack forced the coalition commanders to deploy their main special operations forces sooner than they intended and to launch the main offensive two days early.[45] On the day after the failed-decapitation strike, the shock and awe campaign began in earnest. The US launched massive air-and missile strikes on Baghdad and other key targets. During the first two days of the campaign, some 3,000 bombs and missiles struck Iraqi targets. Meanwhile, some 100,000 allied troops launched their ground invasion.[46] The first allied casualties of the campaign were the result of a helicopter crash which killed eight British and four American service personnel.

The Ground War

Coalition forces made considerable progress during the opening days of the campaign. By 22 March, American forces had swept inward past the city of Nasiriya and captured two crossings over the Euphrates River. Coalition special operations commandos captured the Ramallah oil fields and were able to prevent the regime from setting fire to the oil wells as Saddam had done during the 1991 Gulf War.[47] In addition, British forces had captured the Faw Peninsula. By 28 March, the British were able to begin landing relief supplies at the port of Umm Qasr for Iraqi civilians fleeing the fighting. American infantry and armored units met little significant resistance. In just three days, American forces were able to advance some 200 miles into Iraq.

Although the Fourth Infantry Division had been barred from Turkey, the coalition still launched a limited northern offensive. Airborne and air assault forces landed in Kurdish areas of northern Iraq and helped secure oil fields and transportation links. They also directed coalition air- and pesh merga ground-attacks on the terrorist group Ansar al-Islam which had camps in the north (Ansar al-Islam had links with a range of radical Islamic terrorist groups). By 30 March, coalition and Kurdish forces had overrun the main terrorist camps and began to advance on the main Kurdish cities of Kirkuk and Mosul.

Coalition forces did encounter heavy resistance. Allied planners had hoped that Shiites in cities such as Basra would rise against the regime. However, the lessons of the previous Gulf War, when they rose only to be slaughtered because the allies did not support them, prevented any such revolt. Instead, the town was surrounded by British troops and cut-off. The British laid siege against the Baathists, but avoided urban combat and its potential casualties. The rapid advance of the coalition also caused problems as Fedayeen Saddam units began attacking allied supply columns and convoys. One attack, on 23 March, left twelve Americans dead or captured.[48] Coalition units also ran into trouble when a wave of sand storms disrupted supply lines and limited aerial operations. Attacks on convoys and advancing units continued. The military began to refer to the Fedayeen as "dead-enders" in acknowledgement of their decision to fight-it-out to the bitter end.

Quagmire Fears

In order to improve the security of the supply lines, the advance on Baghdad was slowed in order for US commanders to reallocate forces from the advance to guard the logistics trail. The slowdown of the shock and awe campaign was perceived by many to be a sign that the invasion was in trouble and that the coalition had misjudged the strength of Iraqi resistance. In addition, unlike the 1991 Gulf War, the Iraqis were not surrendering in large numbers, something that shock and awe should have prompted. The deputy commander of coalition forces, Lieutenant General John Abizaid, in response to a question about this phenomenon, implied that the reason Iraqis were not surrendering was that they were instead deserting:

> I think the main reason that there haven't been a lot of mass surrenders on the same scale as in 1991 is that the Iraqi forces really were trapped in Kuwait. They were far away from home. They had no where to melt back to. Here in the areas that we've been encountering regular Iraqi forces, by far the majority of units have just melted away. We find a substantial amount of abandoned equipment on the field, and in the regular army there is clearly very, very little will to fight. True, we've captured 2,000 prisoners thus far, but the units that we have expected to find in various locations and put up resistance really haven't done so.[49]

Many analysts and politicos began to decry the war plans and assert that the coalition was already in a quagmire. Lawrence Korb, a defense official in the Reagan administration, and then a member of the Council on Foreign Relations exclaimed in a interview that the Bush administration "didn't anticipate the fighting in the south, didn't anticipate problems getting humanitarian aid in, didn't anticipate the guerrilla tactics," and that "[t]o say this is going according to plan is nonsense."[50] Many commentators asserted that the American public had been mislead by overly optimistic predictions from the Pentagon and the administration. Perceptions were not helped by some comments from the frontlines. For instance, Lieutenant General William Wallace who commanded the Army units in Iraq stated on 27 March, that "the enemy we're fighting is a bit different than the one we war-gamed against."[51]

Franks even felt obliged to publicly proclaim on 30 March that the advance had not been halted because of Iraqi resistance. In addition, the daily Pentagon press briefings also contained lively defenses of the ongoing invasion. On 31 March, Pentagon spokeswoman Victoria Clarke noted that coalition troops were only 50 miles from Baghdad and summarized some of the differences form the 1991 Gulf War:

Unlike the Gulf War, no Iraqi Scud missiles have been fired into Israel. Unlike the Gulf War, the oil fields have not been turned into a huge bonfire, wreaking enormous economic and environmental damage. There has been, thus far, no humanitarian crisis or mass exodus of refugees. There has, as yet, been no Iraqi use of weapons of mass destruction. Of course, bad things may still occur. Some of the toughest fighting, as we have indicated, may well lie ahead. But the fact that none of the predicted disasters has happened yet is good news in itself, and testimony to the progress we're making.[52]

The speed of the US advance was partially due to the deployment of the main Iraqi ground units. Saddam did not have large concentrations of troops along the border with Kuwait, but instead had his main Republican Guard and Special Republican Guard units deployed in a semi-circle around Baghdad. As coalition ground forces paused and solidified their lines of supply, these Iraqi units came under intense aerial bombardment. By the time coalition ground forces resumed their attack, only 19 out of an original 850 Republican Guard tanks were still operable and only 40 of 550 artillery pieces were operational.[53]

One American officer, Colonel Michael Longoria, commander of a unit that helped coordinate air strikes on ground units noted about the shock and awe of the air assault that: "I don't know if we are going to understand how significant this effort was until we do more analysis. But when you can destroy over three divisions worth of heavy armor in a period of about a week and reduce each of these Iraqi divisions down to even 15, 20 percent of their strength, it's going to have an effect."[54] The Iraqis sought, with some success, to reinforce the main divisions defending Baghdad. Having learned that massed convoys and columns were easily destroyed from the air, they moved their forces in small groups, and mostly by night. A US Air Force officer compiling statistics on the results of aerial bombing reported that: "[w]e never caught them in a big convoy where they just go on the highway. The Iraqis over the past 12 years have done a very good job of learning how to move and hide and keep themselves safe, but not as good a job of learning how to fight."[55]

The shock and awe of the aerial campaign turned-out to be more precise than blunt. Coalition forces attacked specific targets that were prioritized by headquarters units. Each day, teams of planners at the Prince Sultan Air Base in Saudi Arabia were given lists of targets, sorted by classification. Hence, there were teams that specialized in military targets or infrastructure or command and control elements. The teams generated a joint integrated prioritized target list which reflected NCW doctrines by integrating incoming daily intelligence, resources and on-the-ground needs.[56] For instance, after the target list was developed, operational commands then matched munitions, aircraft and target type. There were even efforts made to minimize potential collateral damage. Colonel Gary Crowder discussed this process to reporters early during the war by explaining that through the use of projection tools

you can better understand the environment and the immediate neighborhood of where you're dropping that munition, and then you can do an examination of various things that might include changing the size of the weapon; changing when the weapon fuses, to perhaps fuse the weapon underground, to mitigate that explosion even more; or even changing the direction of your attack axis, because if you attack from one way, you might completely mitigate all effects, if things work properly, but if you attack from another, there might be no way.[57]

Within a few days of the start of the campaign, it became apparent that the aerial portion resembled other, more traditional, campaigns. The shock and awe campaign was intentionally limited after consultations between the British and American air commands. American military planners cut the number of strikes planned for infrastructure targets in half after the British insisted that a massive attack would cause political problems between the coalition and Arab states of the Gulf and that heavy destruction would complicate the rebuilding process. The senior British air officer in the theater, Air Marshal Brian Burridge forced Franks to eliminate a range of targets. Burridge also retained a veto over future specific missions.[58] British military officials repeatedly noted that they opposed the shock and awe concept and one officer stated that "[n]one of us [British officers] ever approved of the phrase Shock and Awe because it painted totally the wrong picture, but it was the Pentagon's favorite slogan."[59]

Targets were carefully chosen and instead of a massive and overwhelming attack across the entire country, specific targets were subject to the concentrated firepower needed to destroy or disrupt that particular entity. As a result, the coalition forces were able to destroy particular units and targets, but minimize civilian and collateral damage. Longoria noted that "as the air power weighed into them [the Iraqi military] and the more destruction we caused to the military vehicles, the buildings, the command and control facilities, I think it did set the tone that probably helped the Iraqi desertion rate."[60]

On to Baghdad

Unbeknownst to the world's press, the administration held a major meeting on 29 March. Bush and his main military and security advisors met at Camp David and held a teleconference with the senior commanders overseeing operations. At issue was whether the coalition should pause while reinforcements made their way to the front units. One argument was that airpower could keep the Iraqis from regrouping or counterattacking while new troops, particularly the Fourth Infantry Division, bolstered the advance units. This would allow the coalition even more time to shore-up its exposed supply lines and rear bases and troops could engage in offensive operations against the Fedayeen and other guerilla forces operating behind coalition lines. The air campaign was doing considerable damage to Iraqi infrastructure and to frontline units, but it had only limited impact on the coalition efforts to fight the stubborn Fedayeen. In his work, *Immaculate Warfare*, Stephen D. Wrage notes that "precision-guided munitions are most effective against fixed civilian infrastructure targets, less effective against opposing military forces, and least effective against irregular forces operating without fixed bases and home societies to be put at risk."[61] To deal with the Fedayeen and other irregulars, the coalition needed more troops, and, therefore, the need for the pause.

On the other hand, Rumsfeld and Franks asserted that a pause would reinvigorate Iraqi troops who had low morale because of the bombing campaign. Many Iraqis were now deserting in large numbers. Intelligence also showed that the main Republican and Special Republican Guard units were so degraded, that they would fall apart once confronted with ground forces. Bush agreed with the second argument and ordered the advance to continue.

Once the coalition ground forces began to exert pressure on the remaining Republican and Special Republican Guard units, they rapidly collapsed. On 1 April, the coalition began its final push toward Baghdad. The Iraqi forces protecting the capital quickly dissolved as their troops either deserted or surrendered. The advance demonstrated the importance of combined air- and ground-operations. Robert A. Pape notes: "Caught in a vise between air strikes and ground attacks, most Iraqi troops deserted."[62] Pape also relates a quote from Brigadier General Allen Peck of the coalition air command: "Ground troops forced the enemy's hand. If they [the Iraqis] massed, air power could kill them. If they scattered they would get cut through by the ground forces."[63] Once the coalition advance resumed, there was no stopping the allied troops.

On 3 April, American units made their way into Saddam Hussein International Airport. By the next day, US troops controlled the airport which was situated on the outskirts of Baghdad. American armored units then made a foray into the heart of the capital, as coalition forces moved to within three miles of the city center. Meanwhile, the British were able to capture Basra, while other American troops captured the city of Karbala. In desperation, Saddam issued an edict that promises $100 for each coalition soldier killed and $200 for each one captured.

Nonetheless, the coalition advance continued. Baghdad was caught between a US Army division on the west and a Marine division on the East. On 9 April, Iraqis and US forces toppled a giant statue of Saddam in the heart of Baghdad, signaling an end to major combat in the city. Five days later, US forces completed the capture of Tikrit, Saddam Hussein's home town and the center of the Baathist Party. US troops and pesh merga continued operations in the north for several more days, but it was clear that the coalition had won in a war that lasted little more than three weeks. As Frum and Perle point out: "In Iraq, US forces overthrew Saddam Hussein's entire regime with half the troops and in half the time it took to shove Saddam out of Kuwait in 1991."[64]

Although Saddam, his sons and many senior regime figures remained at large, there are no major combat engagements after the fall of Tikrit. Over the next several weeks, a number of regime figures are captured as the US publishes a list of its 55-most-wanted (popularized by placing their pictures and information on a deck of cards). By May, the coalition had killed or captured 17 of the 55. On April 21, retired General Jay Garner, who Bush picked to handle the reconstruction and rebuilding, arrived in Iraq. On 1 May, on the deck of the aircraft carrier, the USS *Abraham Lincoln*, Bush declared an end to major combat operations in Iraq. He thanks the members of the US and coalition militaries for their service and he linked the war in Iraq to the broader war on terror: "The liberation of Iraq is a crucial advance in the campaign against terror. We've removed an ally of Al Qaeda, and cut off a source of terrorist funding. And this much is certain: No terrorist network will gain weapons of mass destruction from the Iraqi regime, because the regime is no more."[65] Bush also noted that there were many challenges remaining in Iraq:

> We have difficult work to do in Iraq. We're bringing order to parts of that country that remain dangerous. We're pursuing and finding leaders of the old regime, who will be held to account for their crimes. We've begun the search for hidden chemical and biological weapons and already know of hundreds of sites that will be investigated. We're helping to rebuild Iraq, where the dictator built palaces for himself, instead of hospitals and schools. And we will stand with the new leaders of Iraq as they establish a government of, by, and for the Iraqi people. The transition from dictatorship to democracy will take time, but it is worth every effort. Our coalition will stay until our work is done. Then we will leave, and we will leave behind a free Iraq.[66]

Indeed, the transition to a free Iraq would prove considerably more difficult than the Bush administration may have perceived. Within a short period of time, the euphoria over the fall of Saddam began to dissipate as Iraqis chafed under the coalition occupation and Bush's representative, Garner, would soon find himself replaced by Paul Bremer.

The Lessons and Challenges

In spite of limitations on the planned shock and awe campaign, Operation Iraqi Freedom demonstrated the military utility of the NCW style of warfare. In fact, since it grudgingly limited the air campaign against Iraqi infrastructure targets, the US military concurrently limited the number of civilian casualties. Estimates of civilian casualties vary, but even anti-war groups such as the Project on Defense Alternatives estimate that total losses were about 3,750 for the period from 19 March to 1 May. During the length of the entire 1991 Gulf War, Iraqi civilian casualties were estimated to be about 3,500, and, of course, coalition forces did not campaign extensively in Iraq as was the case in the 2003 conflict.[67]

A comparison of the two US-led wars against Iraq attests to the military success of Rumsfeld's strategy. In the first war, the US deployed 500,000 troops, supported by 160,000 allied forces. In the second war, the US deployed about 250,000 with an additional 50,000 allied troops. In the first war, there were 300 US service personnel killed in combat and 65 allied troops. During the second war, the US lost 129 (only 84 due to hostile fire) and the coalition partners lost 31. The first conflict cost $70 billion and lasted 48 days, while the second conflict cost $20 billion and lasted 26 days.[68] Furthermore, during the 1991 war, the Iraqi military lost about 10,000 killed, while losses in the second war were only about 2,700 killed in action.

The campaign reinforced the image of the US as the world's military hegemon. In spite of predictions of heavy casualties, and despite forecasts that the coalition was bogged down during the early days of the war, the allies were able to defeat the Iraqi Army and topple the regime of Saddam Hussein with relatively light casualties. In addition, as the coalition advanced, the brutality of the Saddam regime was displayed for the world as numbers of mass graves were uncovered. By the end of the campaign, coalition authorities received reports that there were approximately 270 mass graves. By the summer of 2003, they were able to confirm 53 of these. Human Rights Watch estimated that 290,000 people had been "disappeared" by the regime.[69] As the investigations into the regime's brutality continued, more bodies were discovered. On 20 November 2003, British Prime Minister Tony Blair declared that: "We've [the coalition] already discovered just so far the remains of 400,000 people in mass graves," and he noted that additional bodies were likely to be found.[70]

Unfortunately for Bush and Blair, while the coalition forces did discover mass graves, they did not immediately discover substantial evidence of a WMD program in Iraq. A special covert US task force was deployed with the original invasion force in order to secure evidence before the Iraqi's could move or destroy traces of the WMD programs.[71] This unit, the 75th Exploitation Task Force, was unable to find evidence and was recalled after six weeks of relatively fruitless searches.[72] The coalition was able to capture General Amer Hammoudi al-Saadi, the head of Saddam's chemical weapons program, on 12 April 2003, soon after the fall of Baghdad. However, they initially gained little significant information from the General and, after testing, what was perceived to be evidence of chemical or biological weapons proved not to be.[73] The failure to find clear and convincing evidence of Saddam's WMD program, further undermined the credibility of the coalition to both Iraqis and countries around the world.

No Afghan Model

While the military plans for the 2003 Iraq War proved highly effective and flexible, the after-combat strategies of the US lacked depth and foresight. The coalition forces seemed ill-prepared to deal with the collapse of authority within Iraq. Even before major combat operations were declared over, there was widespread looting and chaos as Iraqis sought revenge on Baathist officials or tried to gain access to food and other supplies. UN Secretary General Kofi Annan voiced official concern that "[f]rom what we have seen in the reports, it appears there is no functioning government in Iraq at the moment," and that "[w]e have also seen scenes of looting, and obviously law and order must be a major concern."[74] Major aid organizations reported difficulties in conducting operations and distributing supplies. In addition, a decade of sanctions had already severely degraded the infrastructure of Iraq; weeks of looting after the fall of the regime destroyed even more of the needed water plants, food distribution centers, power and telephone lines, and so forth. Meanwhile, coalition troops were forced to continue combat patrols and operations to counter continuing guerilla activity by irregulars such as the Fedayeen. The Bush administration was criticized for not having military police or stabilization forces prepared to move into the major cities in the aftermath of the fall of Saddam's regime.

In many ways, the success of the US-led coalition in Afghanistan made the administration ill-prepared for Iraq. After the fall of the Taliban in Afghanistan, the Northern Alliance was able to move into the capital and ensure some degree of order, while other nations quickly pledged troops for a UN-sanctioned stabilization force (the International Security Assistance Force, or ISAF, which initially numbered 5,000 multinational troops). In addition, in Hamid Karzai, the US had a readily acceptable indigenous leader who was able to establish both his legitimacy and his authority as the interim leader of the country.[75] In Afghanistan, the US was able to deliberately limit the scope of its involvement in law and order operations and avoid the mission creep which ran counter to the main tenets of the Weinberger-Powell Doctrine.[76]

In Iraq, there was no sudden influx of multinational troops to relieve US troops of the main responsibility for providing law and order and ensuring stability. Instead, the US slowly built a small coalition of peace-enforcement troops. At this point, the problems of the coalition of the willing became apparent. The US was able to point to the support of a range of countries; Bush correctly stated at a news conference with Blair that the US had "a huge coalition. As a matter of fact, the coalition that we've assembled today is larger than one assembled in 1991 in terms of the number of nations participating."[77] Bush went on to say that "I'm very pleased with the size of our coalition. I was down yesterday at CENTCOM and met with many of the generals from the countries represented in our coalition, and they're proud to be side-by-side with our allies. This is a vast coalition that believes in our cause, and I'm proud of their participation. "[78] The problem was that while the size of the coalition was larger than the one of 1991 or of the one assembled for Operation Enduring Freedom, it included a range of countries that either could not or would not contribute troops to a post-Saddam stabilization force. This would include countries such as Micronesia or Palau. In fact, tiny Palau's Ambassador to the US, Hersey Kyota, even noted that its participation was "largely symbolic" and included an offer of the island's harbors and airports if needed (they were not).[79] Hence, when the war ended, there was nothing like ISAF to supplement the US combat troops on the ground.

A New Coalition of the Willing

As the major combat operations ended, the US was forced to seek a new coalition of the willing to develop a stabilization force and restore order to Iraq. The recognition of the US and Great Britain as the occupying powers by the UN, and the subsequent legal status that designation incurred, prompted a range of states to make small contributions to the peace-enforcement effort and the economic plans to rebuild Iraq.

After the fall of the regime, the US divided Iraq into three zones. Two continued to be under the command of US forces, the third was placed under the command of the British and included a multinational division. US forces stabilized at about 130,000 in the immediate aftermath of the end of major hostilities and there were 110,000 left after one year. British forces were initially drawn-down from 11,000 to 8,220. Other states contributing forces to the coalition included: Italy (2,950), Ukraine (1,650),

Spain (1,300), and the Netherlands (1,300). In addition, more than 20 countries contributed small contingents of troops (less than 1,000 each).

The US finally had a significant coalition of the willing, but even the increased numbers fell short of administration requests. The period after May 2003 would prove to be critical to the success of Operation Iraqi Freedom as considerable debate swirled in the press and political discourse over the notion that the US had "won" the war, but "lost" the peace. Nonetheless, events over the summer and fall of 2003 brought both victories and setbacks in the US effort as more of the former regime members were killed (including Saddam's two sons) or captured (including Saddam, himself), and as economic and social conditions improved even as insurgents mounted continuing guerilla and terrorist operations. Meanwhile, the administration worked to improve Iraq's international standing by seeking recognition for the state and by leading efforts to erase a large portion of Iraq's considerable debt. The administration also sought to hold elections and allow the transition to a national governing authority along the lines of the Afghan model.

Notes

[1] US, Secretary of Defense, "Public Affairs Guidance on Embedding Media During Possible Future Operations/Deployments in the US Central Command and Area of Responsibility," SECDEF MSG Washington (3 February 2003), online at http://www.defenselink.mil/news/Feb2003/d20030228pag.pdf. Rumsfeld's directive noted that the purpose of the embedding system was that "media coverage of any future operation will, to a large extent, shape public perception of the national security environment now and in the years ahead," ibid.

[2] Michael O'Hanlon, "The Afghani War: A Flawed Masterpiece," in Art and Waltz, 270.

[3] Ibid.

[4] See Richard A. Melanson, *Reconstructing Consensus: American Foreign Policy Since the Vietnam War* (New York: St. Martin's 1991); or Walter LeFeber, *America, Russia and the Cold War* (New York: McGraw-Hill, 1997). The Weinberger Doctrine contained six formal components:

- Do not commit forces unless deemed vital to our national interests.
- Intend to win and commit the necessary resources to do so.
- Have clearly defined political and military objectives.
- Continuously reassess the relationship between objectives and forces committed.
- Have reasonable assurance of public support.
- Force should be the last resort.

Cited in Council on Foreign Relations, "The Weinberger/Powell Doctrine: Still Relevant or Fit For the Dustbin of History?," Study Group/Roundtable Report (28 October 2002), online at http://www.cfr.org/publication.php?id=5147.

[5] Caspar W. Weinberger, *Fighting for Peace, Seven Critical Years in the Pentagon* (New York: Warner Books, 1990), 159.

[6] Colin Powell, quoted in Nathan, 149.

[7] George P. Shultz, *Turmoil and Triumph, My Years as Secretary of State* (New York: Charles Scribner's Sons, 1993), 646.

[8] Cited in Arnold R. Isaacs, *Vietnam Shadows, The War, Its Ghosts, and Its Legacy* (Baltimore: Johns Hopkins University Press, 1997), 72-73.

[9] Council on Foreign Relations.

[10] Jeffrey Record, "Perils of Reasoning by Historical Analogy: Munich, Vietnam and the American Use of Force Since 1945," *Occasional Paper*, no. 4 (Montgomery, AL: Center for Strategy and Technology, March 1998), 24.

[11] Adam Roberts, "Humanitarian War: Military Intervention and Human Rights," *International Affairs*, 69/3 (July 1993), 439.

[12] Ramesh Thakur, "From Peacekeeping to Peace Enforcement: The UN Operation in Somalia," *The Journal of Modern African Studies*, 32/3 (September 1994), 388.

[13] On the impact of US popular opinion on presidents' willingness to use force and to accept casualties, see Miroslav Nincic, "Loss Aversion and the Domestic Context of Military Intervention," *Political Science Quarterly*, 50/1 (March 1997): 97-120; or Scott Sigmund Gartner and Gary M. Segura, "Opening Up the Black Box of War: Politics and the Conduct of War," *The Journal of Conflict Resolution*, 42/3 (June 1998): 278-300.

[14] Quoted in Bernard Lewis, "The Revolt of Islam," *The New Yorker* (19 November 2001), 62-63.

[15] Thad Cochrane, quoted in Rowan Scarborough, "Pentagon Brief Details Iraq's Arms Capability," *The Washington Times* (26 August 2002), 1.

[16] Eric Schmitt and James Dao, "Air Power Alone Can't Defeat Iraq, Rumsfeld Asserts," *The New York Times* (31 July 2002), 1.

[17] Ibid.

[18] This included a shipment in early September of 70 tanks and heavy vehicles aboard a commercial charter cargo ship; Alex Belida, "Pentagon/Gulf," *Voice of America* (4 September 2002), online at http://www.globalsecurity.org/wmd/library/news/iraq/2002/iraq-020904-375db3e9.htm.

[19] Lawrence Freedman and Efraim Karsh, *The Gulf Conflict, 1990-1991: Diplomacy and War in the New World Order* (Princeton: Princeton University Press, 1993), 321; and Thomas A. Keaney and Eliot A. Cohen, *Revolution in Warfare? Airpower in the Persian Gulf* (Annapolis, MD: Naval Institute Press, 1995), 67.

[20] Frank J Cilluffo, Ronald A. Marks, and George C. Salmoiraghi, "The Use and Limits of US Intelligence," in Loch K. Johnson and James J. Wirtz, eds., *Strategic Intelligence: Windows Into a Secret World* (Los Angeles: Roxbury Publishing, 2004), 33.

[21] Keaney and Cohen, 71.

[22] Rick Atkinson, *Crusade: The Untold Story of the Persian Gulf War* (Boston: Houghton Mifflin, 1993), 345.

[23] Charles Horner quoted in Richard Mackenzie, "A Conversation With Chuck Horner," *Air Force Magazine* 74 (June 1991), 17; cited in Marolda and Schneller, 197.

[24] Ibid.

[25] Frederick W. Kagan, "War and Aftermath," *Policy Review*, 120 (August/September 2003), 6.

[26] David S. Alberts, John J, Gartska, and Frederick P. Stein, *Network Centric Warfare: Developing and Leveraging Information Superiority*, 2nd ed. (Vienna, VA: CCRP Publications, 1999), cited in ibid., 6-7.

[27] See Edward Allen Smith, *Effects Based Operations: Applying Network Centric Warfare in Peace, Crisis, and War* (Vienna, VA: CCRP Publications, 2002).

[28] For a detailed analysis of the concept of rapid dominance, see Harlan Ullman and James Wade, et al., *Shock and Awe: Achieving Rapid Dominance* (Washington, D.C.: National Defense University, 1996), online at http://www.globalsecurity.org/military/library/report/1996/shock-n-awe_index.html; or Harlan Ullman and James Wade, *Rapid Dominance, A Force for all Seasons: Technologies and*

Systems for Achieving Shock and Awe: A Real Revolution in Military Affairs (London: Royal United Services Institute for Defence Studies, 1998).

[29] Ullman and Wade, *Shock and Awe: Achieving Rapid Dominance.*

[30] Ibid.

[31] Timothy Noah, "Meet Mr. Shock and Awe," *Slate* (1 April 2003) online at http://slate.msn.com/id/2081008.

[32] Ibid.

[33] Ibid.

[34] Ibid.

[35] Cited in Michael Tackett, "'Shock, Awe' Means More than Bombs," *Chicago Tribune* (24 March 2003), 1.

[36] Ibid.

[37] Norman Friedman, "Both Gulf Wars Offer Lessons," *Proceedings of the Naval Institute*, 129/5 (May 2003), 61.

[38] Steve Bowman, *Iraq: Potential Military Operations*, Congressional Research Service RL 31701 (13 January 2003), 7.

[39] Anthony Cordesman, *If We Fight Iraq: Iraq and the Conventional Military Balance* (Washington, D.C.: CSIS, 2002), 3.

[40] Ibid.

[41] Ibid.

[42] Bowman, 7.

[43] Max Boot, "The New American Way of War," *Foreign Affairs*, 82/4 (July/August 2003), 44.

[44] Daalder and Lindsey, 145-46.

[45] Ibid., 146.

[46] A large number of US troops were not even in position as the Fourth Infantry Division was still in the process of transferring troops and equipment which had been expected to be deployed in Turkey. Franks decided the timing to launch the invasion and chose to attack without the Fourth Infantry. This was to both surprise the Iraqis, who expected the attack only after the Fourth was in place, and to avoid the worst of the summer heat; ibid., 45.

[47] During the 2003 Iraq War, only 10 oil wells were set ablaze, compared with over 700 wells that fired during the 1991 Iraq War; Jennifer D. Kibbe, "The Rise of the Shadow Warriors," *Foreign Affairs*, 83/2 (March/April 2004), 102.

[48] This was the attack that resulted in the capture of Private Jessica Lynch.

[49] US, Department of Defense, "CENTCOM Operation Iraqi Freedom Briefing" (23 March 2003), online at http://www.centcom.mil/CENTCOMNews/Transcripts/20030323a.htm.

[50] Pat Towell, "'Shock and Awe' Optimism Yields to Slogging Reality," *CQ Weekly* 61/13 (29 March 2003), 744.

[51] Wallace's comments were exacerbated when newspaper and other reports dropped the "a bit" segment of the quote making the comment seem more damaging to the administration; see ibid.; Boot, 48.

[52] Victoria Clarke quoted in US, Department of Defense, "DoD News Briefing" (31 March 2003), online at http://www.defenselink.mil/transcripts/2003/t03312003_t0331asd.html.

[53] Robert A. Pape, "The True Worth of Air Power," *Foreign Affairs*, 83/2 (March/April 2004), 128.

[54] Quoted in Stephen J. Hedges, "Precision, Volume of Air Strikes Were Key to Winning War Quickly," *The Chicago Tribune* (24 April 2003), 28.

[55] Ibid.

[56] See US, Department of Defense, *Network Centric Warfare: A Department of Defense Report to Congress, Appendix* (Washington, D.C.: Department of Defense, 27 July 2001), online at http://www.defenselink.mil/nii/NCW/ncw_appendix.pdf.

[57] Gary Crowder quoted in US, Department of Defense, "Effects Based Operations Briefing: Gary Crowder," *Defenselink*, Washington (19 March 2003), online at http://www.defenselink.mil/news/Mar2003/t03202003_t0319effects.html.

[58] David Charter and Michael Evans, "Britain Reined in US Military's Shock and Awe Strategy," *The Times* (2 May 2003), 18.

[59] Ibid.

[60] Hedges.

[61] Stephen D. Wrage, "Conclusion," Stephen D. Wrage, ed., *Immaculate Warfare: Participants Reflect on the Air Campaigns Over Kosovo and Afghanistan* (Westport: Praeger, 2003), 101.

[62] Pape, 128.

[63] Allen Peck quoted in ibid.

[64] Frum and Perle, 11.

[65] George W. Bush, "President Bush Announces that Major Combat Operations in Iraq Have Ended," White House Press Release (1 May 2003), online at http://www.whitehouse.gov/news/releases/2003/05/iraq/20030501-15.html.

[66] Ibid.

[67] Carl Conetta, *The Wages of War: Iraqi Combatant and Noncombatant Fatalities in the 2003 Conflict*, Project on Defense Alternatives Research Monograph #8 (20 October 2003), online at http://www.reliefweb.int/w/rwb.nsf/UNID/CFE839B30DF98956C1256DD60038B93C?Open Document.

[68] Boot, 43.

[69] Human Rights Watch, "The Mass Graves of al-Mahawil: The Truth Uncovered," Human Rights Watch Report (May 2003), online at http://hrw.org/reports/2003/iraq0503/.

[70] USAID, "Iraq's Legacy of Terror: Mass Graves" (Washington, D.C.: USAID, 2003), online at http://www.usaid.gov/iraq/pdf/iraq_mass_graves.pdf.

[71] Barton Gellman, "Covert Unit Hunted for Iraqi Arms," *The Washington Post* (13 June 2003), A1.

[72] Three vans that may have been mobile chemical or biological labs were discovered, but tests failed to verify their purpose as WMD labs; Barton Gellman, "Frustrated, US Arms Team to Leave Iraq," *The Washington Post* (11 May 2003), A1.

[73] Peter Beaumont, Patrick Graham, and Antony Barnett, "Saddam's Weapons Chief Surrenders to US Forces," Iraq: Special Report, *The Guardian Unlimited* (13 April 2003), online at http://www.guardian.co.uk/Iraq/Story/0,2763,936012,00.html.

[74] Julian Borger and Nicholas Watt, "Sliding Toward Anarchy," *The Guardian Unlimited* (11 April 2003), online at http://www.guardian.co.uk/Iraq/Story/0,2763,934261,00.html.

[75] Tom Lansford, *A Bitter Harvest: US Foreign Policy and Afghanistan* (Aldershot: Ashgate, 2003), 179.

[76] Ibid., 178.

[77] George W. Bush, "Press Conference With British Prime Minister Tony Blair," Camp David, Maryland, White House Press Release (27 March 2003), online at http://www.whitehouse.gov/news/releases/2003/03/20030327-3.html.

[78] Ibid.

[79] Dana Milbank, "Many Willing, But Only a Few Are Able," *The Washington Post* (25 March 2003), A7.

Chapter 6

Rebuilding and Reconstruction

Introduction

The foreign policy challenges to which American presidential administrations must respond typically reflect the security threats facing the United States at a particular historical juncture. Such threats are usually a product of the structure of the international system and characteristics of the actors, whether of the state or non-state variety, interacting therein. Countering any threat, in turn, requires the use of a range of economic, political and military tools that are applied over the short medium and long terms by one administration (or, perhaps, two, three, four or more) depending on the nature, scope and longevity of the individuals or governments controlling the entity or entities presenting that threat.

During the Cold War, most dangers the United States had to counter grew out of its adversarial relationship with the Soviet Union. Since the end of that bipolar struggle, by contrast, American presidents and their advisors have had to respond to challenges related primarily to the emergence of "failing" and "failed states" that threaten military security, economic vitality and political stability in regions deemed vital to the interests of the United States and its allies. Examples range from the Balkans to the Greater Middle East generally and Bosnia-Herzegovina to Afghanistan specifically. These entities have been of particular concern to the most recent two administrations—those presided over by William J. Clinton and George W. Bush. Both intervened militarily in states that could be defined as either "failing" or "failed" in terms of governmental maintenance of, control over, or humane treatment of, their populations. The former took action in Bosnia in 1995 and Kosovo in 1999 and the latter in Afghanistan in 2001 and Iraq in 2003. In each case, the use of force was followed by the conduct of post-conflict operations that have since been defined as "nation building" endeavors.

Given that it was employed effectively in the transformation of Germany and Japan from dictatorships to democracies in the aftermath of World War II, nation building is by no means a new concept. However, both the frequency of the application of nation building operations and the threats such projects are designed to counter have changed markedly in the 1990s and 2000s. The primary purpose of the Clinton administration's participation in nation building operations in the Balkans—one paralleling that of America's European allies—was to ensure political stability in a region adjacent to the borders of member states of the North Atlantic Treaty Organization (NATO) and European Union (EU). The Bush administration, on the other hand, has supported nation building in Afghanistan and played the lead role in those endeavors within Iraq as a means to reduce the threats posed to US interests by transnational terrorist organizations and their state sponsors in two ways: first, by replacing regimes that supported Al Qaeda either directly or indirectly; and, second, by improving the standard of living of, and affording political freedom to, the people of the Greater Middle East.

Notwithstanding the relevance of ongoing nation building operations under NATO auspices in Afghanistan, the physical and economic reconstruction and political democratization of Iraq is absolutely indispensable to the broader transformation of the Islamic world. That much Bush and his advisors have emphasized repeatedly since the elimination of former Iraqi President Saddam Hussein's regime in April 2003 and commencement of reconstruction operations the ensuing month. In April 2004, for instance, Bush stressed that "a free Iraq will stand as an example to reformers across the Middle East. A free Iraq will show that America is on the side of Muslims who wish to live in peace, as we have already shown in Kuwait [by way of the conduct of the 1990-91 Persian Gulf War] and Kosovo, Bosnia and Afghanistan. A free Iraq will confirm to a watching world that America's word, once given, can be relied upon, even in the toughest of times."[1]

Bush's remarks came in the context of an opening statement prior to the start of a nationally televised press conference addressing the many challenges of a nation building project that had cost the lives of more than 600 US servicemen. Above all, the President's remarks were demonstrative of two fundamental points. First, Bush recognized at that juncture that the democratization of Iraq continued to present economic, military and political challenges that were likely, if not certain, to require years, rather than weeks or months to overcome. Second, he emphasized that he was determined to see nation building operations in Iraq through to completion and implied that subsequent administrations should maintain the commitment to the broader transformation of the Greater Middle East over the long term. In particular, he concluded that

America's commitment to freedom in Iraq is consistent with our ideals, and required by our interests. Iraq will either be a peaceful, democratic country, or it will again be a source of violence, a haven for terror and a threat to America and to the world. By helping to secure a free Iraq, Americans serving in that country are protecting their fellow citizens. Our nation is grateful to them all and to their families. … Above all, the defeat of violence and terror in Iraq is vital to the defeat of violence and terror elsewhere; and vital, therefore, to the safety of the American people. Now is the time and Iraq is the place, in which the enemies of the civilized world are testing the will of the civilized world. We must not waver.[2]

With these observations providing a useful contextual point of departure, this chapter will address the issue of nation building in Iraq through the presentation of six sections that unfold in the following manner. The first section examines in general terms the most relevant approaches to post-conflict reconstruction and nation building in the 1990s and 2000s. The second section discusses the Bush administration's rationale for, and offers an overview of the implementation of, nation building operations in Iraq. The third section examines the security challenges associated with nation building operations in Iraq. The fourth and fifth sections examine the economic and political aspects, respectively, of those endeavors. The concluding section discusses the future implications of the success or failure of nation building in Iraq.

General Approaches to Post-Conflict Reconstruction and Nation Building

History has demonstrated that conflict is a regular, if not inevitable, byproduct of interaction between actors in the international system, whether individuals, nation-states or groups of states. The outbreak of conflict, in turn, demands that foreign policy practitioners develop effective ways to reconstruct states once military action, diplomatic negotiations or a combination of the two have brought hostilities to an end. In response to that demand, scholars and policymakers have developed a distinct sub-field of international relations over the past half-century in particular, one associated with the conduct of post-conflict reconstruction projects. The objectives of such projects are relatively straightforward: to establish post-conflict states—and, at times, broader geographic regions—that are economically vibrant, politically free and stable, and militarily secure. Achieving those objectives, on the other hand, requires intervening actors to meet a broad range of daunting challenges that, above all, relate to the causes, characteristics and consequences of the conflict that the inhabitants of a particular state or region have just endured.

In general terms, there are three types of conflicts that call for the subsequent conduct of reconstruction operations—inter-state wars conducted at the global and regional levels, respectively; and intra-state wars between two or more distinct groups within a given domestic context. Essentially, the reconstruction processes in Western Europe broadly and the Western half of occupied Germany specifically following World War II served as a test case upon which to build the field of post-conflict studies. In short, those processes demanded substantial economic and political commitments from the United States in order to facilitate reconciliation between the Germans and their former adversaries, excluding the Soviet Union.[3]

The lack of a global war as destructive as World War II in the years since its conclusion in 1945 has confined contemporary post-inter-state war reconstruction projects to conflicts played out at the regional level, most notably so in the Greater Middle East in general and Iraq in particular. The majority of reconstruction operations carried out in the 1990s and 2000s, by contrast, have come in response to intra-state conflicts pitting groups determined to fight to preserve their often disparate cultural identities, whether defined in terms of ethnicity, race, religion, ideology or a combination of one or more of the preceding characteristics. Unfortunately, recovery from these types of conflicts almost always proves more challenging than is true of the inter-state variety in light of the profound differences between the former warring parties.

The most significant development associated with post-conflict reconstruction operations since the end of the Cold War has been the proliferation of entities referred to as "failing" or "failed" states. For example, John Hamre and Gordon Sullivan, who serve as co-chairs of the Post-Conflict Reconstruction Project, cite statistics suggesting that 15 percent of the world's states presently fall into one these categories. They note that such states typically lack a government with the democratic legitimacy, political will and military power to control their territory, and the economic capacity to ensure the physical survival of their people. Those weaknesses are rooted in—and have been progressively exacerbated by—the resurgent religious rivalries that have proven the rule rather than the exception during the post-Cold War era.[4]

There is not necessarily one geographic region in which most or all "failing" or "failed" states have already—or are, in the future, likely—to emerge. In recent years, such entities have emerged in regions as geographically wide-ranging as the Balkans (Bosnia and Kosovo), Western Africa (Sierra Leone, Liberia and the Democratic Republic of the Congo) and Central Asia (Afghanistan). What is certain is that these entities will continue to provide both challenges and opportunities for the conduct of post-conflict reconstruction projects with an emphasis on nation building in the future. Ultimately, when those situations do arise, the incentive for intervention is likely to be greater than was the case prior to Al Qaeda's attacks on the World Trade Center in New York and the Pentagon on the outskirts of Washington on 11 September 2001. The reason, as Hamre and Sullivan among others have cautioned, is simple. As illustrated by the case of Afghanistan in the 1990s, states on the brink of failure serve as ideal bases for terrorist groups to organize devastating attacks against their foes, a fact Al Qaeda demonstrated on 9/11.[5]

One means to that end is through the use of nation building operations, a tool on which the United States has become increasingly reliant over the past decade.[6] Prior to engaging an a detailed examination of the nation building project the Bush administration has placed a considerable emphasis on—that of Iraq—it is instructive to review the concept in broader terms. This balance of this section does so through a four-part discussion that focuses on the military, economic and political aspects of nation building operations, and the interplay among individuals, ethnic and religious communities, states, international organizations and non-governmental organizations in contexts of such projects.

The maintenance of security is central to any nation building project. Achieving that end, in turn, demands the application of military tools designed to apprehend or liquidate members of former warring parties who are determined to undermine the peace in a nascent state, build a domestic police force to provide for its internal security and safeguard it against external threats over the long term. Put bluntly, the first stage entails the removal of troublemakers—especially those wanted for war crimes—from the scene through military or judicial means, or, in some instances, a combination of the two. Serbian President Slobodan Milosevic's 2001 extradition to The Hague for trial before the International Criminal Tribunal for the Former Yugoslavia is one notable example; the killing of Saddam's sons, Uday and Qusay, by

US forces in July 2003 and capture of the Iraqi dictator himself in mid-December 2003 are two others.

Once potential troublemakers have been dealt with, intervening actors can begin to devote more attention to the development of enduring security guarantees for an emerging nation-state. Threats to internal and external security are often interrelated. As a result, safeguards against such threats must, in many cases, be put into place concurrently. Ultimately, the challenge is for occupying forces (those under either unilateral or multilateral international control) to gradually hand over responsibility for a state's security to domestic bodies to the extent feasible in light of the potential threats presented by neighboring powers.

Above all, the development of a sound economy is indispensable to the success of any nation building project. In short, lacking the capacity to support its people, no state is likely to survive for long. The development of that capacity usually unfolds in three broad stages of economic recovery and reconstruction, which are undertaken by a combination of states and governmental and non-governmental institutions in a particular context.

The first stage entails the provision of the requisite support to ensure the survival of the civilian population in the immediate aftermath of a conflict, whether of the inter- or intra-state variety. The means to achieve that end include treating the injured, feeding the hungry and preventing the spread of disease by burying the dead and setting up basic sanitation facilities for the living. Most significantly, such measures help to provide a basic foundation for the development of a sustainable economic system. The second stage features the reconstruction of whatever physical infrastructure was destroyed during the previously prevailing conflict and is deemed critical to future economic productivity (most notably power grids, major transportation arteries and natural resource processing facilities). The length of this stage, in turn, is conditioned by the size of the nation to be rebuilt and the scope (and degree of destruction) of the conflict from which it has just emerged.

Once a state has recovered sufficiently from the short-term humanitarian and physical consequences of hostilities, intervening actors then have a better opportunity to establish a viable long-term economic system. Ideally, such a system should seek to avoid past shortcomings (most often those associated with state-centric economics and governmental corruption). As a result, contemporary nation-building projects typically involve the construction of a free-market system under Western auspices with the capacity to survive, if not thrive, in the increasingly global economy of the 2000s. The administration of each of these stages demands the involvement of outside actors. These actors include occupying states and coalitions as well as intervening international institutions and Non-Governmental Organizations (NGOs). Depending on the circumstances, they have the potential to cooperate—or refrain from doing so—along an interactive continuum ranging from unilateralism to selective multilateralism to unequivocal collaboration.

Coinciding with the aforementioned economic reconstruction processes is a related series of political undertakings that usually unfolds in three distinctive phases: governance by outside actors, whether occupying states or international organizations, in the short term; mixed rule by an intervening power and a transitional domestic body in the medium term; and the establishment of an democratically elected and fully independent government that proves enduring over the long term.

In the immediate aftermath of an inter- or intra-state conflict that ends as a result of outside intervention, the task of establishing the requisite political order to govern the people residing in the former war zone falls to the occupying powers (states, international organizations or a combination of the two). Most significantly, those in charge—military officers and civilian officials alike—must allow at least some measure of participatory democracy as soon as possible in order to begin to earn the trust of the population of the territory under occupation. The time that elapses before the establishment of an interim authority short of an independent government is a product of the extent of stability prevailing in an occupied state or region. Once the launch of such a body becomes feasible, it is essential that it is at least broadly representative of the cultural composition of the society over which its members will preside. Understandably, the degree of difficulty in constructing a transitional government tends to correspond to the number of distinctive ethnic and religious groups involved in the process.

The ultimate political objective in carrying out a nation-building project is the creation of an enduring democratic state. The administrative mechanisms therein certainly need not be identical in each case so long as they produce democratic rather than autocratic governing bodies. In the end, whether a state has a presidential system, a parliamentary system or a combination of the two is not nearly as important as its long-term viability. At its core, the development of useful economic and political institutions in areas recently torn by conflict is dependent on the maintenance of security—and thus stability—therein while the reconstruction processes needed to facilitate those outcomes are in progress. Providing that security is the responsibility of military officers serving at the behest of the states and institutions engaging in nation-building projects.

The formulation and implementation of effective economic, political and military nation-building operations typically entails interaction among a variety of actors at the domestic and international levels, ranging from individuals and culturally distinctive interest groups to international organizations and NGOs. Domestically, for example, the stabilization of a state or region in the aftermath of a conflict often requires collaboration between military forces under the command of a global power such as the United States and a proverbial alphabet soup of international organizations (i.e. NATO and the United Nations) and NGOs (i.e. the Red Cross, CARE and Doctors Without Borders).

Economic and military burden-sharing in the contexts of the ensuing economic and reconstruction projects often proves equally challenging, as does the taking of decisions on precisely who should represent the myriad ethnic and religious groups on transitional governing bodies in places like Iraq and Afghanistan. At the international level, regional and global disputes leading up to a given conflict often complicate the nation-building projects that follow. The imbroglio pitting the United States and United Kingdom against fellow Security Council members France and Russia over the former pair's decision to use military force to liquidate Saddam's regime in 2003, for instance, continues to hamper ongoing nation-building efforts in Iraq.

Rationale for and Overview of Nation Building Operations in Iraq

There are two interconnected reasons why nation building is indispensable to the Bush administration's policy toward the Greater Middle East generally and Iraq specifically. First, the elimination of Saddam's regime through the conduct of the Second Iraq War from March to May 2003 created a power vacuum that needed to be filled expeditiously in order to avoid the failure of the nascent post-conflict Iraqi state. Without an American commitment to the military stabilization of Iraq and subsequent establishment of representative political institutions and a free market economy, that nascent state would itself likely fail and become a base for terrorist groups in the future. As scholar Robert I. Rotberg notes, "in the wake of September 11, the threat of terrorism has given the problem of failed nation-states an immediacy and importance that transcends its previous humanitarian dimension. ... The existence of these kinds of countries, and the instability that they harbor, not only threatens the lives and livelihoods of their own peoples but endangers world peace."[7] Second, any overarching strategy must begin somewhere. With respect to Bush's promised democratization of the Greater Middle East, the point of departure was—and remains—Iraq.[8]

As is true of most nation building projects, the present US-led endeavor in Iraq features interconnected economic, military and political components. Policies associated with each of those components have been—and will continue to be—applied in distinctive (and, to some extent, overlapping) stages played out over the short, medium and long terms. The first step in the process was post-conflict stabilization. In the case of Iraq, pursuit of that end has entailed the deployment of military forces—primarily, albeit not exclusively, those from the United States and United Kingdom—to safeguard the security of individuals ranging from Iraqi civilians to humanitarian aid workers, which will, in turn, help to foster political stability. As evidenced by the myriad attacks carried out against proponents of (and participants in) reconstruction operations to date—including, most notably, a series of attacks on coalition forces and civilians in the Spring of 2004—the challenges to enduring stability in Iraq remain daunting.

The principal objective in the medium term is the development of transitional economic and political institutions, whose officials are broadly representative of that state's ethnic and religious composition. Ideally, the leaders and staffs of such institutions will then collaborate with outside actors (states as well as international organizations and NGOs) to help facilitate the eventual emergence of a democratically elected government capable of supporting its population economically and maintaining political and military control over its territory.

The construction of a fully democratic and independent Iraqi state is necessarily a long-term goal. The timetable for the realization of that objective is at present—and will likely remain—at least somewhat ambiguous. But as a general rule, one need only consider the length of past and contemporary nation building projects across the globe. In the aftermath of World War II, for example, four years elapsed between the commencement of reconstruction efforts in occupied Germany and the establishment of an independent Federal Republic in May 1949. Similarly, nation building efforts in the Balkans began in December 1995 in Bosnia and very clearly remain a work in progress.

The economic, political and military aspects of the reconstruction of Iraq broadly parallel many of the general characteristics of nation building touched on in the previous section. However, as one would expect, many of the specificities associated with the planning and implementation of those components of nation-building operations in Iraq reflect that state's distinctive history, geography and natural resources, as well as its ethnic, religious and tribal diversity.

Economically, Iraq is unique in that it possesses the requisite natural resources (in the form of vast petroleum reserves) for the construction of a vibrant economy. Yet, for that to occur, occupying forces—and eventually the Iraqis themselves—must supply the security necessary to rebuild and maintain the physical infrastructure to use those resources productively. Once the infrastructure is at least relatively free from the threat of sabotage by loyalists to Saddam's now-defunct regime and transnational terrorist organizations, domestic and international officials and the institutions they administer can begin instituting the deeper free-market reforms required for Iraq to compete both regionally and globally. Such reforms include safeguards against centralized state control over the economy and the accompanying fiscal profligacy, government corruption and income inequality.

Similarly, the political aspects of nation building in Iraq can be compartmentalized in a series of stages. First, the administration of temporary governmental institutions by the military and civilian occupation forces of the United States, United Kingdom and their coalition partners. Second, the development of local and national transitional bodies composed of Iraqis reflective of the ethnic and religious diversity of the domestic population, deemed reliable by the occupying forces and accepted to whatever extent is feasible by neighboring Persian Gulf states. And third, the establishment of an independent Iraq with democratic electoral and governmental systems, the variants of which have been discussed in great detail by scholars Anthony Cordesman and Joseph Braude among others.[9]

For either economic or political reconstruction to proceed in an expeditious—and ultimately successful—fashion, the long-term deployment of American, British and, perhaps, international peacekeepers and peace-enforcers is essential. Those forces have been (and will continue to be) relied upon to pursue and apprehend those insurgents determined to disrupt nation-building operations, and also to protect both the Iraqis and foreigners carrying out such operations.

Put simply, the conduct of nation-building operations in Iraq requires interaction among a variety of actors, ranging from individuals, extended families, political parties and religious groups to states, international institutions, terrorist organizations and NGOs. The interplay of these actors has—and will continue to—manifest itself at both the domestic and international levels within and outside of the Persian Gulf region. The stiffest challenges to reconstruction efforts in Iraq have grown out of two sets of domestic-level relationships, those between representatives of the US-led nation-building coalition and the Iraqi population, and among members of the Kurdish, Shiite and Sunni ethnic and religious groups in that context.

The level of stability, or lack thereof, in the former set of relationships—and within the post-war state itself—is conditioned largely by the extent to which those who suffered when Saddam was in charge believe their lives have improved since the fall of the Iraqi dictator's regime. Building that trust hinges on the capacity of the nation builders (American civilian administrator Paul Bremer and those under his command within the Coalition Provisional Authority [CPA] in particular) to minimize the domestic security threats posed by Saddam loyalists on one hand, and power struggles among Kurds, Shiites and Sunnis on the other.

Complicating each of the aforementioned domestic relationships are international interactions that reflect geopolitical disagreements, most notably those pertaining to American policies at the broader Middle Eastern and global levels. French and German refusal to condone the use of force against Saddam, for instance, produced a fracture in the transatlantic alliance. As a result, the United States has secured only limited international involvement in nation building operations, a shortcoming that has increased the overall costs to Washington in particular.

Muslim distrust of the United States rooted in the Israeli-Palestinian conflict has been equally problematic. Notwithstanding American efforts to forge a settlement between Israel and the Palestinian Authority via a "Road Map" to peace sponsored collectively by the United States, Russia, European Union (EU) and UN, transnational terrorist organizations have continued to use Washington's perceived favoritism of the Jewish state in encouraging their followers to launch strikes against US forces, as well as representatives of international organizations and NGOs, attempting to rebuild Iraq.

As is the case with any nation building project, the ongoing effort in Iraq has both costs and benefits that are most usefully articulated contextually in terms of economics, politics and security. The following assessment of those costs and benefits, in turn, is intended—and should be considered—as a point of departure for the in-depth discussions that follow in the ensuing three sections.

Economically, the costs and benefits of rebuilding Iraq are interdependent. In short, those states, international organizations and NGOs participating in nation-building operations in that state must pay a stiff financial cost in the short term—estimates range from dozens to hundreds of billions of dollars annually—that may or may not pay off over the long term. In the end, the degree to which investment in the development of Iraq's petroleum resources reaps benefits will likely hinge both on the level of internal security and the durability of free-market reforms at the domestic level.

The most relevant political costs and benefits of American-led nation-building in Iraq are international in orientation. Above all else, the credibility of the United States is at stake on two levels. First, Bush has consistently promised to replace Saddam's autocratic regime with enduring democratic institutions, irrespective of the economic and physical costs (in dollars and lives, respectively). Second, he has pledged to achieve that objective with—or without—economic and military assistance from US allies and the broader international community. Breaking either of those promises would undermine Washington's credibility at home and abroad—and, perhaps, appear as a sign of weakness in the context of the ongoing war against terrorism. The realization of any, if not all, of the above benefits demands the maintenance of a reasonably stable security environment in Iraq. Regrettably, the pursuit of that objective will result in the loss of lives of individuals participating in nation-building operations throughout the emerging democratic Iraqi state. The continuation of those operations, in turn, is sure to remain contingent on the willingness of participants in the process, whether individuals, states, international organizations or NGOs, to shoulder those burdens in order to create a stable and productive Iraq—and, perhaps a safer world—over the long term.

Security Component of Nation Building in Iraq ⴕ

At its core, the success or failure of any nation building project hinges on the capacity of the intervening actors—and, eventually, the reconstituted government of the state under reconstruction—to provide for the physical security of the population. The pursuit of that objective, in turn, typically unfolds in a series of stages. With respect to the case of Iraq, one can identify three such stages:

- The period between the end of major combat operations in May 2003 and the handover of authority from the CPA to an interim Iraqi government on 30 June 2004.
- The gradual assumption of greater security responsibilities by Iraq's nascent police and armed forces in the medium term from June 2003 through elections for a transitional Iraqi government by January 2005.
- The long-term handover of some, albeit certainly not most or all, responsibility for Iraq's internal and external security from coalition partners such as the United States and United Kingdom to a permanent government expected to be in place in Baghdad by the end of December 2005.[10]

The initial security challenges faced by coalition forces in the aftermath of the fall of Baghdad in April 2003 grew primarily out of the desire of many Iraqis to strike out against members of Saddam's Baath Party by looting the dictator's palaces and the government ministries formerly administered by his minions. Unfortunately, the subsequent inability or unwillingness of the United States and its coalition partners to take decisive action to prevent the looting contributed to a sense that the liberators had lost control of the situation. The resulting instability led to widespread criticism of the Bush administration such as that expressed by Peter Galbraith, a former American Ambassador to Croatia in testimony before Congress in June 2003: "When the United States entered Baghdad on April 9, it entered a city largely undamaged by a carefully executed military campaign. However, in the three weeks following the US takeover, unchecked looting effectively gutted every important public institution in the city—with the notable exception of the oil ministry."[11]

Yet, in the end, looting proved to be just the first of many obstacles to the stabilization of Iraq during the CPA's 14 months administering the country. The most daunting of those obstacles have been erected by two sets of insurgents, those with internal and external roots. There are two principal sources of internal opposition to the CPA—former Baath Party members still loyal to Saddam, nearly all of whom practice the Sunni strain of Islam; and dissatisfied Shiites willing to support radical clerics such as Muqtada al-Sadr, a 30-year-old firebrand with ties to the theocracy in neighboring Iran. External foes include a range of terrorist operatives, most of whom are aligned with Al Qaeda and have entered Iraq since the end of major combat operations as a result of lax controls along the Iranian, Saudi Arabian and Syrian borders.[12] Allowing either to succeed in preventing the democratization of Iraq would have disastrous implications for that state as well as in the context of the Bush administration's war on terror. As Steven Metz, director of research at the US Army War College's Strategic Studies Institute explains,

> The stakes in Iraq are immense. The conflict there will help determine whether the world continues its difficult and uneven movement toward a global system based on open governments and economies or fractures into a new bipolarity. The Arab world is the region most resistant to the US vision of open economies and governments. If it can work there, it can work anywhere. Iraq is the beachhead, the test case, the laboratory.[13]

The task of preventing domestic and international insurgents from permanently destabilizing Iraq has fallen primary to American military forces, some 135,000 of which have been deployed in Iraq throughout the postwar period to date. Consequently, the costs of conducting counter-insurgency operations since May 2003 have been borne primary by Americans. Collectively, in excess of 800 US servicemen had died and more than 3,500 had been injured wounded (including approximately 2,500 through hostile action) by the end of April 2004, with the vast majority of those casualties occurring since 1 May 2003.[14] In addition, estimates indicate that as many as 1,400 members of the nascent Iraqi security services had perished in a variety of attacks carried out by terrorists and other opponents of the CPA and Iraqi Governing Council (IGC) by late April 2004.[15]

The aforementioned casualties were generated through two types of encounters from May 2003-April 2004: those designed to bring members of the Iraqi regime to justice—most notably 55 leading Baathists, of whom all but 43 were dead or in coalition custody by the end of April 2004, including Saddam (captured) and his sons (killed);[16] and those conducted against the insurgents. Notwithstanding the many successes in the former operations, the latter have produced mixed results, in large part because of the terrorists' ability to strike soft targets such as the UN compound in Baghdad with relative impunity. The resulting fear generated among Iraqi civilians,

NGO representatives and private contractors among others when that brand of attack is successful and its subsequent proliferation by the international news media has further complicated the task at hand for both coalition and Iraqi security forces.

Unfortunately, the problem of terrorist violence has had a tendency to grow progressively worse as positive developments in the economic and political situations in Iraq (the subjects of the ensuing two sections) have convinced insurgents to escalate their attacks in an effort to derail the democratization process while they still can. In April 2004, for instance, simultaneous eruptions of violence in the Sunni Baathist stronghold of Fallujah and among al-Sadr loyalists in Najaf and Kufa led to the deaths of more than 100 coalition soldiers. It was the single most violent month since nation building operations commenced.[17]

Cordesman, Arleigh A. Burke Chair in Strategic at the Center for Strategic and International Studies, noted that as of April 2004, neither the Fallujah or al-Sadr uprisings represented dire threats to the overall stability of Iraq at that juncture. More pointedly, he asserted that,

> The fighting around Fallujah is serious, but the brunt is being borne by 3,000 US troops dealing with a mix of insurgents that probably have a core strength of less than 1,000 in a city that has at most 300,000 people or a little over 1% of Iraq's population. ... Similarly, Sadr seems to remain a force that can call up substantial crowds, but not popular masses. His militia seems to be about 5,000-10,000, and has far less experienced military cadres than the Sunnis.[18]

On the other hand, should more direct collusion develop among Sunni and Shiite insurgents and foreign fighters—especially those loyal to Ansar al-Islam, a terrorist organization linked to Al Qaeda associate Abu Musab al-Zarqawi[19]—on a broader scale, it would likely create serious problems for the coalition as it attempts to pass on more security responsibilities to the transitional Iraqi government over the balance of 2004. Concerns over that probability have already prompted US Secretary of Defense Donald Rumsfeld to postpone for three months a planned June 2004 drawdown of American forces in Iraq from 135,000-115,000. Others have suggested that even Rumsfeld's extension is not nearly long enough to guard against the medium and long term threats posed by insurgents. Neo-conservatives Robert Kagan and William Kristol, for instance, warn that "even more troops may be required to fully pacify the country. It would be useful to have as many of those troops as possible there sooner rather than later."[20]

The need to maintain a substantial US force presence through the establishment of a permanent elected government by the end of 2005—and, most likely, for considerably longer—is primarily the product of the unlikelihood that the Iraqis will be able to provide for their own security for the foreseeable future. While the CPA spent much of its year in control of the new Iraq attempting to build a set of viable domestic security institutions—including a police force of 75,000 and civil defense corps of 40,000—the vast majority of individuals serving in those capacities by the end of April 2004 had yet to receive adequate training.[21]

The challenge over the medium term is for the US-led coalition, which had forces from 31-35 states on the ground for most of the period between May 2003 and June 2004,[22] to collaborate with the Iraqis in improving their security forces' collective capacity to limit the instability caused by the insurgents and developing more effective border controls. Both these steps are indispensable to preventing an escalation of the terrorist threat to Iraq in 2004-05. As Amir Taheri, an Iranian-born journalist and scholar of Middle Eastern politics, asserts, terrorism in Iraq "is, in fact, a security problem, which must be combated with policing methods."[23] The problem is that widespread terrorist strikes have the potential to reduce the will of the police to remain at their posts on a consistent basis.

Once a permanent Iraqi government has assumed power, it will eventually need to acquire armed forces of a sufficient strength to safeguard its interests against external threats, whether those dangers are presented by neighboring countries, transnational terrorist groups, or—as is perhaps the most probable scenario—combinations of the two. CPA plans call for the establishment of Iraqi military forces numbering 40,000, of which just over 5,000 were in place as of April 2004.[24] Early difficulties in building the size of that force were largely attributable to Bremer's decision not to rehire members of Saddam's army upon assuming control of the CPA in May 2003.[25] While critics have questioned that decision, it was at least partially justifiable given both public distrust for Saddam loyalists in the military and the potential logistical difficulty of recalling forces that had dispersed and faded into the general population in the wake of the launch of Operation Iraqi Freedom in March 2003.

Economic Aspects of Nation Building in Iraq

As is the case with the security component of nation building in Iraq, the economic aspects of that project are best addressed contextually in terms of short-, medium- and long-term needs and objectives. The timeline associated with those needs and objectives is as follows:

- CPA-administered reconstruction and rehabilitation of infrastructure and industries either damaged or destroyed during Operation Iraqi Freedom or, as is true in most cases, ravaged by the mismanagement and corruption of Saddam's regime.
- Management of Iraq's economy in a manner sufficient to meet the needs of its people during the transition from interim to permanent governance in Iraq from June 2004-December 2005.
- Planning for the long-term restructuring of the Iraqi economy under free market auspices from 2006 onward.

There are two sets of economic costs associated with the initial stage of the nation building process in Iraq—that administered by the CPA politically and the US-led coalition militarily. One relates to the expenses generated through maintaining a military force presence in excess of 160,000 for a period that will eventually be measured in years rather than months. Another pertains to the direct needs of an Iraqi populace struggling to recover from the conflict that removed the Saddam from power and its immediate aftermath as well as from the misdeeds of his regime over the past quarter-century.

Above all, providing for the economic needs of Iraqis requires a secure environment, one in which there is a sense that threats to life and property are declining rather than increasing on a daily basis. The development of that type of environment will entail a significant financial cost, especially with respect to the US force presence in Iraq. That much became evident when, in September 2003, the Bush administration submitted a request to Congress for supplemental funding of $87 billion ($67 billion for the American military and $20 billion for the reconstruction of Iraq), one that was approved a month later.[26] The military segment of the request equated to more than $4 billion a month to maintain US forces in excess of 135,000 through the end of 2004. Beyond that, additional appropriation requests are all but a certainty, as indicated by Gen. Richard Myers, Chairman of the Joint Chiefs of Staff, in April 2004.[27]

The task of attempting to lay the foundation for Iraqi economic growth fell primarily to the CPA, which was administered for just over a month by retired American Gen. Jay Garner before Bremer took over. Coupled with a lack of sufficient planning for nation building in the run-up to—and during the conduct of—Operation Iraqi Freedom, the switch from Garner to Bremer resulted in a less than efficient start to CPA efforts to jump-start the economy. In addition, Saddam's use of oil profits for conventional military and WMD projects and the enrichment of the Baath Party from the 1980s-2000s left the economy in a state of utter disrepair by 2004.[28] As Cordesman concludes, between 1991 and 2003, "a command economy turned into a command kleptocracy, where the Baath elite took what it wanted, significant financial resources went to securing the regime and the people took what they could simply to survive."[29]

Understandably, redressing the excesses of the past is an objective that will require years, if not decades, rather than months to achieve. Initial infusions of cash in the first stage of that process were earmarked for humanitarian aid and the reconstruction of infrastructure in the fields of oil production and electricity generation. Subsequent injections of funds have been reserved primarily for the training and payment of salaries for members of the nascent Iraqi security forces and government ministries as well as for the refurbishment of schools and payment of teachers. The logic behind these measures is two-pronged: invest in infrastructure (especially the oil industry) that will enhance Iraq's capacity to generate greater revenues in the future, while putting its citizens to work with money drawn from external sources in the short term.

The sources from which the CPA drew funds during its year administering Iraq included the aforementioned US infusion to help meet reconstruction needs, in addition to pledges of some $18 billion from other states and institutions (most notably the IMF and World Bank), and $13 billion from Iraqi oil revenues and seizures of the assets of Saddam's regime.[30] The problem is that the vast majority of these monies had yet to enter the economy prior to the transition from CPA to Iraqi interim governmental control on 30 June 2004. As a result, progress has been limited with respect to electricity generation in particular. For example, a year after the end of Operation Iraqi Freedom, the level of electricity available across Iraq generally and within Baghdad specifically had yet to surpass pre-war levels.[31]

The prospects for growth in the medium term, by contrast, are considerably more encouraging. One positive indicator pertains to the issue of job creation. Between April 2003 and March 2004, the unemployment rate in Iraq dropped from 50-60 percent to 25-35 percent.[32] In addition, those numbers are likely to fall further as reconstruction aid enters the economy over the balance of 2004 and Iraq's capacity for generation of autonomous revenues increases. More precisely, Bill Block, a US Treasury Department economist working for the CPA, has predicted that the GDP of Iraq will reach $24-25 billion by the end of 2004.[33] Collectively, these indicators—positive and negative alike—demonstrate that while all has certainly not proceeded smoothly in the economic context, there is reason for at least a measured degree of future optimism. As Cordesman notes,

A lot of money and activity is in the pipeline, and the results should be much more visible as projects begin to be completed from early summer onwards. It is clear, however, that much needs to be done and the critical tasks of rehabilitating the petroleum, industrial and agricultural sectors of the economy have just begun. Furthermore, progress needs to be measured in far less Stalinized terms than gross measures of "inputs" like power, gross unemployment and project starts. The issue is what key projects are completed, how well services meet actual needs, how much employment is coming from real and lasting jobs and how the Iraqi economy is progressing by sector and region.[34]

Ultimately, progress in each of the general issue areas Cordesman raises will have to be assessed over both the medium and long terms. At this juncture, on the other hand, it is possible only to touch on expectations such as those outlined in the 2004 budget and projections for the 2005 and 2006 budgets of the Iraqi Finance Ministry (IFM). In short, the IFM places emphases on two points. First, because of Saddam's legacies of economic mismanagement and war, Iraq faces "immediate reconstruction and redevelopment needs well in excess of available resources," which will force it to run a deficit of $590 million in 2004. Second, by taking advantage of infusions of aid to compensate for most of the reconstruction shortfalls and refraining from excessive borrowing or printing of New Iraqi Dinars (NID) in the future, the IFM anticipates balancing the budget in both 2005 and 2006.[35]

Most significantly, the 2004 budget was designed to demonstrate that Iraq can build a tradition of fiscal responsibility, one based on five fundamental principles, those associated with economic openness, private sector development, international integration, public sector transparency and the establishment and maintenance of a safety net for the poor.[36] Furthermore, the IFM projects that, by focusing on those principles and capitalizing on the sales of Iraq's plentiful petroleum resources, revenues will rise from $12.8 billion in 2004 to $19.2 billion in 2006.[37] Those increases in revenue, in turn, are likely to serve as a point of departure for more robust economic growth in the future. Block, for one, concludes that such increases will contribute to GDP growth of 7-9 percent annually over the next decade.[38]

Political Aspects of Nation Building in Iraq

Perhaps to an even greater extent than was the case with the previous sections on the security and economics of nation building in Iraq, the democratization of that state is best described in terms of in the following three stages, each of which is examined in the balance of this section:

- Laying the rudimentary foundation for the development of an enduring democracy in Iraq under CPA auspices from May 2003 through its handover to an interim domestic governing body in June 2004.
- Managing the transition from interim to permanent Iraqi governmental rule from June 2004 through December 2005.
- Assessing the prospects for the development of an enduring Iraqi democracy over the long term.

Any useful discussion of the political aspects of the ongoing nation building project in Iraq must begin with a primer that touches both on the ethnic and religious diversity prevalent in that context and also on the political legacy of Saddam's Baathist regime. Ethnically, the Iraqi population is divided primarily among Arabs (75-80 percent) and Kurds (15-20 percent) and a range of other groups, including Turkomen and Assyrians (five percent). With respect to religion, it is 97 percent Muslim (60-65 percent Shiite and 32-37 percent Sunni) and approximately three percent Christian.[39] Geographically, the Kurds reside in the north near Iraq's borders with Turkey and Iran, while most Shiites and Sunnis live in the south and north-central sections of the country. Historically, members of these groups have rarely mixed socially and continue to remain suspicious of each other.

Complicating the contemporary relationships among Sunnis, Shiites and Kurds further is the legacy of Saddam's quarter-century in power. During that time, Saddam and his Sunni-dominated Baath Party systematically repressed and exterminated hundreds of thousands of Kurds, Shiites and other political opponents. Perhaps the most brutal period of repression came in the aftermath of the 1990-91 Persian Gulf War when Saddam's army crushed Kurdish and Shiite revolts that were encouraged but not supported by the George H.W. Bush administration. Since the end of Operation Iraqi Freedom, for example, coalition forces have uncovered more than 300,000 bodies in mass graves across Iraq. That number is all but sure to increase substantially given that nearly one million Iraqis disappeared concurrent with Baathist repression of Saddam's opponents in the 1980s and 1990s.[40] As Sandy Hodgkinson, a US State Department expert who spent a year working on the issue of mass graves in Iraq, explains, "There will be graves people haven't seen or don't remember. It will be a long time before we determine how many sites there are and where they are."[41]

Once Saddam's regime had been eliminated, it was left to the CPA (and, as of May 2003, Bremer in particular) to establish the basis for an enduring representative democracy in Iraq. He spent his year at the head of the CPA working on two major political projects. First, he orchestrated a process through which an initial Iraqi Governing Council (IGC) composed of members from each of Iraq's principal ethnic and religious groups (the Shiites, Sunnis and Kurds) drafted an interim constitution to serve as the foundation for long-term democratization. Second, he developed a plan for the progression from an interim Iraqi governing body in June 2003 to a transitional government by January 2005 to a permanent elected government by the end of December 2005.[42]

Upon assuming power, Bremer correctly insisted that no one with even marginal ties to Saddam's regime would be allowed to hold a politically influential position, most notably so on the 25-member IGC, which held its initial meeting in July 2003 and was charged with drafting an interim constitution. Among those named to the IGC was Ahmed Chalabi, a prominent Shiite exile who headed the Iraqi National Congress, an ethnically and religiously diverse group that opposed Saddam from abroad between 1992 and the conduct of Operation Iraqi Freedom.[43]

Conceived as an interim body with an indeterminate tenure, the IGC had two fundamental weaknesses, both of which reflected deeper challenges to the democratization process within Iraq and neither of which it had fully overcome as of May 2004 when this book went to press. First, while broadly representative of Iraq's diverse ethnic and religious composition, the IGC lacked any leader capable of commanding widespread support among Shiites, Sunnis and Kurds. The one figure capable of generating such respect among majority Shiites, for instance, was (and remains) the Grand Ayatollah Ali Sistani. Yet, as is the case with most mainstream Shiite clerics, he prefers to focus on religion and play a more indirect role at the political level within Iraq. According to Reuel Marc Gerecht, a fellow at the American Enterprise Institute and expert on Shiism, "clerics like Sistani ... understand that clerics cannot become politicians without compromising their religious missions."[44]

Second, the divergent interests of its members—and their respective constituencies—complicated the interim constitution drafting process. Initially opposed by the IGC's five Shiite members, the constitution was eventually approved via negotiated compromises to include a provision on minority rights for the Kurds, Sunnis and women, and another recognizing Islam as the central source of Iraqi law in March 2004, the constitution's long-term viability remains very much in question.[45] As Cordesman notes, the "risk of confessional struggles between Sunni and Shiite is obvious, as is the risk of some form of power struggle between Arab and Kurd. The role of Islam in the state also remains undefined and could become a serious issue. At the same time, Iraqis have so far shown they are fully aware of the risks of such divisions, and are willing to compromise to avoid them."[46]

The constitutional dilemma is one of the more problematic issues that either Bremer or his de facto successor—John Negroponte, who Bush appointed as the first post-Saddam US Ambassador to Iraq—will have to help either the IGC or, more likely, a yet to be appointed (as of late April 2004) interim Iraqi government to address effectively.[47] Others include the aforementioned timetable for the progression from interim to transitional to permanent governance in Iraq between June 2003 and December 2005 and what role, if any, the UN will play in that process. The imperative for UN involvement is that, of course, the world body could help legitimate the transition and any future Iraqi government.

The timetable settled on by the CPA and IGC in the fall of 2003 called for the selection of an interim Iraqi government by the end of May 30 2004. That interim body, which UN envoy Lahdar Brahimi and CPA officials were in the process of assembling in the spring of 2004, is scheduled to serve from 30 June 2004 through the establishment of a transitional National Assembly and executive and judicial governing councils by 31 January 2005. The executive will be composed of a three-member Presidency Council to include a prime minister responsible for the day-to-day management of governmental affairs. The Presidency Council will appoint both the prime minister and a nine-member Supreme Court.

Ultimately, the 275-member National Assembly will be responsible for drafting a permanent constitution, which must be approved in a national referendum no later than 15 October 2005. Assuming that deadline is met, elections for a permanent government will follow, with the members of that body scheduled to assume office by 31 December 2005 and manage the future of the new Iraq thereafter. Whether that timeline is followed to the letter remains open to question and will likely be a product of both the security environment in Iraq and economic progress—or lack thereof—in that context in 2005.[48] What is clear, however, is that the character of the political entity that emerges in Iraq and its maintenance over the long term will be conditioned primarily by the relationships among and decisions made by the Iraqis themselves. Writing while Saddam was still in power, historian Charles Tripp perhaps captured Iraq's predicament the best:

> The political history of the Iraqi state is a continuing one. However dominant the present order in Iraq has been during the past thirty years and however much it has exerted itself to eliminate possible alternatives, time will erode and destroy it. With its passing, new spaces will open up and new possibilities will be created for other narratives to assert themselves in the shaping of Iraqi history. This does not mean that all traces of the present regime will vanish. They will continue to exist both in the processes and structures which it has developed and in the conditions and attitudes which allowed it to emerge. The population of Iraq is not condemned to repeat this history since certain key players and factors will have changed significantly. However, those who are seeking to develop new narratives for the history of Iraq must recognize the powerful legacies at work in the country if they do not want to succumb to their logic.[49]

Conclusions

This chapter was designed to discuss the issue of nation building in Iraq by addressing five related issues. First, it focused on the centrality of nation building operations to the pursuit of American interests in the post-9/11 era in order to provide a useful contextual foundation for its subsequent examination of the case of Iraq. Second, it provided an overview of the challenges associated with the reconstruction of Iraq in the aftermath of Operation Iraqi Freedom. Third, it presented an in-depth examination of the security situation in Iraq, placing an emphasis on the extent to which maintaining a stable environment in the Persian Gulf region is certain to entail substantial costs over the short, medium and long terms. Fourth, it explored the economic aspects of nation building in Iraq and assessed the prospects for future prosperity in that nascent state. Fifth, it discussed the CPA's progress in laying a foundation for the democratization of Iraq, but also touched on the uncertainty of achieving that objective over the medium and long terms.

The following conclusions grow out of the evidence presented in examining each of those fundamental issues. First, the Bush administration has acknowledged the indispensability of nation building to the war on terrorism as evidenced by the commitment it has made to the establishment of an enduring democracy in Iraq since the elimination of Saddam's regime. In short, the administration has recognized that following the reconstruction of Iraq through to completion is its only prudent course of action, particularly given the potential for that state to develop into in base for terrorist organizations should nation building fail. Second, it is clear that providing the necessary security safeguards to allow for the emergence of a vibrant economy and stable representative political system over the medium term and the maintenance of both over the long term will be difficult. The eruption of insurgent violence in April 2004 was particularly illustrative of that point. Third, Bush's resolute commitment to nation building in Iraq has already entailed—and will undoubtedly continue to generate—substantial economic and physical costs. The more those costs (especially the loss of American lives and funds to maintain the military presence) rise, the greater the pressure to reduce the US commitment will grow. Nonetheless, irrespective of who occupies the White House from 2005-09, Bush or Democratic challenger John Kerry, abandoning Iraq is simply not a realistic option given that American credibility is on the line. Fourth, so long as the United States maintains its commitment, the situation is likely to improve rather than deteriorate over the long term. The aforementioned projections for economic growth suggest as much. Fifth, should nation building in Iraq succeed, it certainly has the potential to serve as a foundation for the broader democratization of the Greater Middle East, albeit over a period of decades rather than years.

Notes

[1] George W. Bush, "Address to the Nation in Prime Time Press Conference," *White House Office of the Press Secretary* (13 April 2004).

[2] Ibid.

[3] For a detailed examination of post-conflict reconstruction operations in Germany and at the broader Western European level in the aftermath of World War II, see Geir Lundestad, *Empire by Integration: The United States and European Integration, 1945-1997* (New York: Oxford University Press, 1998).

[4] John J. Hamre and Gordon R. Sullivan, "Toward Postconflict Reconstruction," *Washington Quarterly* (Autumn 2002): 85-86.

[5] Ibid., 85.

[6] For two particularly useful recent studies on nation building in the post-9/11 world, see James Dobbins, "Nation Building: The Inescapable Responsibility of the World's Only Superpower," *RAND Review* (Summer 2003) and Marina Ottaway, "Think Again: Nation Building," *Foreign Policy* (September/October 2002).

[7] Robert I. Rotberg, "Failed States in a World of Terror," *Foreign Affairs* (July/August 2002): 127.

[8] For two particularly useful recent studies on the Bush administration's efforts to democratize the Greater Middle East through a combination of the preemptive use of force followed by the implementation of nation building operations, see John Lewis Gaddis, *Surprise, Security and the American Experience* (Cambridge: Harvard University Press, 2004) and Ivo H. Daalder and James M. Lindsay, *America Unbound: The Bush Revolution in Foreign Policy* (Washington, DC: Brookings Institution Press, 2003).

[9] For comprehensive accounts of nation building operations in Iraq, see Anthony H. Cordesman, "One Year On: Nation Building in Iraq," *Center for Strategic and International Studies* (8 April 2004) and Joseph Braude, *The New Iraq: Rebuilding the Country, its People, the Middle East and the World* (New York: Basic Books, 2003).

[10] Cordesman, "One Year On," 10-11; Stephen Lanier, "Low Intensity Conflict and Nation-Building in Iraq: A Chronology," *Center for Strategic and International Studies* (14 April 2004).

[11] Quoted in James Fallows, "Blind Into Baghdad," *Atlantic Monthly* (January/February 2004): 73.

[12] Steven Metz, "Insurgency and Counterinsurgency in Iraq," *Washington Quarterly* (Winter 2003-04): 25-30.

[13] Ibid., 26.

[14] "Iraqi Coalition Casualty Count," <http://lunaville.org/warcasualties/Summary.aspx> (21 April 2004).

[15] Cordesman, "One Year On," 7-9.

[16] Ron Coddington and James West, "Most-wanted Iraqis," *USA Today* (19 April 2004).

[17] Lanier, "Low Intensity Conflict and Nation Building in Iraq"; "Iraqi Coalition Casualty Count."

[18] Anthony H. Cordesman, "The Situation in Iraq: The Impact of President Bush's Speech," *Center for Strategic and International Studies* (16 April 2004).

[19] "Results in Iraq: 100 Days Toward Security and Freedom," *White House Office of the Press Secretary* (8 August 2003): 5. According to the Bush administration, Abu Musab al-Zarqawi traveled to Baghdad for medical treatment in May 2002, along with some two-dozen Al Qaeda operatives, who have been in Iraq ever since.

[20] Robert Kagan and William Kristol, "Too Few Troops," *Weekly Standard* (26 April 2004): 7.

[21] Cordesman, "A Year On," 25-28.

[22] The number of coalition members with forces on the ground in Iraq has fluctuated at the margins since the end of major combat operations on 1 May 2003 and stood at 32 in May 2004.

[23] Amir Taheri, "What to Do: The Problem in Iraq is neither political nor military; it is a security problem," *National Review* (24 November 2003): 18.

[24] Cordesman, "A Year On," 26-28.

[25] Fred Barnes, "The Essential Bremer: What the American Administrator in Iraq has Accomplished," *Weekly Standard* (12-19 April 2004): 11-12.

[26] Matthew Continetti, "Brother, Can You Spare $87 Billion," *Weekly Standard* (27 October 2003): 10-12; "Iraq and a Hard Place," *Economist* (20 September 2003).

[27] Jonathan Weisman, "Iraq War May Require More Money Soon," *Washington Post* (21 April 2004).

[28] Cordesman, "One Year On," 14-15; "Republic of Iraq: 2004 Budget," *Coalition Provisional Authority/Iraqi Finance Ministry* (October 2003): 8-10.

[29] Cordesman, "One Year On," 15.

[30] Cordesman, "One Year On," 16; Michael E. O'Hanlon and Adriana Lins de Albuquerque, "Iraq Index: Tracking Variables of Reconstruction and Security in Post-Saddam Iraq," *Brookings Institution* (21 April 2004): 15.

[31] O'Hanlon and Lins, "Iraq Index," 17.

[32] Cordesman, "One Year On," 15.

[33] Fred Barnes, "The Bumpy Road to Democracy in Iraq," *Weekly Standard* (5 April 2004): 21-23.

[34] Cordesman, "One Year On," 19.

[35] "Republic of Iraq: 2004 Budget," 4-5.

[36] Ibid., 10-11.

[37] Ibid., 16.

[38] Barnes, "The Bumpy Road to Democracy," 23.

[39] "Iraq," *CIA World Factbook 2003*.

[40] Fred Barnes, "Uncovering Saddam's Crimes: The Legacy of a Mass Murderer," *Weekly Standard* (26 April 2004): 22-25.

[41] Quoted in ibid., 23.

[42] Cordesman, "One Year On," 10-11.

[43] Charles Tripp, *A History of Iraq* (Cambridge, UK: Cambridge University Press, 2000), 275-76.

[44] Reuel Marc Gerecht, "Democratic Anxiety," *Weekly Standard* (2 February 2004): 24.

[45] Lanier, "Low Intensity Conflict and Nation-Building in Iraq."

[46] Cordesman, "One Year On," 9.

[47] "President Announces Intention to Nominate Ambassador to Iraq," *White House Office of the Press Secretary* (19 April 2004).

[48] Cordesman, "One Year On," 10-11.

[49] Tripp, *A History of Iraq*, 293.

Conclusion

The Future of US Iraq Policy

Introduction

In the aftermath of World War II in 1945, American President Harry S. Truman's administration conceived and implemented the strategy of containment as a means through which to conduct the Cold War against the Soviet Union. Over the ensuing three decades, US administrations led by Democrats as well as Republicans used several variants of that basic strategy in developing their policies toward Moscow. Ultimately, the bipolar confrontation lasted nearly a half-century and was brought to a conclusion favorable to the United States as a direct result of President Ronald Reagan's proactive stance toward the Soviet Union during the 1980s, one characterized by a robust effort to "roll back" its influence across the globe.

Nearly a decade after the implosion of the Soviet Union in December 1991 signaled the formal end of the Cold War, the United States faced its first major challenge comparable in scope to the one encountered by the Truman administration in 1945. Al Qaeda's strikes on the World Trade Center and Pentagon on 11 September 2001 left President George W. Bush to determine how best to respond to the threats to American interests at home and abroad posed by transnational terrorist organizations and their state sponsors.

Following the events of 9/11, the President struck a balance between the approaches of Truman and Reagan. First, Bush impressed upon the American people the fact that Al Qaeda had attacked the United States and, as a result, Washington would be at war with Osama bin Laden and his supporters, whether states or non-state actors, over the long term. Similar to the Truman administration's characterization of the Cold War, he emphasized that the struggle against Al Qaeda would be of an indeterminate length. Second, Bush stressed that it was essential for the United States to fight that war in a proactive rather than reactive manner. His subsequent promulgation of a doctrine of preemption designed to eliminate potential threats to American interests ahead of time was similar to Reagan's "rollback" approach, especially in terms of its somewhat revolutionary nature and the assertive manner of its expression.

The practical implications of that doctrine, which the Bush administration articulated in its National Security Strategy (NSS) in September 2002, were demonstrated through the conduct of the Second Iraq War in 2003 and will likely continue to condition US foreign policy in the context of nation building operations in Iraq over the long term. This closing chapter examines the future of Washington's relationship with the new Iraq and its likely impact upon the prosecution of the war on terrorism and democratization of the Greater Middle East therein. It does so through the presentation of four related sections. The first section reviews the most significant points made in the six main chapters of the book. The second section discusses the prospects for the future of nation building in Iraq. The third section examines the potential for the democratization of the Greater Middle East. The final section addresses the broader issue of the evolution of the relationship between Islam and the West during and beyond the 2000s.

Review of Book's Central Points

At its core, the book was designed to address the issue of US foreign policy and the Second Iraq War by exploring the following three clusters of issues, each of which is discussed broadly within this section:

- The impact of the events of 9/11 on American foreign policy and national security strategy.
- The manners in which the United States constructed a coalition of the willing to confront Saddam Hussein and then liquidated his regime through the conduct of the Second Iraq War.
- The objectives associated with nation building operations in Iraq and the hurdles the United States must clear to achieve those goals.

When Al Qaeda attacked the World Trade Center and Pentagon, it altered markedly the perception of threats to the United States in the minds of American policymakers and citizens alike. The loss of a sense of invulnerability to external threats demanded an alteration in the strategy through which the Bush administration would attempt to mitigate, if not eliminate, terrorist threats in the future. The expression and practical implementation of that change required both short and medium term action. As a result, the administration first signaled that it would hold both Al Qaeda and its sponsors responsible for the events of 9/11 by conducting Operation Enduring Freedom, through which it eliminated the Taliban regime in Afghanistan and put Al Qaeda on the defensive in the fall of 2001. Next, Bush formalized a more sweeping adjustment in strategy by expressing an American willingness to take preemptive measures against adversaries before the threats they pose become imminent, an approach articulated in the NSS.

For any strategy to be deemed credible, decisive action to back rhetorical promises is essential. That is why the Bush administration's release of the NSS coincided with the President's issuance of an ultimatum to Saddam to disarm and desist from sponsoring terrorist organizations, one he put forward in a speech before the United Nations (UN) General Assembly in September 2002. Following that address, Bush and his foreign policy team set to work assembling a coalition to confront Saddam— most notably by demanding that he prove in a verifiable manner that Iraq did not possess any nuclear, biological or chemical weapons of mass destruction (WMD). Their diplomatic offensive, which was carried out over the fall of 2002 and winter of 2002-03 failed to produce the necessary international consensus to secure unambiguous UN Security Council approval for the use of force to remove Saddam from power. While that lack of consensus failed to hamper the US-led coalition militarily, as evidenced by its liquidation of the Baathist regime in Iraq in less than a month's time in March and April 2003, it did open the most serious rift in transatlantic relations in nearly four decades. The Franco-American and German-American relationships in particular sustained damage that has yet to be fully repaired at a most inopportune time given that the European Union (EU) and North Atlantic Treaty Organization (NATO) moved forward with their latest—and perhaps most challenging—set of enlargements to date in 2004.

In addition to the discord the Bush administration's selectively multilateral action against Iraq helped to generate between Washington and two of three most influential members of the EU, it also forced the United States to shoulder nearly all of the military and economic burdens associated with the conduct of a nation building project in Iraq. The purpose of that project is both noble and revolutionary: the development of an economically prosperous and politically free Iraq as the first step in the democratization of the Greater Middle East. However, achieving these objectives in Iraq, let alone at the broader regional level, will entail a long-term commitment that has already resulted in a substantial loss of American lives and growing financial burden on US taxpayers. In short, if enduring economic growth and political reform are to become realities in Iraq, the maintenance of a more secure environment than was prevalent from May 2003 through April 2004 will be essential over the medium and long terms.

Future of Nation Building in Iraq

The 1990s featured the emergence of entities that gradually came to be referred to by scholars and policymakers as "failing" and "failed" states. Perhaps the most notable example was Bosnia-Herzegovina, an ethnically and religiously diverse stillborn state embroiled in civil war from 1992-95. NATO intervention under American leadership in Bosnia in the summer of 1995 laid the foundation for the conduct of a nation building project in that context, one that continues at present. Essentially, that project reflected an assessment by President William J. Clinton that nation building was an indispensable tool for use in the conduct of US foreign policy in the post-Cold War era. The Bush administration reached the same conclusion in the aftermath of the 9/11 attacks and hopes to use the economic reconstruction and political democratization of Iraq as a springboard for similar transformations of the broader Middle Eastern and Islamic worlds.

As noted earlier in the book, the initial year of nation building operations in Iraq yielded somewhat mixed results in terms of progress in the economic, political and security contexts. Put simply, the challenges in each of those issue areas are likely to remain daunting in the future as well. Economically, for instance, Iraq possesses considerable potential for growth in the form of substantial petroleum reserves, and projections of GDP increases in 2005 and 2006 are encouraging. However, much remains to be achieved vis-à-vis the modernization, if not total reconstruction, of Iraq's electricity grid and also with respect to the extraction of a progressively larger proportion of its oil over time. Similar to the aforementioned example of Bosnia, the political obstacles are equally, if not more problematic, in Iraq. In both instances, the aftermath of a conflict left three distinctive groups—the Shiites, Sunnis and Kurds in the latter case—with shared control over an interim governmental body (the Iraqi Governing Council) that did not enjoy the full support of the population. In Iraq in particular, Kurdish and Shiite suspicions of the Sunnis are deeply rooted after a quarter-century of repression and slaughter at the hands of Saddam's Baathist regime. Nor do most Kurds or Sunnis welcome the prospect of a Shiite controlled government with the potential to develop into an Islamic theocracy under Iranian auspices.

Notwithstanding the hurdles to surmount in the economic and political contexts, those challenges are all but insignificant when compared to the security threats faced by coalition forces, private contractors and the Iraqi population at large. In short, there are three sets of insurgencies with which the US military and its allies will have to grapple with through the end of 2004 at the least and, most likely, well beyond that date: loyalists to Saddam's now extinct regime; radical elements within the lower classes of the Shiite majority, especially those who choose to support extremists such as cleric Muqtada al-Sadr; and foreign fighters aligned with Al Qaeda. All three slowed reconstruction efforts by attacking coalition forces and—more importantly— the nascent Iraqi police in 2003-04. While their strikes did not destabilize the entire country at a given juncture, they did create a chaotic environment in selected geographic pockets, most notably so in the north-central Sunni triangle surrounding Baghdad. The selective targeting—and eventual extermination—of each of these insurgent groups will prove indispensable to developing the secure environment necessary to allow for economic growth and political stability within Iraq over the long term.

Prospects for Democratization of the Greater Middle East

At the core of insurgent efforts to undermine nation building operations in Iraq is the fear that the United States will ultimately achieve its objectives and thus establish an enduring free market economy and representative government in that context. That outcome could eventually lead to two developments that dictatorial regimes and terrorist groups alike would abhor: an improved standard of living for members of the lower classes of society; and the creation of a political atmosphere in which individuals are free to elect and, if they choose, criticize those in power. With Iraq as a model, other countries possessing comparably autocratic characteristics to those of Saddam's former dictatorship (examples range from Islamic states such as Saudi

Arabia and Iran to more secular oriented states like Egypt and Syria) could be the next candidates for regime change and subsequent economic and political transformation.

In particular, the above outcomes scare the leaders of terrorist organizations including, but not limited to, Al Qaeda for two reasons. First, those groups thrive on discontent, if not outright desperation, to recruit members willing to sacrifice their lives to battle the adversaries they blame for the dearth of economic growth and political freedom prevalent across much of the Islamic world. One such adversary (the United States) is perceived by many Muslims to be responsible for the majority of these shortcomings. Should Bush—or, for that matter, any other American president— prove able to use a successful transformation of Iraq to start the engine of reform at the broader regional level, the pool of terrorist recruits would decrease substantially. Second, while men such as bin Laden also seek the elimination of the present governments in control of states throughout the Middle East, they would prefer that those changes come under their auspices. That would, of course, allow them to take control and install equally repressive regime, which they could then administer in a style similar to that of the Taliban in Afghanistan. The establishment of representative democracies, by contrast, would allow for the free expression of dissent to prevent the development of any type of autocracy, whether Islamic or secular in character.

Assuming that the democratization of the Greater Middle East is a realistic long-term objective, a topic on which there is considerable debate, the Bush administration deserves credit for taking the initial step toward its achievement. However, it is also essential to recognize that the pursuit of such a revolutionary transformation will entail substantial costs and require a commitment that lasts for decades rather than years. Most significantly, those costs will grow out of the myriad challenges associated with the transformation Bush has suggested the United States should pursue. Such challenges are primarily ethnic and religious in orientation, each set of which is addressed briefly below.

Broadly articulated ethnic differences between groups tend to complicate reconstruction efforts at the national level, most notably as pertains to the creation and subsequent administration of economic and financial institutions in a given domestic environment. When individuals of one ethnic persuasion are appointed to leadership positions in such institutions, their counterparts from other groups understandably demand equitable treatment that, while morally just in theory, may slow the recovery process in practice. The reluctance of members of a particular ethnic group to accept advice from, and thus place their trust in, foreigners, is equally problematic. When those foreigners represent institutions perceived to be in business simply to do the bidding to the United States (say the International Monetary Fund or World Bank), earning that trust can be exceedingly difficult within the developing world generally and the Greater Middle East specifically.

Challenges related to linguistic differences and intra-ethnic familial and tribal rivalries typically prove even more daunting at the local level. Even if, for instance, one ethnic group is represented on a transitional economic or political body at the national level, it is by no means certain that decisions taken by that entity will be accepted by the leaders of tribes or villages thousands of miles from the capital. And, in those cases where local leaders agree to help administer humanitarian aid in an area under their control, communications are not always smooth between starving civilians and the foreign soldiers or Non-Governmental Organization (NGO) workers distributing foodstuffs.

As is true of the aforementioned political and ethnic hurdles, religious impediments to the economic and financial aspects of nation building manifest themselves in interactions among individuals, states and institutions at several different levels. Inter- and intra-denominational differences, for instance, are often evident locally and nationally, as well as regionally and globally. Domestically, inter- and intra-denominational religious disputes have the potential to undermine both the political and economic aspects of reconstruction projects. In addition to rivalries among adherents to distinctive faiths and denominations, more general contradictions between religious and secular belief systems have the potential to hamper the construction of modern financial institutions. Consider the holy book of Islam (the Koran), the most radical interpretations of which prohibit banks from charging interest and exclude women from playing a productive role in the economy of a given society. Some international religious impediments to nation building grow out of global issues (support from a small but violent minority of Muslims for transnational terrorist organizations, as evidenced by efforts to sabotage reconstruction efforts in Afghanistan and Iraq, is one such example). Others are the result of the use of NGOs to spread one faith (most often Christianity or Islam) in a state or region where the vast majority of the inhabitants already adhere to another.

Putting forward the effort to overcome these hurdles—and accepting the requisite economic, military and political costs that accumulate along the way—will provide an opportunity to change alter the broader relationship between Islam and the West in an equally favorable manner. The United States has embraced similarly daunting challenges in the past, most notably its commitment in the aftermath of World War II to the idea of a Europe whole and free. That project is now nearly 60 years old and gradually nearing completion with the EU and NATO both moving forward with their most recent enlargement processes in 2004. Lacking the economic, military and political sacrifices the Americans and Western Europeans made during the Cold War, the European continent, too, might still lack the freedoms the Bush administration now hopes to spread to the Greater Middle East.

Islam and the West: Cooperation, Confrontation or Ambivalence?

Since the events of 9/11, American scholars, policymakers and laymen alike have focused their attention on a variety of issues related to the terrorist attacks on the World Trade Center and the Pentagon, ranging from the conduct of military operations in Afghanistan and Iraq to the escalating Israeli-Palestinian conflict. While distinctive individually, the particulars of such issues are ultimately the products of the evolving relationships among adherents to the world's three oldest monotheistic religions— Christianity, Islam and Judaism—as played out in the many contexts (whether local, national or international) within which Christians, Muslims and Jews interact on a daily basis.

In order to lay out a useful set of closing observations on the dynamics and practical consequences of these relationships and interactions effectively, it is necessary to address four questions. First, to what extent is the contemporary Islamic world (to include all states with Muslim-majority populations) a homogeneous or heterogeneous entity relative to the West (to include North America and Western Europe)? Second, what is the nature of the relationship between Islam and the West at present and how much has it changed historically? Third, what are the potential interactive courses for Muslim- and Christian-majority states and citizens to follow with respect to one another in the future? Fourth, what steps can American leaders and their Western European counterparts take to increase the likelihood that Islamic-Western relations evolve in a positive rather than a negative manner over the balance of the 21st century?

Regarding the initial question, the world's 1.2 billion Muslims and the states they populate—primarily but not exclusively in North Africa, the Middle East and Central and South Asia—exhibit both homogeneous and heterogeneous characteristics, of which the latter exceed the former markedly. These characteristics are best described in religious, ethnic, political and socio-economic terms. As to religious adherence, Islam is split into two predominant strains of followers—Sunnis (85 percent) and Shias (15 percent)—who profess a shared belief in the five fundamental "pillars" of the faith, but disagree on the historical right to leadership of the Muslim world. Additionally, each strain is interpreted in a variety of ways, leaving room for the governance of believers under myriad auspices, whether traditional, modern, secular, theocratic or a hybrid of these and other socio-religious precepts.

Ethnically, the Islamic world includes states with majority populations ranging from Arabs and Turks to Pakistanis and Uzbeks to Iranians and Indonesians. For example, contrary to popular Western perceptions of Islam as a religion composed almost exclusively of radical Arab fundamentalists, Indonesia is actually the most populous Muslim state in existence at present. Similarly, while Arabic is the language of the Koran, a substantial minority of Islam's adherents do not speak or read Arabic fluently and thus rely on a wide array of interpretations of Koranic text that detract from its ability to deliver a universally accepted message. Such interpretive variety clouds the political landscape across an Islamic world that includes governmental structures as diverse in orientation as absolute military and civilian dictatorships (Libya, Pakistan, Syria and all five former Soviet Central Asian Republics) to putative democracies under de facto military control (Turkey and Algeria) to autocratic conservative religious monarchies (Saudi Arabia and Kuwait) to reforming religious-secular monarchies (Bahrain, Oman, Jordan, Morocco, Oman, Qatar and the United Arab Emirates) to a clerical theocracy (Iran).

There is, on the other hand, at least one issue—the plight of the Palestinians, who have spent more than five decades attempting to carve a contiguous state out of territory presently controlled by Israel—that has consistently drawn the collective support of states and citizens across the Islamic world. This solidarity is largely a result of clever governmental propaganda campaigns emanating from capitals such as Cairo and Riyadh to shift domestic attention from the travails of the most economically marginalized (and thus embittered) elements of Middle Eastern societies to Washington's favoritism of Israel (albeit more often real than simply perceived) at the expense of the Palestinian Authority. However, notwithstanding the prevalence of anti-American sentiments among the lower classes in many Islamic states, global Christian-Muslim relations are not nearly so straightforward as indicated by some Western scholars' Manichean warnings of an impending if not ongoing clash of civilizations.

Historically, interactions among Christians and Muslims have often been adversarial in nature, as evidenced by Islamic invaders' capture of and eventual expulsion from the Iberian Peninsula between the 8th and 15th centuries and subsequent conflicts pitting Western and Central Europeans against the forces of the Ottoman Empire. In fact, the conception of European identity was itself in part a response to the initial appearance of Islam on the continent through the Umayyads' invasion of Spain in 711. Yet, the relationship between Islam and the West has grown perpetually more complex over time, most notably so as a result of the interconnected colonization and de-colonization of wide swaths of the Greater Middle East by European powers and the subsequent migration of individuals from those areas to states across Western Europe over the latter half of the 20th century. There are, for instance, as many as 15 million Muslims residing in EU member states at present, a number that is expected to grow to at least 23 million by 2015.

Although interactions among adherents to the Islamic and Christian faiths have, on balance, proven adversarial in these contexts, such conflicts usually grow out of intra- as opposed to inter-civilizational issues. Examples range from attacks by far-right groups on Muslims in Western Europe to terrorist strikes against American interests— commercial, military and political alike—in states situated in the Greater Middle East. And, despite the fact that Islamic-Western relations have taken a turn for the worse over the past seven months (beginning with the events of 9/11 and continuing with the conduct of Operation Enduring Freedom and Operation Iraqi Freedom), there remain three potential courses for interfaith interactions in the future, whether measured at the global, regional, national, local or individual level: cooperation, confrontation or ambivalence.

Ultimately, in order to influence the character of the Islamic-Western relationship in a positive manner, one that pushes it toward cooperation rather than confrontation— and at least ensures ambivalence manifested in peaceful coexistence—American and European leaders would be prudent to consider six policy prescriptions in the future:

- First, the United States must maintain its commitment to the democratization of Iraq through nation building operations in that context until that objective has been achieved.
- Second, the United States must take a carrot-and-stick approach to its relationships with states across the Islamic world, maintaining a hard line in

confronting Iran over its development of WMD and missile systems and sponsorship of terrorist groups, but also remaining open to economic and political engagement with both moderate Muslim regimes and those trouble states willing to take substantive action to alter their behavior favorably and verifiably.

- Third, Western governments and institutions must develop and maintain an even-handed approach in attempting to negotiate an end to the most recent flare-up in Israeli-Palestinian violence and an eventual settlement of the two sides' myriad differences through collaborative transatlantic mediation rather than either American or European unilateralism. Ideally, the EU will serve as an interlocutor to represent the collective interests of its member states in this process.

- Fourth, Western European governments—especially those of France, Germany and the United Kingdom—must make concerted efforts to more fully integrate the presently marginalized Muslims residing within their borders, a perpetually increasing proportion of which hold EU citizenship. Coordination among municipal, national and EU officials and representatives from Islamic communities is the necessary point of departure toward achieving that end.

- Fifth, the United States must do a better job in representing American tolerance of a variety of Islamic interpretive viewpoints—provided they are expressed peacefully rather than via acts of terrorism within and beyond the Greater Middle East—to Muslims residing within states throughout both the Islamic and Western worlds. Islamic leaders in the West in particular could assist the Bush administration in implementing this approach, which would add a constructive element of dual interest in and responsibility for a positive outcome.

- Sixth, American and European leaders must consistently press their counterparts in the Greater Middle East to take some of the difficult but necessary steps to further democratize their own societies. Deflecting criticism over backward domestic economic and social policies by shifting popular focus to the plight of the Palestinians is a short-term fix that will only further radicalize lower- and-to some extent-middle-class Muslims to the long-term detriment of both the Islamic and the Western worlds.

Bibliography

Documents and Official Sources

Albania, Bulgaria, Estonia, Croatia, Latvia, Lithuania, Macedonia, Romania, Slovakia, and Slovenia. "Statement of the Vilnius Group Countries in Response to the Presentation by the United States Secretary of State to the United Nations Security Council Concerning Iraq." New York (5 February 2003).

Aznar, Jose Maria, Jose-Manuel Durão Barroso, Silvio Berlusconi, Tony Blair, Vaclav Havel, Peter Medgyessy, Leszek Miller and Anders Fogh Rasmussen. "United We Stand." (30 January 2003).

Blix, Hans. "An Update on Inspection." Report of the Executive Chairman of UNMOVIC to the United Nations Security Council, New York (27 January 2003). Blix, Hans. "Briefing of the Security Council." Report of the Executive Chairman of UNMOVIC to the United Nations Security Council, New York (14 February 2003).

Bush, George W. Addresses and Speeches (various).

_____. *A National Security Strategy for a New Century*. White House Office of the Press Secretary (17 September 2002).

Clinton, William. *A National Security Strategy for a New Century*. White House Office of the Press Secretary (December 1999).

NATO, Press Releases (various editions).

The North Atlantic Treaty ("The Washington Treaty"). Washington, D.C. (4 April 1949).

UN Department of Public Information. Press Releases (various).

UN *Security Council Resolution 660*. S/RES/660 (2 August 1990).

UN *Security Council Resolution 678*. S/RES/678 (29 November 1990).

UN *Security Council Resolution 1441*. S/2002/1198 (8 November 2002).

US Department of Defense. *Network Centric Warfare: A Department of Defense Report to Congress, Appendix*. Washington, D.C.: Department of Defense, 27 July 2001.

US Department of Defense. Press Releases and Availabilities (various).

US Department of State. *Department of State Bulletin* (various editions).

US Department of State. *Foreign Broadcast Information Service/Middle East and North Africa* (various editions).

US Department of State. *Foreign Relations of the United States (FRUS), The Near East, South Asia, and Africa*. Washington, D.C.: GPO (various years).

US White House. *National Strategy for Homeland Security* (September 2002).

US White House. *Organization of the National Security Council*. National Security Presidential Directive 1 (14 February 2001).

US White House. Press Releases (various).

US White House. Press Releases and Availabilities (various).

US White House. State of the Union Address (various).

Newspapers, News Sources and Serials

ABC News
Agence-France Presse
Air Force Magazine
Anadolu Agency
Associated Press
The Atlantic Monthly
British Broadcasting Corporation (BBC)
The Christian Science Monitor
CNN
CQ Weekly
The Daily Telegraph
Defense Link
The Economist
Europe
The Financial Times
The Guardian
The International Herald Tribune
The National Review
The New Republic
The New York Times
The New Yorker
The San Francisco Chronicle
Slate
The Times
USA Today
Voice of America
The Wall Street Journal
The Washington Post
The Weekly Standard

Books

Art, Robert J., and Kenneth N. Waltz, eds. *The Use of Force: Military Power and International Politics*, 6th ed. New York: Rowman and Littlefield, 2004.

Atkinson, Rick. *Crusade: The Untold Story of the Persian Gulf War.* Boston: Houghton Mifflin, 1993.

Bell, Coral. *The Reagan Paradox: American Foreign Policy in the 1980s.* New Brunswick: Rutgers University Press, 1989.

Bergen, Peter L. *Holy War, Inc.: Inside the Secret World of Osama bin Laden.* New York: The Free Press, 2001.

Brands, H. W. *TR: The Last Romantic.* New York: Basic Books, 1997.

Braude, Joseph. *The New Iraq: Rebuilding the Country, its People, the Middle East and the World.* New York: Basic Books, 2003.

Brody, Richard. *Assessing the Presidency: The Media, Elite Opinion, and Public Support.* Stanford: Stanford University Press, 1991.

Brown, Seyom. *Faces of Power: United States Foreign Policy From Truman to Clinton.* New York: Columbia University Press, 1994.

Brzezinski, Zbigniew. *Out of Control: Global Turmoil on the Eve of the Twenty-first Century.* New York: Touchstone Books, 1993.

Burton, David. *Theodore Roosevelt: Confident Imperialist.* Philadelphia: University of Pennsylvania Press, 1968.

Bush, George. *We Will Prevail: President George W. Bush on War Terrorism and Freedom.* New York: Continuum, 2003.

Callahan, Patrick. *Logics of American Foreign Policy: Theories of America's World Role.* New York: Longman, 2004.

Campbell, Colin, and Bert A. Rockman. *The Bush Presidency: First Appraisals.* Chatham, NJ: Chatham House, 1991.

Choudhry, Mashhud H. *Coalition Warfare: Can the Gulf War-91 Be the Model for Future?* Carlisle Barracks: U.S. Army War College, 1992.

Cordesman, Anthony S. *The Gulf and the Search For Strategic Stability.* Boulder: Westview Press, 1984.

Cordesman, Anthony S., and Ahmed S. Hashim. *Iran: Dilemmas of Dual Containment.* Boulder: Westview, 1997.

Cordesman, Anthony S., and Ahmed S. Hashim. *Iraq: Sanctions and Beyond.* Boulder: Westview, 1997.

Coughlin, Con. *Saddam: King of Terror.* New York: HarperCollins, 2002.

Craig, Theodore. *Call for Fire: Sea Combat in the Falklands and the Gulf War.* London: John Murray, 1995.

Daalder, Ivo H., and James M. Lindsay. *America Unbound: The Bush Revolution in Foreign Policy.* Washington, D.C.: The Brookings Institute, 2003.

De Jong, Frederik and Bernd Radtke, eds. *Islamic Mysticism Contested: Thirteen Centuries of Controversies and Polemics.* Leiden: Brill, 1999.

Dunnigan, James P., and Austin Bay, *From Shield to Storm: High-Tech Weapons, Military Strategy, and Coalition Warfare in the Persian Gulf.* New York: Morrow, 1992.

Eksterowicz, Anthony J., and Glenn P. Hastedt, eds. *The Post-Cold War Presidency.* New York: Rowman & Littlefield, 1999.

Finaly, David, Ole Hosti and Richard Fagen. *Enemies in Politics.* Chicago: Rand McNally, 1967.

Freedman, Lawrence, and Efraim Karsh. *The Gulf Conflict, 1990-1991: Diplomacy and War in the New World Order.* Princeton: Princeton University Press, 1993.

Frum, David, and Richard Perle. *An End to Evil: How to Win the War on Terror.* New York: Random House, 2003.

Fukuyama, Francis. *The End of History and the Last Man.* New York: Avon, 1993.

Gaddis, John Lewis. *Strategies of Containment: A Critical Appraisal of Postwar American National Security Policy.* New York: Oxford University Press, 1982.

_____. *Surprise, Security and the American Experience.* Cambridge: Harvard University Press, 2004.

Garthoff, Raymond L. *Reflections on the Cuban Missile Crisis.* Washington, D.C.: Brookings Institute, 1987.

George, Alexander, and William E. Simmons, eds. *The Limits of Coercive Diplomacy.* Boulder: Westview Press, 1994.

Haass, Richard N. *The Reluctant Sheriff: The United States After the Cold War.* New York: Council on Foreign Relations, 1997.

Haass, Richard, ed. *Economic Sanctions and American Diplomacy.* New York: Council on Foreign Relations, 1998.

Hanson, Victor Davis. *Ripples of Battle: How Wars of the Past Still Determine How We Fight, How We Live and How We Think.* New York: Doubleday, 2003.

Harrison, Michael M., and Mark G. McDonough. *Negotiations on the French Withdrawal From NATO: FPI Case Studies, No. 5.* Washington, D.C.: Johns Hopkins, 1987.

Hartmann, Frederick. *The Relations of Nations*, 3rd ed. New York: Macmillan, 1967.

Hayden, Patrick, Tom Lansford and Robert P. Watson, eds. *America's War on Terror.* Aldershot: Ashgate, 2003.

Huntington, Samuel P. *The Clash of Civilizations and the Remaking of World Order.* New York: Simon & Schuster, 1996.

Isaacs, Arnold R. *Vietnam Shadows, The War, Its Ghosts, and Its Legacy.* Baltimore: Johns Hopkins University Press, 1997.

Johnson, Loch K., and James J. Wirtz, eds. *Strategic Intelligence: Windows Into a Secret World.* Los Angeles: Roxbury Publishing, 2004.

Kaplan, Lawrence F., and William Kristol. *The War Over Iraq: Saddam's Tyranny and America's Mission.* San Francisco: Encounter Books, 2003.

Keaney, Thomas A., and Eliot A. Cohen. *Revolution in Warfare? Airpower in the Persian Gulf.* Annapolis, MD: Naval Institute Press, 1995.

Lagon, Mark P. *The Reagan Doctrine: The Sources of American Conduct in the Cold War's Last Chapter.* Westport, CT: Praeger, 1994.

Lansford, Tom. *The Lords of Foggy Bottom: American Secretaries of State and the World They Shaped.* New York: International Encyclopedia Society, 2001.

_____. *All for One: Terrorism, NATO and the United States.* Aldershot: Ashgate Publishing Limited, 2002.

_____. *A Bitter Harvest: US Foreign Policy and Afghanistan.* Aldershot: Ashgate Publishing Limited, 2003.

LeFeber, Walter. *America, Russia and the Cold War.* New York: McGraw-Hill, 1997.

Lowry, Rich. *Legacy: Paying the Price for the Clinton Years.* Washington, D.C.: Regnery Publishing, Inc., 2003.

Lundestad, Geir. *Empire by Integration: The United States and European Integration, 1945-1997.* New York: Oxford University Press, 1998.

Marks, III, Frederick W. *Velvet on Iron: The Diplomacy of Theodore Roosevelt.* Lincoln: University of Nebraska Press, 1979.

Marola, Edward J., ed. *Theodore Roosevelt, the US Navy, and the Spanish American War.* New York: Palgrave, 2001.

Melanson, Richard A. *Reconstructing Consensus: American Foreign Policy Since the Vietnam War.* New York: St. Martin's 1991.

Meyer, William H. *Security, Economics and Morality in American Foreign Policy: Contemporary Issues in Historical Context.* Upper Saddle River, NJ: Pearson Prentice Hall, 2004.

Miniter, Richard. *Losing Bin Laden: How Bill Clinton's Failures Unleashed Global Terror.* Washington, D.C.: Regnery Publishing, Inc., 2003.

Morgenthau, Hans J. *Politics Among Nations: The Struggle for Power and Peace*, 4th ed. New York: Knopf, 1967.

Morris, Dick. *Off With Their Heads: Traitors, Crooks & Obstructionists in American Politics, Media & Business.* New York: ReganBooks, 2003.

Mylroie, Laurie. *Study of Revenge: The First World Trade Center Attack and Saddam Hussein's War against America.* Washington, D.C.: The AEI Press, 2001.

Nathan, James A. *Soldiers, Statecraft, and History: Coercive Diplomacy and International Order.* Westport: Praeger, 2002.

Nye, Jr., Joseph S. *Bound to Lead: The Changing Nature of American Power.* New York: Basic Books, 1991.

_____. *The Paradox of American Power: Why the World's Only Superpower Can't Go it Alone.* New York: Oxford University Press, 2002.

Patrick, Stewart, and Shepard Foreman, eds. *Multilateralism & US Foreign Policy: Ambivalent Engagement.* Boulder: Lynne Rienner, 2002.

Pollack, Kenneth M. *The Threatening Storm: The Case for Invading Iraq.* New York: Random House, 2002.

Powell, Colin, with Joseph E. Persico, *My American Journey.* New York: Random House, 1995.

Rapkin, David P., ed. *World Leadership and Hegemony.* Boulder: Lynne Rienner, 1990.

Reckner, James R. *Teddy Roosevelt's Great White Fleet.* Annapolis: Naval Institute Press, 1988.

Renshon, Stanley A., and Deborah Welch Larson, eds. *Good Judgment in Foreign Policy: Theory and Application.* New York: Rowman & Littlefield, 2003.

Rodman, Peter. *More Precious Than Peace: The Cold War Struggle for the Third World.* New York: Charles Scribner's Sons, 1994.

Ruggie, John G., ed. *Multilateralism Matters: The Theory and Praxis of an Institutional Form.* New York: Columbia University, 1993.

_____. *Winning the Peace: America and World Order in the New Era.* New York: Columbia University, 1996.

Sammon, Bill. *Fighting Back: The War on Terrorism — From Inside the Bush White House.* Washington, D.C.: Regnery Publishing, Inc., 2002.

Schissler, Mark. *Coalition Warfare: More Power or More Problems?* Newport: U.S. Naval War College, 1993.

Serfaty, Simon. *After Reagan: False Starts, Missed Opportunities & New Beginnings.* Washington, D.C. : Johns Hopkins University School of Advanced International Studies, 1988.

Shull, Steven, ed. *The Two Presidencies.* Chicago: Nelson Hall, 1991.

Shultz, George. *Turmoil and Triumph: Diplomacy, Power and the Victory of the American Ideal.* New York: Charles Scribner's Sons, 1993.

Sick, Gary S., and Lawrence G. Potter, eds. *The Persian Gulf at the Millennium: Essays in Politics, Economy, Security, and Religion.* New York: St. Martin's, 1997.

Smith, Edward Allen. *Effects Based Operations: Applying Network Centric Warfare in Peace, Crisis, and War.* Vienna, VA: CCRP Publications, 2002.

Smith, Tony. *America's Mission: The United States and the Worldwide Struggle for Democracy in the Twentieth Century.* Princeton: Princeton University Press, 1994.

Spikes, Daniel. *Angola and the Politics of Intervention.* Jefferson, NC: McFarland and Company, Inc., Publishers, 1993.

Stein, Arthur A. *Why Nations Cooperate: Circumstance and Choice in International Relations.* London: Cornell University, 1990.

Sutterlin, James S. *The United Nations and the Maintenance of International Security: A Challenge to be Met,* 2nd ed. Westport, Conn: Praeger, 2003.

Theodoulou, S. Z., and M. A. Cahn, eds. *Public Policy: The Essential Readings.* Englewood Cliffs, NJ: Prentice Hall, 1984.

Ullman, Harlan, and James Wade. *Rapid Dominance, A Force for all Seasons: Technologies and Systems for Achieving Shock and Awe: A Real Revolution in Military Affairs.* London: Royal United Services Institute for Defence Studies, 1998.

Ullman, Harlan, James Wade, et al. *Shock and Awe: Achieving Rapid Dominance.* Washington, D.C.: National Defense University, 1996.

Weinberger, Caspar W. *Fighting for Peace, Seven Critical Years in the Pentagon.* New York: Warner Books, 1990.

Wittkopf, Eugene R., and James M. McCormick, eds. *The Domestic Sources of American Foreign Policy: Insights and Evidence,* 4th ed. New York: Rowman and Littlefield, 2004.

Woodward, Bob. *Bush at War.* New York: Simon & Schuster, 2002.

Wrage, Stephen D., ed. *Immaculate Warfare: Participants Reflect on the Air Campaigns Over Kosovo and Afghanistan.* Westport: Praeger, 2003.

Journal Articles, Reports and Essays

Albright, Madeleine. "Bridges, Bombs, or Bluster?" *Foreign Affairs* 82/5 (September/October 2003): 2-18.

Bennet, Andrew, Joseph Lepgold and Danny Unger. "Burden-sharing in the Persian Gulf War." *International Organization* 48/1 (Winter 1994): 39-75.

Biddle, Stephen. "Afghanistan and the Future of Warfare." *Foreign Affairs* 82/2 (March/July 2003): 31-46.

Boot, Max. "The New American Way of War." *Foreign Affairs* 82/4 (July/August 2003): 41-59.

Bowman, Steve. *Iraq: Potential Military Operations.* Congressional Research Service RL 31701 (13 January 2003).

Byman, Daniel and Matthew Waxman. *Confronting Iraq: U.S. Policy and the Use of Force Since the Gulf War.* Santa Monica: Rand 2000.

Cohen, Eliot A. "Constraints on America's Conduct of Small Wars." *International Security* 9/2 (Fall 1984): 151-81.

Conetta, Carl. *The Wages of War: Iraqi Combatant and Noncombatant Fatalities in the 2003 Conflict.* Project on Defense Alternatives Research Monograph #8 (20 October 2003).

Cordesman, Anthony. *If We Fight Iraq: Iraq and the Conventional Military Balance.* Washington, D.C.: CSIS, 2002.

_____. "One Year On: Nation Building in Iraq." Center for Strategic and International Studies (8 April 2004).

Council on Foreign Relations. "The Weinberger/Powell Doctrine: Still Relevant or Fit For the Dustbin of History?" Study Group/Roundtable Report (28 October 2002).

Dimuccio, Ralph B. A. "The Study of Appeasement in International Relations: Polemics, Paradigms, and Problems." *Journal of Peace Research* 35/2 (March 1998): 245-59.

Dulles, John Foster. "Policy for Security and Peace." *Foreign Affairs* 32 (April 1954).

Friedman, Norman. "Both Gulf Wars Offer Lessons." *Proceedings of the Naval Institute* 129/5 (May 2003).

Gartner, Scott Sigmund, and Gary M. Segura. "Opening Up the Black Box of War: Politics and the Conduct of War." *The Journal of Conflict Resolution* 42/3 (June 1998): 278-300.

Gause, III, F. Gregory. "Getting It Backwards on Iraq." *Foreign Affairs* 78/3 (May/June 1999): 54-65.

Haass, Richard N. "The Squandered Presidency: Demanding More From the Commander-in-Chief." 79/3 *Foreign Affairs* (May/June 2000).

Hechter, Michael. "Karl Polanyi's Social Theory: A Critique." *Politics and Society* 10/4 (Fall 1981): 401- 25.

Hellmann, Gunther and Reinhard Wolf. "Neorealism, Neoliberal Institutionalism, and the Future of NATO." *Security Studies* 3/1 (Autumn 1993).

Human Rights Watch. "The Mass Graves of al-Mahawil: The Truth Uncovered." Human Rights Watch Report (May 2003).

Huntington, Samuel P. "The Erosion of American National Interests." *Foreign Affairs* 76/5 (September/October 1997): 28-49.

_____. "The Lonely Superpower." *Foreign Affairs*, 78/2 (March/April 1999): 35-49.

Huth, Paul and Bruce Russett. "Deterrence Failure and Crisis Escalation." *International Studies Quarterly* 32/1 (March 1988): 29-45.

Ikenberry, G. John. "The Future of International Leadership." *Political Science Quarterly* 111/3 (Fall 1996): 385-402.

Jervis, Robert. "Deterrence and Perception." *International Security* 14/1 (Summer 1989): 5-49.

Kagan, Frederick W. "War and Aftermath." *Policy Review* 120 (August/September 2003).

Khalilzad, Zalmay. "The United States and the Persian Gulf: Preventing Regional Hegemony." *Survival* 37/2 (Summer 1995): 95-120.

Kibbe, Jennifer D. "The Rise of the Shadow Warriors." *Foreign Affairs* 83/2 (March/April 2004): 102-115.

Lanier, Stephen. "Low Intensity Conflict and Nation-Building in Iraq: A Chronology." Center for Strategic and International Studies (14 April 2004).

Lieber, Robert J. "No Transatlantic Divorce in the Offing." *Orbis* 44, no. 4 (Fall 2000): 571-85.

Mearsheimer, John J. "Back to the Future: Instability in Europe After the Cold War." *International Security* 15/2 (Summer 1990): 5-56.

Mearsheimer, John J., and Stephen M. Walt. "Can Saddam Be Contained? History Says Yes." *Occasional Paper.* Belfer Center for Science and International Affairs Security Program (12 November 2002).

Metz, Steven. "Insurgency and Counterinsurgency in Iraq." *Washington Quarterly* (Winter 2003-04): 25-30.

Mueller, John and Karl Mueller, "Sanctions of Mass Destruction," *Foreign Affairs* 78/3 (May/June 1999):43-53.

Murray, Shoon Kathleen, and Jason Meyers. "Do People Need Foreign Enemies: American Leaders' Beliefs After the Soviet Union." *Journal of Conflict Resolution* 43/5 (October 1999): 555-569.

Nacos, Brigitte Lebens. "Presidential Leadership During the Persian Gulf Conflict." *Presidential Studies Quarterly* 24/3 (Summer 1994): 543-62.

Nincic, Miroslav. "Loss Aversion and the Domestic Context of Military Intervention." *Political Science Quarterly* 50/1 (March 1997): 97-120.

Nye, Jr., Joseph S. "Redefining the National Interest." *Foreign Affairs* 78/ 4 (July/August 1999): 22-35.

Pape, Robert A. "The True Worth of Air Power." *Foreign Affairs* 83/2 (March/April 2004): 116-130.

Post, Jerrold M., and Amatzia Baram. "Saddam is Iraq: Iraq is Saddam." *Counterproliferation Papers: Future Warfare Series* no. 17 (November 2002).

Putnam, Robert. "Diplomacy and Domestic Politics: The Logic of Two-Level Games." *International Organization* 42 (Summer 1988): 427-61.

Razi, Hossein G. "Legitimacy, Religion, and Nationalism in the Middle East." *American Political Science Review* 84/1 (March 1990): 69-91.

Record, Jeffrey. "Perils of Reasoning by Historical Analogy: Munich, Vietnam and the American Use of Force Since 1945," *Occasional Paper*, no. 4 (Montgomery, AL: Center for Strategy and Technology, March 1998).

Richter, James G. "Perpetuating the Cold War: Domestic Sources of International Patterns of Behavior." *Political Science Quarterly* 107/2 (Summer 1992): 271-301.

Roberts, Adam. "Humanitarian War: Military Intervention and Human Rights." *International Affairs* 69/3 (July 1993).

Rotberg, Robert I. "Failed States in a World of Terror." *Foreign Affairs* (July/August 2002): 127-40.

Rubin, James P. "Stumbling into War." *Foreign Affairs* 82/5 (September/October 2003): 46-66.

Rubner, Michael. "The Reagan Administration, the 1973 War Powers Act, and the Invasion of Grenada." *Political Science Quarterly* 100/4 (Winter 1985-1986): 627-647.

Ruggie, John G. "Third Try at World Order? America and Multilateralism After the Cold War." *Political Science Quarterly* 109 (Fall 1994): 553-70.

Skillet, Wayne A. Skillet. "Alliance and Coalition Warfare." *Parameters* 23 (Summer 1993): 74-85.

Snyder, Glenn H. "Alliance Theory: A Neorealist First Cut." *International Affairs* 44/1 (Spring 1990): 103-24.

Thakur, Ramesh. "From Peacekeeping to Peace Enforcement: The UN Operation in Somalia." *The Journal of Modern African Studies* 32/3 (September 1994): 387-410.

Treacher, Adrian. "Europe as a Power Multiplier for French Security Policy: Strategic Consistency, Tactical Adaptation." *European Security* 10/1 (Winter 2001/2002): 22-44.

Walt, Stephen M. "Alliance Formation and the Balance of World Power." *International Security* 9/4 (Spring 1985): 225-41.

Waltz, Kenneth. "The Emerging Structure of International Politics." *International Security* 18/2 (Fall 1993): 44-79.

Index